Chinese

An Essential Grammar

Second Edition

This new edition of *Chinese: An Essential Grammar* is an up-to-date and concise reference guide to modern Chinese (Mandarin) grammar.

Refreshingly jargon free, it presents an accessible description of the language, focusing on the real patterns of use today. This *Grammar* aims to serve as a reference source for the learner and user of Chinese, irrespective of level, setting out the complexities of the language in short, readable sections.

It is ideal either for independent study or for students in schools, colleges, universities and adult classes of all types.

Features include:

- a new chapter on paragraph development
- Chinese characters, as well as the *pinyin* romanisation, alongside all examples
- literal and colloquial translations into English to illustrate language points
- detailed contents list and index for easy access to information
- a glossary of grammatical terms.

Yip Po-Ching is former Lecturer in Chinese Studies at the University of Leeds. **Don Rimmington** is Emeritus Professor of East Asian Studies and former Head of the East Asian Studies Department at the University of Leeds.

Routledge Essential Grammars

Essential Grammars are available for the following languages:

Chinese
Czech
Danish
Dutch
English
Finnish
Modern Greek
Modern Hebrew
Hungarian
Norwegian
Polish
Portuguese
Serbian
Spanish
Swedish
Thai
Urdu

Other titles of related interest published by Routledge:

The Chinese Lexicon
By Yip Po-Ching

Basic Chinese: A Grammar and Workbook
By Yip Po-Ching and Don Rimmington

Intermediate Chinese
By Yip Po-Ching and Don Rimmington

Colloquial Chinese: A Complete Language Course
By Kan Qian

Colloquial Chinese (Reprint of the first edition)
By Ping-Cheng T'ung and David E. Pollard

Basic Cantonese: A Grammar and Workbook
By Virginia Yip and Stephen Matthews

Cantonese: A Comprehensive Grammar
By Stephen Matthews and Virginia Yip

Colloquial Cantonese: A Complete Language Course
By Keith S. T. Tong and Gregory James

Chinese

An Essential Grammar

Second Edition

**Yip Po-Ching and
Don Rimmington**

 Routledge
Taylor & Francis Group

LONDON AND NEW YORK

First published 1997
by Routledge
2 Park Square, Milton Park Abingdon, Oxon OX14 4RN

Simultaneously published in the USA and Canada
by Routledge
270 Madison Ave, New York, NY 10016
Reprinted 1998, 2000, 2001, 2003 (twice)
2nd edition 2006

Routledge is an imprint of the Taylor & Francis Group, an informa business

© 1997, 2006 Yip Po-Ching and Don Rimmington

Typeset in 10/12pt Sabon by Graphicraft Limited, Hong Kong
Printed and bound in Great Britain by The Cromwell Press, Trowbridge, Wiltshire

British Library Cataloguing in Publication Data
A catalogue record for this book is available from the British Library

Library of Congress Cataloging in Publication Data
Yip, Po-Ching, 1935–
    Chinese : an essential grammar / Yip Po-Ching and Don Rimmington. – 2nd ed.
        p.   cm. – (Routledge essential grammars)
    Includes index.
    ISBN 0-415-38026-X (hbk.) – ISBN 0-415-37261-5 (pbk.)
    1. Chinese language–Grammar. 2. Chinese language–Textbooks for foreign
speakers–English. I. Rimmington, Don. II. Title. III. Series: Essential grammar.
    PL1107.Y57 2006
    495.1'82421–dc22
                                                                    2005025872

ISBN10: 0-415-38026-X (hbk)
ISBN10: 0-415-37261-5 (pbk)
ISBN10: 0-203-96979-0 (ebk)

ISBN13: 978-0-415-38026-3 (hbk)
ISBN13: 978-0-415-37261-9 (pbk)
ISBN13: 978-0-203-96979-3 (ebk)

Contents

Contents

Preface

This book aims to identify the basic features of the grammar of Mandarin Chinese. It should therefore be of use not only to students and teachers of Chinese, but also to those with a general interest in languages and linguistics. While we hope our analysis is based on sound linguistic principles, we have endeavoured to keep technical terminology to a minimum to allow as wide a readership as possible access to the material. Where it has been necessary to use specialist terminology, we have offered explanations which we hope will be intelligible to the general reader. A 'Glossary of grammatical terms' is also included (pp. 226–229) for reference.

Our approach has been eclectic: we have used both traditional and modern forms of analysis, and for maximum clarity both syntactic and semantic categories. Our concern has been twofold. First, we have sought to provide a structural description of Mandarin Chinese, starting with the noun and its modifiers; moving to the verb and its fundamental characteristics, including pre-verbal adverbials and post-verbal complements; then discussing the sentence, where the subject and its verbal predication are very much geared to a pragmatic use of word order and sentence particles; and finally looking at the paragraph, in which the component sentences can be seen to acquire extemporaneous features of abbreviation and additional structural flexibility brought about by the context or cotext. Second, we have been conscious of functional needs; we have therefore, where possible, shaped our analysis in the form of meaningful units and provided a wide range of practical vocabulary to illustrate language usage.

The language examples in the book are in most cases provided with both a literal (*lit.*) and a colloquial translation into English. The literal translations include a limited number of grammatical symbols representing functional words as follows:

asp	aspect marker	phon	phonaestheme
int	intensifier	onom	onomatopoeia
mw	measure word	cv	coverb
p	particle	interj	interjection

Two other symbols used in the text are:

> meaning 'changes into'

* indicating incorrect usage

We are deeply indebted to Li Quzhen for extensive assistance with the provision of Chinese script in the examples, paragraphs, and texts. We also appreciate support given by Sophie Oliver, senior editor, and Elizabeth Johnston, editorial assistant, at Routledge. The contents of the book are, of course, entirely our responsibility.

Yip Po-Ching and Don Rimmington

Introduction

The Chinese language

The Chinese language, or group of related languages, is spoken by the Hans, who constitute 94 per cent of China's population. One word for the language in Chinese is *Hanyu*, the Han language. Different, non-Han languages are spoken by the remaining 6 per cent of the population, the so-called minority peoples, such as the Mongols and Tibetans.

The Chinese language is divided into eight major dialects (with their numerous sub-dialects). Speakers of different dialects in some cases find each other unintelligible, but dialects are unified by the fact that they share a common script. This book describes the main dialect, which is known by various names: Mandarin, modern standard Chinese, or *Putonghua* ('common speech'). It is spoken in various sub-dialect forms by 70 per cent of Hans across the northern, central and western regions of the country, but its standard pronunciation and grammar are associated with the Beijing region of north China, though not Beijing city itself. The seven other Chinese dialects are Wu (spoken in Jiangsu and Zhejiang, including Shanghai, by 8.4 per cent of Han speakers), Xiang (Hunan, 5 per cent), Cantonese (Guangdong, 5 per cent), Min (Fujian, 4.2 per cent), Hakka (northeast Guangdong and other southern provinces, 4 per cent) and Gan (Jiangxi, 2.4 per cent).

Cantonese, Min and Hakka are widely spoken among overseas Chinese communities. In Taiwan a form of Min dialect is used, though the official language is Mandarin, brought over by the Nationalists in 1949 and called there *Guoyu* ('national language'). Mandarin is also widely used in Singapore, where it is known as *Huayu* ('Chinese language'). The Chinese population of Britain, which comes largely from Hong Kong, uses mainly Cantonese.

Written Chinese employs the character script, which existed virtually unchanged in China for over two thousand years, until a range of simplified forms began to be introduced by the mainland Chinese government in the 1950s. Words in Chinese are made up of one or more syllables, each of which is represented by a character in the written script. Since the last century, Chinese has also been transcribed into Western alphabetic scripts, and this book makes use of the standard romanisation *pinyin*.

Note: Mandarin is China's official language, transmitted nationally by radio and television, and therefore understood by virtually everyone in the country.

 Mandarin pronunciation

Syllables can be divided into initials (consonants) and finals (vowels or vowels followed by -n or -ng). Below is a full list of initials and finals, with some guidance on pronunciation. Where possible, the closest equivalents in English pronunication have been given, but care should be taken with these and confirmation sought, if necessary, from a native Chinese speaker.

Initials

f, l, m, n, s, (w) and **(y)** – similar to English
p, t and **k** – pronounced with a slight puff of air, like the initials in *pop*, *top* and *cop*
h – like *ch* in the Scottish *loch*, with a little friction in the throat
b, d and **g** – not voiced as in English, but closer to *p* in *spout*, *t* in *stout*, and *c* in *scout*, than to *b* in *bout*, *d* in *doubt* and *g* in *gout*
j – like *j* in *jeep*
q – like *ch* in *cheap*
x – like *sh* in *sheep*

The three above are pronounced with the lips spread as in a smile.

ch – like *ch* in *church*
sh – like *sh* in *shirt*
zh – like *j* in *judge*
r – like *r* in *rung*

The four above are pronounced with the tip of the tongue curled back.

c – like *ts* in *bits*
z – like *ds* in *bids* (but not voiced)

Finals

a – as in *father*

ai – as in *aisle*

an – as in *ran*

ang – as in *rang*, with the *a* slightly lengthened as in *ah*

ao – like *ou* in *out*

e – as in *her*, *the*

ei – as in *eight*

en – as in *open*

eng – like **en** + *g*

er – like *err*, but with the tongue curled back and the sound coming from the back of the throat

i – with initials **b, d, j, l, m, n, p, q, t** and **x**, as in *machine*, or like *ee* in *see* (but pronounced differently with other initials, see below)

ia – i followed by **a**, like *ya* in *yard*

ian – similar to *yen*

iang – i followed by **ang**

iao – i followed by **ao**, like *yow* in *yowl*

ie – like *ye* in *yes*

in – as in *thin*

ing – as in *thing*

iong – i merged with *ong*

iu – like *yo* in *yoga*

i – with initials **c, r, s, z, ch, sh** and **zh**, somewhat like *i* in *sir*, *bird* (but pronounced differently with other initials, see above)

o – as in *more*

ou – as in *dough*, or like *oa* in *boat*

ong – like *ung* in *lung*, but with lips rounded

u – as in *rule*, or like *oo* in *boot*

ua – **u** followed by **a**

uai – **u** followed by **ai**, like *wi* in *wild*

uan – **u** followed by **an**

uang – **u** followed by **ang**, like *wang* in *twang*

ueng – **u** followed by **eng**, which exists only with zero initial as **weng**

ui – **u** followed by **ei**, similar to *way*

un – **u** followed by **en**, like *uan* in *truant*

uo – **u** followed by **o**, similar to *war*

u/ü – with initials **j, q** and **x** (as u) and with initials **l** and **n** (as ü) like *i* in *machine*, pronounced with rounded lips, and similar to *u* in French *une* or *ü* in German *über*

uan – **u/ü** followed by **an**, only with initials j, q and x

ue or üe – with initials **j, q** and **x** (as ue) and with initials **l** and **n** (as üe), u/ü followed by **e** as above

un – **u/ü** with **n**, like French **une**, only with initials j, q and x

Most finals can be used without an initial (zero initial), and finals beginning with **i** (as in *machine*) and **u/ü** (like the French *une*) are written in the *pinyin* romanisation with **y** as the first letter, and those beginning with **u** (as in *rule*) with **w** as the first letter:

-i	>	**yi**	**-ie**	>	**ye**
-ia	>	**ya**	**-in**	>	**yin**
-ian	>	**yan**	**-ing**	>	**ying**
-iang	>	**yang**	**-iong**	>	**yong**
-iao	>	**yao**	**-iu**	>	**you**
-u/ü	>	**yu**	**-ue/üe**	>	**yue**
-uan	>	**yuan**	**-un**	>	**yun**
-u	>	**wu**	**-uang**	>	**wang**
-ua	>	**wa**	**-ui**	>	**wei**
-uai	>	**wai**	**-un**	>	**wen**
-uan	>	**wan**	**-uo**	>	**wo**

Note the vowel changes with **-iu** (> **you**), **-ui** (> **wei**) and **-un** (> **wen**).

Note: Strictly speaking, in the *pinyin* system the hand-written form 'a' is used instead of the printed version 'a', but this book has adopted 'a' throughout.

Tones

In Chinese each syllable (or character) has a tone, and in Mandarin there are four tones. In the *pinyin* romanisation, the mark above a syllable indicates its tone: ¯ first tone, ´ second tone, ˇ third tone and ` fourth tone. Some words have unstressed syllables which are toneless and therefore are not given tone marks. Structural words like particles are also often unstressed and are similarly unmarked.

First tone	high, level pitch; constant volume
Second tone	rising quite quickly from middle register and increasing in volume
Third tone	starting low and falling lower before rising again; louder at the beginning and end than in the middle
Fourth tone	starting high, falling rapidly in pitch and decreasing in volume

In speech, when a third tone precedes another third tone it changes to a second tone. Also, the pronunciation of 一 **yī** 'one' and 不 **bù** 'not' varies according to their context. **Yī** 'one' is first tone in counting but otherwise is fourth tone **yì**, except if followed by a fourth tone when it changes to second tone **yí**. Similarly, **bù** 'not' is fourth tone but changes to second tone **bú** when it comes before a fourth tone. However, since these tonal adjustments are all rule-governed, they will not be indicated in our example sentences. That is to say, **yī** will always be shown as first tone and **bù** as fourth tone.

The Chinese vocabulary

A large number of words in everyday vocabulary are of one syllable:

我 **wǒ** 'I', 你 **nǐ** 'you', 他/她/它 **tā** 'he/she/it', 天 **tiān** 'sky', 海 **hǎi** 'sea', 街 **jiē** 'street', 跑 **pǎo** 'run', 买 **mǎi** 'buy'

Structural particles are also almost always monosyllabic:

了	**le**	aspect marker and sentence particle
的/地/得	**de**	indicator of attributives, adverbials or complements
吗	**ma**	signifier of general questions

In general, however, the vocabulary is full of disyllabic words or expressions which combine monosyllables in one way or another. These words or expressions derive their meaning explicitly or implicitly from the words or syllables that make them up:

电 **diàn** 'electricity' + 梯 **tī** 'ladder'	= 电梯 **diàntī** 'lift'; 'elevator'
海 **hǎi** 'sea' + 洋 **yáng** 'ocean'	= 海洋 **hǎiyáng** 'ocean'
大 **dà** 'big' + 家 **jiā** 'family'	= 大家 **dàjiā** 'everybody'
打 **dǎ** 'to hit' + 断 **duàn** 'to break'	= 打断 **dǎduàn** 'to interrupt', 'to break in two'
房 **fáng** 'house' + 子 **zi** suffix	= 房子 **fángzi** 'house'
玩 **wán** 'to play' + 儿 **er** suffix	= 玩儿 **wánr** 'to have fun', 'to enjoy oneself'
走 **zǒu** 'to walk' + 路 **lù** 'road'	= 走路 **zǒulù** 'to go on foot'
跑 **pǎo** 'to run' + 步 **bù** 'step'	= 跑步 **pǎobù** 'to run', 'to jog'

跳 **tiào** 'to jump' + 高 **gāo** 'high' = 跳高 **tiàogāo** 'high jump'

扫 **sǎo** 'to sweep' + 兴 **xìng** 'interest' = 扫兴 **sǎoxìng** 'to disappoint'

投 **tóu** 'to throw' + 资 **zī** 'funds' = 投资 **tóuzī** 'to invest (money)'

后 **hòu** 'behind' + 来 **lái** 'to come' = 后来 **hòulái** 'afterwards'

国 **guó** 'nation' + 家 **jiā** 'family' = 国家 **guójiā** 'nation'

火 **huǒ** 'fire' + 车 **chē** 'vehicle' = 火车 **huǒchē** 'train'

首 **shǒu** 'head' + 都 **dū** 'capital' = 首都 **shǒudū** 'capital (of a country)'

Words or expressions of three or more syllables can also be formed:

邮 **yóu** 'postal' + 递 **dì** 'to pass on' + 员 **yuán** 'person' = 邮递员 **yóudìyuán** 'postman'

科学 **kēxué** 'science' + 家 **jiā** 'expert' = 科学家 **kēxuéjiā** 'scientist'

打 **dǎ** 'to hit' + 电话 **diànhuà** 'telephone' = 打电话 **dǎ diànhuà** 'to make a telephone call'

明 **míng** 'open' + 信 **xìn** 'letter' + 片 **piàn** 'piece' = 明信片 **míngxìnpiàn** 'postcard'

自 **zì** 'self' + 行 **xíng** 'to walk' + 车 **chē** 'vehicle' = 自行车 **zìxíngchē** 'bicycle'

圣 **shèng** 'saint' + 诞 **dàn** 'birth' + 节 **jié** 'festival' = 圣诞节 **Shèngdànjié** 'Christmas'

出租 **chūzū** 'to hire out' + 汽车 **qìchē** 'car' = 出租汽车 **chūzū qìchē** 'taxi'

百货 **bǎihuò** 'hundred goods' + 商店 **shāngdiàn** 'shop' = 百货商店 **bǎihuò shāngdiàn** 'department store'

The lists above show how the majority of Chinese words are constructed in accordance with grammatical principles. Chinese word-formation is therefore in a sense Chinese syntax in miniature. For example:

1   花 **huā** 'flower' + 园 **yuán** 'plot (of land)' = 花园 **huāyuán** 'garden'
    is a *modifier* + *modified* structure

2 头 **tóu** 'head' + 痛 **tòng** 'to be painful' = 头痛 **tóutòng** 'headache' is a *subject* + *verb* structure

3 学 **xué** 'to learn' + 习 **xí** 'to practise' = 学习 **xuéxí** 'to study' is a *juxtapositional* structure where two synonymous items are placed side by side

4 唱 **chàng** 'to sing' + 歌 **gē** 'song' = 唱歌 **chànggē** 'sing' is a *verb* + *object* structure

5 吵 **chǎo** 'to make a noise' + 醒 **xǐng** 'to wake up' = 吵醒 **chǎoxǐng** 'to wake (somebody) up (by making a noise)' is a *verb* + *complement* structure

The
Chinese
vocabulary

Part I

Nouns

 Introduction

In this section we discuss nouns and pronouns in Chinese. In particular we will look at the different types of nouns and those elements closely associated with them: numerals, demonstratives, measure words and attributives.

Nouns in Chinese generally have one or two syllables. A few have three syllables, but four-syllable nouns are quite rare. Some nouns are identifiable by the suffixes 子-**zi**, 儿-(e)**r** or 头-**tou**, but most are not obviously distinguishable from other word classes.

Nouns do not change for number. An unqualified noun can therefore be singular or plural, though out of context it is likely to be plural. The plural suffix 们-**men** is used with pronouns, and in particular circumstances with human nouns.

Numerals are placed before nouns to specify number, but a measure word must be inserted between the numeral and the noun. Similarly, a measure word must be placed between a demonstrative and a noun. There is a general measure word 个 **gè**, but most measure words are specific to particular nouns or sets of nouns.

Adjectives or other qualifying elements also come before the nouns they qualify. If the qualifier is monosyllabic, it is usually placed directly before the noun. If the qualifier is of two or more syllables, the particle 的 **de** will come after the qualifier and before the noun.

Definite and indefinite reference for Chinese nouns is not signified by articles like *the* or *a(n)* in English, though the demonstratives and the numeral 一 **yī** 'one' when used with a noun (with a measure) may indicate respectively definiteness and indefiniteness. Perhaps more important is the location of the noun in the sentence, since a pre-verbal position is normally definite and a post-verbal position indefinite.

Pronouns are naturally of definite reference. The third person pronoun **tā** in its spoken form may signify any of the three genders: masculine, feminine or neuter. The written forms make the distinction clear:

他 'he', 她 'she', and 它 'it'. However, 它 **tā** as a neuter pronoun indicating an inanimate entity is rarely present as the subject or object of a sentence, since its sense is usually understood from the context or cotext.

1 Nouns

1.1 Noun features

In Chinese *nouns* may consist of one or more syllables, each syllable being represented by a written character. Nouns with two syllables are by far the most numerous in the vocabulary, though in everyday speech monosyllabic nouns are likely to be as frequent as disyllabic ones. A noun of more than one syllable is usually formed by building meaning-related syllables around a headword. For example:

笔	**bǐ**	pen	
铅笔	**qiānbǐ**	pencil	(*lit.* lead-pen)
毛笔	**máobǐ**	writing brush	(*lit.* hair-pen)
圆珠笔	**yuánzhūbǐ**	biro, ball-point pen	(*lit.* round-pearl-pen)
笔名	**bǐmíng**	pen name, pseudonym	(*lit.* pen-name)
笔试	**bǐshì**	written examination	(*lit.* pen-examination)
笔记	**bǐjì**	notes	(*lit.* pen-note)
笔记本	**bǐjìběn**	notebook	(*lit.* pen-note-book)

Nouns do not change for number or case. That is, they remain the same whether they are singular or plural (the distinction usually indicated by context or, more obviously, by use of numbers), and whether they are the subject or the object of a verb. For example:

一支笔	**yī zhī bǐ**	one/a *pen*
很多笔	**hěn duō bǐ**	a lot of *pens*
笔在这儿。	**Bǐ zài zhèr.**	*The pen is here.*
我有笔。	**Wǒ yǒu bǐ.**	*I have got a pen.*

Nouns may be divided into the following categories:

(a) Proper nouns: 中国 **Zhōngguó**, China; 长城 **Chángchéng**, The Great Wall; 圣诞节 **Shèngdànjié**, Christmas

(b) Common nouns: 足球 **zúqiú**, soccer; 火车 **huǒchē**, train;
词典 **cídiǎn**, dictionary

(c) Abstract nouns: 印象 **yìnxiàng**, impression; 意见 **yìjiàn**,
opinion; 能力 **nénglì**, ability

(d) Material nouns: 水 **shuǐ**, water; 塑料 **sùliào**, plastics;
煤气 **méiqì**, gas

(e) Collective nouns: 车辆 **chēliàng**, vehicles; 人口 **rénkǒu**, population; 信件 **xìnjiàn** correspondence (letters)

| 1.2 | **Proper nouns** |

Proper nouns are names of people, places, institutions, etc. Contrary to
English practice, the names of individuals in Chinese are in the order of
first surname, which is usually one syllable, and then chosen name,
which can be either one or two syllables.

李惠明 **Lǐ Huìmíng**, in which 李 **Lǐ** is the surname and 惠明 **Huìmíng**
the chosen name

张兰 **Zhāng Lán** in which 张 **Zhāng** is the surname and 兰 **Lán** the
chosen name

Note: There is a relatively small number of surnames in Chinese; some of
the most common, as well as 李 Lǐ and 张 Zhāng, are 王 Wáng, 黄 Huáng,
赵 Zhào, 孙 Sūn, 马 Mǎ, 吴 Wú, 胡 Hú, 钱 Qián, 徐 Xú.

In forms of address, nouns denoting title or status follow the surname:

王先生	**Wáng xiānsheng**	Mr Wang
李小姐	**Lǐ xiǎojie**	Miss Li
周总理	**Zhōu zǒnglǐ**	Prime Minister Zhou
高校长	**Gāo xiàozhǎng**	Headmaster Gao
赵经理	**Zhào jīnglǐ**	Manager Zhao

Note: People are addressed in Chinese by their occupational title far more than
in English. It would therefore be normal to address someone as Headmaster
高 Gāo, Manager 赵 Zhào, etc.

The names of places can also be followed by a status noun such as
县 **xiàn** 'county', 镇 **zhèn** 'town', 市 **shì** 'city', 地区 **dìqū** 'district' or
省 **shěng** 'province'. For example:

北京市	**Běijīng shì**	the City of Beijing
河北省	**Héběi shěng**	Hebei Province
顺德县	**Shùndé xiàn**	Shunde County

Similarly, in the names of institutions the place name is followed by a noun indicating institutional function:

| 上海师范大学 | **Shànghǎi Shīfàn Dàxué** | Shanghai Normal University |
| 广东省公安局 | **Guǎngdōngshěng Gōng'ānjú** | Guangdong Provincial Public Security Bureau |

In the case of postal addresses, the sequence of wording is the opposite of English with the largest entity coming first and the smallest last:

中国	**Zhōngguó**	Mr Ming Li
山东(省)	**Shāndōng (shěng)**	[c/o Miss Huiming Zhang]
济南(市)	**Jǐnán (shì)**	Department of Chinese
济南大学	**Jǐnán Dàxué**	Jinan University
中文系	**Zhōngwénxì**	Jinan
张惠明小姐转 李明先生收/启	**[Zhāng Huìmíng xiǎojiě zhuǎn] Lǐ Míng xiānsheng shōu/qǐ**	Shandong Province CHINA

A direct translation of the Chinese address would be:

CHINA

Shandong (province) Jinan (city)

Jinan University

Department of Chinese

[Zhang Huiming Miss to transfer]

Li Ming Mr to receive/to open (formal)

Note: 收 *Shōu* 'to receive' or 启 qǐ 'to open (formal)' is conventionally added after the name of the recipient, and 转 zhuǎn 'to transfer' is generally used where the letter is c/o somebody else.

This principle of the large coming before the small is applied elsewhere in Chinese. Dates, for instance, are in the order of year, month and day. (See 10.2.1.)

1.3 Common nouns

Common nouns make up a large part of the language's vocabulary. Some incorporate conventional monosyllabic suffixes such as: 子-zi, 儿-(e)r, or 头-tou; others have more meaningful monosyllabic suffixes such as: 员-yuán 'person with specific skills or duties', 者-zhě 'person concerned with an activity', 家-jiā 'specialist', etc. For example:

孩子	**háizi**	child	瓶子	**píngzi**	bottle
鸟儿	**niǎor**	bird	花儿	**huār**	flower
砖头	**zhuāntou**	brick	馒头	**mántou**	bun
运动员	**yùndòngyuán**	athlete	驾驶员	**jiàshǐyuán**	pilot/driver
记者	**jìzhě**	journalist	学者	**xuézhě**	scholar
作家	**zuòjiā**	writer	画家	**huàjiā**	painter

Common nouns by themselves, particularly when they are grammatical objects, are indefinite, singular or plural, unless otherwise specified:

书	**shū**	a book or books
笔	**bǐ**	a pen or pens
学生	**xuésheng**	a student or students
老师	**lǎoshī**	a teacher or teachers

1.3.1 The plural suffix – **men**

Human nouns can be followed by the *plural suffix* 们-*men*; they then take on definite reference. Compare:

学生	**xuésheng**	a student or students
学生们	**xuéshengmen**	*the* students
孩子	**háizi**	a child or children
孩子们	**háizimen**	*the* children

There is usually some implication of familiarity when 们-**men** is used; it often occurs when groups of people are addressed:

| 先生们，
女士们 | **Xiānshengmen,**
nǚshìmen ... | Ladies and gentlemen ... |
| 朋友们好！ | **Péngyoumen hǎo!** | How are you, my friends? |

However, 们-**men** cannot be used with a number:

| 两个学生 | **liǎng gè xuésheng** | two students |
| NOT: *两个学生们 | *liǎng gè xuéshengmen | |

Neither can -**men** be used as a plural suffix for non-human nouns:

| *书们 | *shūmen | *(lit. book + plural suffix) |
| *猫们 | *māomen | *(lit. cat + plural suffix) |

1.3.2 Nouns and definite or indefinite reference

There are no definite or indefinite articles like *the* or *a(n)* in Chinese. Definite or indefinite reference is usually determined by the positioning of the noun before or after the verb. A pre-verbal position normally denotes definite reference, and a post-verbal position indefinite reference. Take, for example, 猫 **māo** 'cat(s)' in the following sentences:

猫在哪儿? **Māo zài nǎr?**	她喜欢猫。 **Tā xǐhuan māo.**
(*lit.* cat be-at where)	(*lit.* she like cat)
Where is/are *the* cat(s)?	She likes *cats*.

1.4 *Nouns and conjunctions*

Two or more nouns may be joined together by the conjunctions 和 **hé** 'and' or 或 **huò** 'or':

刀和叉	**dāo *hé* chā**	knives *and* forks
笔和纸	**bǐ *hé* zhǐ**	pen *and* paper
李惠明 和张兰	**Lǐ Huìmíng** ***hé* Zhāng Lán**	Li Huiming *and* Zhang Lan
信纸、信封 和邮票	**xìnzhǐ, xìnfēng** ***hé* yóupiào**	letter-paper, envelopes *and* stamps

牙膏、牙刷、 毛巾<u>和</u>肥皂	**yágāo, yáshuā,** **máojīn _hé_ féizào**	toothpaste, toothbrush, towel _and_ soap
猫<u>或</u>狗	**māo _huò_ gǒu**	cats _or_ dogs
现金<u>或</u>支票	**xiànjīn _huò_ zhīpiào**	cash _or_ cheque
小李<u>或</u>老王	**Xiǎo Lǐ _huò_ Lǎo Wáng**	Little Li _or_ Old Wang

Note 1: There are other words in Chinese for 'and' used in a similar way to 和 hé, e.g. 跟 **gēn** (preferred by northerners), 同 **tóng** (often used by southerners) and, more formally, 与 **yǔ**: 萝卜跟白菜 **luóbo _gēn_ báicài** 'turnips and cabbage', 姐姐同妹妹 **jiějie _tóng_ mèimei** 'elder sisters and younger sisters', 工业<u>与</u>农业 **gōngyè _yǔ_ nóngyè** 'industry _and_ agriculture'.

Note 2: In familiar speech 小 **xiǎo** 'little' and 老 **lǎo** 'old' are prefixed to surnames or sometimes given names. 小 **Xiǎo** generally indicates that the addressee is younger than the speaker, and 老 **lǎo** the reverse.

Note 3: The conjunctions 和 **hé** (跟 **gēn**, 同 **tóng** and 与 **yǔ**) 'and' and 或 **huò** 'or' may only be used to join words or expressions and NOT clauses:

*她喜欢猫<u>和</u>我喜欢狗。　*Tā xǐhuan māo, _hé_ wǒ xǐhuan gǒu.
*(_lit._ she likes cats, _and_ I like dogs)

1.5	_Common nouns: countability_

One feature of common nouns is that they can be counted. This involves the use not only of numbers (see Chapter 2) but also measure words (see Chapter 3).

2 Numerals and nouns

2.1	_Cardinal numbers_

一	**yī**	one	六	**liù**	six
二/两	**èr/liǎng**	two	七	**qī**	seven
三	**sān**	three	八	**bā**	eight
四	**sì**	four	九	**jiǔ**	nine
五	**wǔ**	five	十	**shí**	ten

Numbers ranging from eleven to ninety-nine are combinations of members of the basic set one to ten:

十一	**shí yī**	eleven		三十	**sānshí**	thirty
十二	**shí èr**	twelve		四十一	**sìshí yī**	forty-one
二十	**èrshí**	twenty		九十九	**jiǔshí jiǔ**	ninety-nine

The system extends itself beyond the basic set with the following:

百	**bǎi**	hundred
千	**qiān**	thousand
万	**wàn**	ten thousand
亿	**yì**	hundred million

For example:

三百六十八	**sānbǎi liùshí bā**	368
九千四百二十七	**jiǔqiān sìbǎi èrshí qī**	9,427
五万八千六百三十一	**wǔwàn bāqiān liùbǎi sānshí yī**	58,631
二十三亿四千五百六十七万八千九百二十一	**èrshísānyì sìqiānwǔbǎiliùshíqīwàn bāqiān jiǔbǎi èrshí yī**	2,345,678,921

Care must be taken with large numbers, since the English number sets a thousand and a million differ from the Chinese 万 **wàn** 'ten thousand' and 亿 **yì** 'hundred million'. A million in Chinese is 一百万 **yībǎiwàn**; ten thousand is 一万 **yīwàn**, NOT *十千 *shíqiān.

If there is a nought (or noughts) in a figure, 零 **líng** 'zero' must be added as a filler. For example:

三百零五	**sānbǎi líng wǔ**	305
三千零五	**sānqiān líng wǔ**	3,005
三千零五十	**sānqiān líng wǔshí**	3,050

| 2.1.1 | Two forms of the number two |

There are two forms of the number two in Chinese: 二 **èr** and 两 **liǎng**. 二 **Èr** is used in counting, or in telephone, room, bus numbers, etc.:

一、二、三、四 …	**yī, èr, sān, sì** …	one, two, three, four . . .
二号	**èr hào**	no. two (house, room, etc.)

二号车	**èr hào chē**	no. two bus
八九二三三六	**bā jiǔ èr sān sān liù**	892336 (telephone number)

二 Èr occurs in compound numbers: 十二 **shí èr** 'twelve', 二十二 **èrshí èr** 'twenty two', 二百 **èrbǎi** 'two hundred', etc. (though 两 **liǎng** can also be used with 百 **bǎi**, 千 **qiān**, 万 **wàn** and 亿 **yì**). 两 **Liǎng** is almost always used with measures (see Chapter 3):

两个人　　**liǎng gè rén**　two people (*lit.* two *mw* person)

NOT: *二个人　*èr gè rén

2.2　*Ordinal numbers*

Ordinal numbers in Chinese are formed simply by placing 第 **dì** before the cardinals. For example:

一	**yī** one	>	第一	**dì yī** first
二	**èr** two	>	第二	**dì èr** second
三	**sān** three	>	第三	**dì sān** third
九十七	**jiǔshí qī** ninety-seven	>	第九十七	**dì jiǔshí qī** ninety-seventh
一百	**yībǎi** hundred	>	第一百	**dì yībǎi** hundredth

When used with nouns, ordinals, like cardinals, need to be followed by measure words (see Chapter 3).

Note: In the following cases Chinese uses ordinal numbers where English employs cardinals:

(1)	dates:	三月一号	**sān yuè yī hào**	March 1st
		五月六号	**wǔ yuè liù hào**	May 6th
(2)	floors/storeys:	二楼	**èr lóu**	(American English) the second floor; (British English) the first floor
		三楼	**sān lóu**	(American English) the third floor; (British English) the second floor

Whereas the British convention is to number floors ground, first, second, etc., in Chinese the ground floor is 地下 **dìxià** (or less commonly 一楼 **yī lóu**) and the floors above are second, third, etc. This means that 'first floor' in British English is 二楼 **èr lóu** (*lit.* two floor) in Chinese, 'second floor' is 三楼 **sān lóu**, etc.

(3)   years of study (at an educational institution):

一年级	**yī niánjí**	first year
三年级	**sān niánjí**	third year

2.3 | *'Half'*

半 **Bàn** 'half' functions as a number and therefore requires a measure word. 半 **Bàn** may also come after the measure word when it follows a whole number:

<u>半</u>个苹果	*bàn gè píngguǒ*	half an apple
<u>半</u>杯啤酒	*bàn bēi píjiǔ*	half a glass of beer
一个<u>半</u>梨	*yī gè bàn lí*	one and a half pears

2.4 | *Fractions, percentages, decimals, multiples, and 'every'*

Other forms of numbers in Chinese are:

(1)   Fractions:

三<u>分之</u>二	*sān fēn zhī èr*	2/3 (*lit.* three *parts'* two)
八<u>分之</u>五	*bā fēn zhī wǔ*	5/8 (*lit.* eight *parts'* five)

(2)   Percentages:

<u>百分之</u>一	*bǎi fēn zhī yī*	1% (*lit.* hundred *parts'* one)
<u>百分之</u>六十	*bǎi fēn zhī liùshí*	60% (*lit.* hundred *parts'* sixty)

(3)   Decimals:

零<u>点</u>五	*líng diǎn wǔ*	0.5 (*lit.* nought *point* five)
一<u>点</u>四	*yī diǎn sì*	1.4 (*lit.* one *point* four)

(4)   Multiples:

两<u>倍</u>	*liǎng bèi*	2 times
十二<u>倍</u>	*shí èr bèi*	12 times

(5) The inclusive 每 **měi** 'every':

每个人	*měi gè rén*	everyone
每天	*měi tiān*	every day

2.5 | *Approximation*

Approximation in Chinese may take the following forms:

(1) 几 **Jǐ** 'several':

几个苹果	*jǐ gè píngguǒ*	a few apples
几个句子	*jǐ gè jùzi*	a few sentences
几个生词	*jǐ gè shēngcí*	a few new words
几十个朋友	*jǐ shí gè péngyou*	a few dozen friends (*lit.* a few tens friends)
几千个警察	*jǐ qiān gè jǐngchá*	a few thousand policemen

几 **Jǐ** can also mean 'or so, and more', when used after 十 **shí** 'ten' or its multiples:

十几个人	*shí jǐ gè rén*	a dozen or so people
三十几个瓶子	*sān shí jǐ gè píngzi*	thirty or so bottles

(2) 来 **lái** 'or so' and 多 **duō** 'just over', placed like 几 **jǐ** after 十 **shí** 'ten' or its multiples. However, while 多 **duō** may also occur after 百 **bǎi** 'hundred', 千 **qiān** 'thousand', or 万 **wàn** 'ten thousand', 来 **lái** is used only after 百 **bǎi**:

十来个老师	*shí lái gè lǎoshī*	ten teachers or so
二十多个学生	*èr shí duō gè xuésheng*	over twenty students
(一)百来/多 个工人	*(yī) bǎi lái/duō gè gōngrén*	a hundred and more workmen
两千多个人	*liǎng qiān duō gè rén*	over two thousand people

Note 1: All these expressions of approximation with 几 **jǐ**, 来 **lái** and 多 **duō** require measure words when used with nouns (see Chapter 3). Also, in these cases, 一 **yī** 'one' is not used before 十 **shí** 'ten', is optional before 百 **bǎi** 'hundred', but is obligatory before 千 **qiān** 'thousand' and 万 **wàn** 'ten thousand'.

Note 2: 多 **Duō** must come after the measure when the number is not ten or a multiple of ten. This is notably the case in expressions relating to age, distance, height, weight, money, etc.

五岁多	**wǔ suì duō**	over 5 (years old)
十六公斤多	**shí liù gōngjīn duō**	over 16 kilo(gram)s
三英里多	**sān yīnglǐ duō**	over 3 miles

(3) two consecutive numbers (from one to nine) in increasing order, either alone or as part of larger numbers:

四五个客人	**sì wǔ gè kèren**	four or five guests
四五十个 男孩子	**sì wǔ shí gè nán háizi**	forty to fifty boys
十七八个 女孩子	**shí qī bā gè nǚ háizi**	seventeen to eighteen girls
五六百(个)人	**wǔ liù bǎi (gè) rén**	five to six hundred people

Note: As we can see in the last example, the measure word 个 gè is optional before 人 rén 'person/people'. This is because 人 rén, apart from being a noun, can be used as a measure word itself.

(4) (大)约 **(Dà)yuē** 'about/around' and 左右 **zuǒyòu** 'more or less', used with any numbers and any of the above forms of approximation:

(a) 大约 **dàyuē** is placed before the 'numeral + measure word + noun' phrase:

大约十五 个大人	**dàyuē shí wǔ gè dàren**	about/around fifteen adults
大约三十来/ 多个来宾	**dàyuē sānshí lái/ duō gè láibīn**	about thirty or so visitors

(b) 左右 **Zuǒyòu** comes after the 'numeral + measure word + noun' phrase:

二十个 孩子左右	**èrshí gè háizi zuǒyòu**	roughly twenty children

Note: 上下 **Shàngxià** functions in a similar way to 左右 zuǒyòu, but its use is limited to approximation about age, height and weight: e.g. 三十岁上下 sānshí suì shàngxià 'around thirty years of age'.

3   Measures for nouns

3.1   *Measures and gè*

When in Chinese a number is used with a noun, a *measure word* must be placed between the number and the noun. This contrasts with English where nouns can be divided into countables and uncountables, the former being used directly with numbers and the latter requiring a measure phrase after the number, e.g. *three students* (countable) and *three loaves of bread* (uncountable). Chinese nouns on the other hand all take measure words:

| 三个学生 | **sān gè xuésheng** | three students |
| 三个面包 | **sān gè miànbāo** | three loaves of bread |

Note: Measure words are sometimes also called classifiers.

Gè is by far the commonest measure and can be used with almost all nouns, including abstract nouns:

一(个)人	**yī (gè) rén**	one/a person
十(个)人	**shí (gè) rén**	ten people
两个姐姐	**liǎng gè jiějie**	two elder sisters
三个手表	**sān gè shǒubiǎo**	three watches
一个花园	**yī gè huāyuán**	one/a garden
四十个字	**sìshí gè zì**	forty Chinese characters
五个月	**wǔ gè yuè**	five months
每个旅客	**měi gè lǚkè**	every passenger
一个印象	**yī gè yìnxiàng**	an impression

However, with time nouns, some of which have monosyllabic and disyllabic alternatives, the occurrence of **gè** is decided with reference to rhythm: **gè** must be omitted before monosyllables but is present before disyllables. For example:

一年	**yī nián/**	*一个年	*yī gè nián	one year
一个月	**yī gè yuè**			one month
两天	**liǎng tiān/**	*两个天	*liǎng gè tiān	two days

三晚	**sān wǎn/**	三个 **sān gè**	three nights
		晚上 **wǎnshàng**	
两个上午	**liǎng gè shàngwǔ**	two mornings	
三个下午	**sān gè xiàwǔ**	three afternoons	
四周	**sì zhōu/**	四个星期 **sì gè xīngqī/**	four weeks
		四个礼拜 **sì gè lǐbài**	(colloq.)
五个	**wǔ gè zhōngtou/**	五(个) **wǔ (gè)**	five hours
钟头	(colloq.)	小时 **xiǎoshí**	

Note: The monosyllabic 月 **yuè** 'month' is nevertheless an exception. This is because without the measure 个 **gè**, 一月 **yī yuè** means 'January'. Similarly, 两个月 **liǎng gè yuè** means 'two months' whereas 二月 **èr yuè** is 'February', 三个月 **sān gè yuè** 'three months' and 三月 **sān yuè** 'March', etc. Also, with the time word 小时 **xiǎoshí** 'hour', 个 **gè** is optional regardless of rhythm.

3.2 | *Other measure words*

In addition to 个 **gè**, there is a wide range of commonly used measure words, which can be divided roughly into the categories below. (In the examples, the numeral 一 **yī** 'one' is used, though any number could appear in its place.)

(1) Shapes: the shape measure words are perhaps the most interesting because they evoke images of their associated nouns.

    (a) 条 **tiáo** (long and flexible):

一条蛇	**yī tiáo shé**	a snake
一条河	**yī tiáo hé**	a river

Other nouns used with 条 **tiáo** include: 裙子 **qúnzi** 'skirt', 裤子 **kùzi** 'trousers', 线 **xiàn** 'thread', 绳子 **shéngzi** 'rope', 'string', 街 **jiē** 'street', etc.

    (b) 支 **zhī** (long and slender):

一支笔	**yī zhī bǐ**	a pen
一支香烟	**yī zhī (xiāng)yān**	a cigarette

Also with 支 **zhī**: 牙膏 **yágāo** '(tube of) toothpaste', 枪 **qiāng** 'pistol; rifle', etc.

    (c) 根 **gēn** (slender):

一根香蕉	**yī gēn xiāngjiāo**	a banana
一根香肠	**yī gēn xiāngcháng**	a sausage

Also with 根 gēn: 头发 tóufa 'hair', 铁丝 tiěsī 'wire', 针 zhēn 'needle', etc.

(d)　张 **zhāng** (flat):

一张纸	**yī zhāng zhǐ**	a piece of paper
一张票	**yī zhāng piào**	a ticket

Also with 张 zhāng: 报纸 bàozhǐ 'newspaper', 邮票 yóupiào 'stamp', 支票 zhīpiào 'cheque', 名片 míngpiàn 'name card', 明信片 míngxìnpiàn 'postcard', 地图 dìtú 'map', 照片 zhàopiàn 'photograph', 唱片 chàngpiàn 'gramophone record', 床 chuáng 'bed', 桌子 zhuōzi 'table', etc.

(e)　颗 **kē** (small and round):

一颗珍珠	**yī kē zhēnzhū**	a pearl
一颗星	**yī kē xīng**	a star

Also with 颗 kē: 糖 táng 'sweets', 心 xīn 'heart', etc.

(f)　粒 **lì** (round and smaller than 颗 **kē**):

一粒米	**yī lì mǐ**	a grain of rice
一粒沙	**yī lì shā**	a grain of sand

Also with 粒 lì: 子弹 zǐdàn 'bullet', 花生 huāshēng 'peanut', etc.

(2)　Associated actions:

(a)　把 **bǎ** (to handle):　一把刀　**yī bǎ dāo**　a knife

一把牙刷　**yī bǎ yáshuā**　a toothbrush

Also with 把 bǎ: 梳子 shūzi 'comb', 椅子 yǐzi 'chair', 锁 suǒ 'lock', 钥匙 yàoshi 'key', 尺子 chǐzi 'ruler', 伞 sǎn 'umbrella', etc.

(b)　封 **fēng** (to seal):　一封信　**yī fēng xìn**　a letter

(3)　Particular sets:

(a)　本 **běn** (for books, etc.):

一本词典	**yī běn cídiǎn**	a dictionary
一本杂志	**yī běn zázhì**	a magazine

(b)　只 **zhī** (for animals, birds and insects):

一只兔子	**yī zhī tùzi**	a rabbit
一只鸟	**yī zhī niǎo**	a bird
一只苍蝇	**yī zhī cāngying**	a fly

There are alternative measure words for some common animals: 一头牛 **yī tóu niú** 'an ox', 一匹马 **yī pǐ mǎ** 'a horse', 一条狗 **yī tiáo gǒu** 'a dog'.

(for utensils):	一只箱子	**yī zhī xiāngzi**	a box/suitcase
	一只碗	**yī zhī wǎn**	a bowl

Also with: 杯子 **bēizi** 'cup', 'glass', 'mug', etc.

(c) 棵 **kē** (for certain plants):

一棵菜	**yī kē cài**	a vegetable
一棵草	**yī kē cǎo**	a tuft of grass

Also with: 树 **shù** 'tree', etc.

(d) 辆 **liàng** (for vehicles):

一辆汽车	**yī liàng qìchē**	a car
一辆火车	**yī liàng huǒchē**	a train

(e) 架 **jià** (for planes):

一架飞机	**yī jià fēijī**	a(n) (aero)plane
一架轰炸机	**yī jià hōngzhàjī**	a bomber
一架喷气机	**yī jià pēnqijī**	a jet plane

(f) 台 **tái** (for machines):

一台机器	**yī tái jīqì**	a machine
一台电视机	**yī tái diànshìjī**	a television

Also with: 电脑 **diànnǎo** 'computer', 缝纫机 **féngrènjī** 'sewingmachine', etc.

(g) 件 **jiàn** (for shirts, coats, etc.):

一件衬衫	**yī jiàn chènshān**	a shirt
一件大衣	**yī jiàn dàyī**	an overcoat

(h) 间 **jiān** (for rooms, etc.):

一间屋子	**yī jiān wūzi**	a room
一间卧室	**yī jiān wòshì**	a bedroom

(i) 所 **suǒ** (for houses, institutions):

一所房子	**yī suǒ fángzi**	a house
一所学校	**yī suǒ xuéxiào**	a school

Also with: 医院 **yīyuàn** 'hospital', etc.

(j)　座 **zuò** (for buildings, mountains, etc.):

一座宫殿	**yī zuò gōngdiàn**	a palace
一座山	**yī zuò shān**	a hill/mountain

　　Also with: 桥 **qiáo** 'bridge', 城市 **chéngshì** 'city', etc.

(k)　场 **chǎng** (for activities, etc.):

一场电影	**yī chǎng diànyǐng**	a film
一场足球赛	**yī chǎng zúqiú(sài)**	a soccer match

Note: The measures associated with particular sets of nouns are too numerous to list. They include: 一朵花儿 yī *duǒ* huār 'a flower', 一顶帽子 yī *dǐng* màozi 'a hat/cap', 一出戏 yī *chū* xì 'a play', 一首歌 yī *shǒu* gē 'a song', etc.

(4)　Containers:

一杯咖啡	**yī bēi kāfēi**	a cup of coffee
一碗饭	**yī wǎn fàn**	a bowl of rice
一桶水	**yī tǒng shuǐ**	a pail/bucket of water

Other containers include: 瓶 **píng** 'bottle', 盘 **pán** 'plate', 罐 **guàn** 'tin'/'can', 盒 **hé** 'small box', 包 **bāo** 'packet', etc.

Note: Cultural artefacts can sometimes dictate different sets of container measures. Take the case of 杯 **bēi** 'cup', 'glass', 'mug':

一杯茶	**yī bēi chá**	a cup of tea
一杯啤酒	**yī bēi píjiǔ**	a glass of beer

(5)　Standard measures:

一公斤苹果	**yī gōngjīn píngguǒ**	a kilo(gram) of apples
一码布	**yī mǎ bù**	a yard of cloth
一加仑汽油	**yī jiālún qìyóu**	a gallon of petrol

Other standard measures include: 英里 **Yīnglǐ** 'mile', 公里 **gōnglǐ** 'kilometre', 米 **mǐ** 'metre', 磅 **bàng** 'pound', 盎司 **àngsī** 'ounce', and the Chinese measures 斤 **jīn** 'catty', 两 **liǎng** 'tael', 尺 **chǐ** 'foot', 寸 **cùn** 'inch'.

(6)　Collections:

一群人	**yī qún rén**	a crowd of people
一套课本	**yī tào kèběn**	a set of textbooks
一沓纸	**yī dá zhǐ**	a pile of paper

Other collection measures include: 串 **chuàn** 'cluster', 堆 **duī** 'pile'/
'heap', 打 **dá** 'dozen', 批 **pī** 'batch', etc.

Note 1: The collection measure 群 **qún** 'group'/'crowd' in Chinese
is matched in English by a range of measures used with different nouns:
一群蜜蜂 **yī qún mìfēng** 'a swarm of bees', 一群牛 **yī qún niú** 'a herd of
cows', 一群狼 **yī qún láng** 'a pack of wolves', 一群羊 **yī qún yáng** 'a flock
of sheep', etc.

Note 2: The notion of *pair* is usually expressed in Chinese by 对 **duì**,
双 **shuāng** or 副 **fù**: 一双鞋 **yī shuāng xié** 'a pair of shoes', 一双筷子 **yī
shuāng kuàizi** 'a pair of chopsticks', 一对耳环 **yī duì ěrhuán** 'a pair of
ear-rings', 一副眼镜 **yī fù yǎnjìng** 'a pair of spectacles/glasses', 一副手套
yī fù shǒutào 'a pair of gloves', etc.

However: a pair of trousers 一条裤子 **yī** *tiáo* **kùzi**, a pair of scissors 一把
剪刀 **yī** *bǎ* **jiǎndāo**.

(7) Portion:

一块蛋糕	**yī kuài dàngāo**	a piece of cake
一片面包	**yī piàn miànbāo**	a slice of bread
一滴水	**yī dī shuǐ**	a drop of water

Note: 块 **kuài** is also used for 肥皂 **féizào** 'soap', 地 **dì** 'land', etc.; 片 **piàn**
for 叶子 **yèzi** 'leaf', etc; 滴 **dī** for 血 **xiě** '(drop of) blood', etc.

(8) Indefinite small numbers or amounts (一些 **yī xiē** 'some'; 一点儿
yī diǎnr 'a little'):

一些书	**yī xiē shū**	some books
一些时间	**yī xiē shíjiān**	some time
一点儿面粉	**yī diǎnr miànfěn**	a little flour

Note 1: 些 **Xiē** can only be used with the numeral 一 **yī** 'one' and with
demonstratives (see 4.3).

Note 2: 一些 **Yī xiē** usually occurs with common nouns (e.g. books) and
material nouns (e.g. water), and 一点儿 **yī diǎnr** with material nouns
(e.g. flour) and abstract nouns (e.g. time, opinion). (See also 3.3 and
3.4 below.)

3.3 Abstract nouns

Abstract nouns in Chinese also take measure words. For example,

一<u>条</u>消息	**yī tiáo xiāoxi**	a piece of news
一<u>个</u>主意/主张	**yī gè zhǔyi/zhǔzhāng**	an idea/a proposal
一<u>件</u>事	**yī jiàn shì**	a matter
一<u>丝</u>笑容	**yī sī xiàoróng**	a smile

The measure word 种 **zhǒng** 'kind, type' is regularly found with abstract nouns:

一种能力	**yī zhǒng nénglì**	a skill
一种方法	**yī zhǒng fāngfǎ**	a method
一种思想	**yī zhǒng sīxiǎng**	a kind of thinking

Abstract nouns may always be used with the indefinite small amount measures 一些 **yī xiē** or 一点儿 **yī diǎnr** 'some':

一些/点儿建议	**yī xiē/diǎnr jiànyì**	some suggestions
一些/点儿印象	**yī xiē/diǎnr yìnxiàng**	some impression

3.4 Material nouns

Material nouns in Chinese, on the other hand, may only occur with standard measures, container measures, portion measures and indefinite small amount measures:

一斤米	**yī jīn mǐ**	a **jin** (i.e. half a kilogram) of rice (standard)
一瓶酒	**yī píng jiǔ**	a bottle of wine/spirits (container)
一块布	**yī kuài bù**	a piece of cloth (portion)
一些水	**yī xiē shuǐ**	some water
一点儿水	**yī diǎnr shuǐ**	a little water

3.5 Collective nouns

Collective nouns are formed by attaching a measure word as a kind of suffix to their related nouns. However, they are established expressions and new forms are rarely coined. For example:

一只船	yī zhī chuán	>	船只	chuánzhī
	a ship			shipping, ships
一本书	yī běn shū	>	书本	shūběn
	a book			books
四口人	sì kǒu rén	>	人口	rénkǒu
	a family of four			population

Note 1: Other collective nouns include: 车辆 chēliàng 'vehicles', 信件 xìnjiàn 'correspondence (letters)', 马匹 mǎpǐ 'horses', 纸张 zhǐzhāng 'paper', 花朵 huāduǒ 'flowers/blossoms', 水滴 shuǐdī 'drops of water', 冰块 bīngkuài 'cubes of ice', 雪片 xuěpiàn 'snowflakes', 人群 rénqún 'crowds of people', etc.

Note 2: 口 Kǒu is used as a measure word for the number of people in a family.

Collective nouns, since they are notionally plural, cannot be used with numerals and measure words. The only excepion is: 两千万人口 liǎngqiānwàn rénkǒu 'a population of twenty million' (no measure word is required).

4 Pronouns

4.1 Personal pronouns

Personal pronouns in Chinese are as follows:

	singular		plural	
1st person	我 wǒ	I	我们 wǒmen	we
2nd person	你 nǐ	you	你们 nǐmen	you
3rd person	他 tā	he	他们 tāmen	they
	她 tā	she	她们 tāmen	
	它 tā	it	它们 tāmen	

As for nouns, there is no case inflection for pronouns; they remain the same whether they are the subject or the object:

我喜欢他。	Wǒ xǐhuan tā.	I like him.
她喜欢我。	Tā xǐhuan wǒ.	She likes me.
我们不喜欢他们。	Wǒmen bù xǐhuan tāmen.	We don't like them.
他们不喜欢我们。	Tāmen bù xǐhuan wǒmen.	They don't like us.

The spoken form of the third person singular is the same for masculine, feminine and neuter genders. In other words, 他 **tā** may mean he/she/it or him/her/it.

Two other personal pronouns are widely used. The first, 您 **nín**, is a polite form of second person singular:

你好	**Nǐ hǎo!** *(lit.* you good)	Hello; how are you?
您好	**Nín hǎo!** *(lit.* polite: you good)	How do you do?

Note: There is no corresponding polite form for the second person plural: 您们 **nínmen*. To address a group politely one can use the phrase: 您几位 **nín jǐ wèi**, where 几 **jǐ** means 'several' and 位 **wèi** is a polite measure word for *people*.

The second, 咱们 **zánmen** meaning 'we'/'us', is used where the speaker intends to include the listener(s) in what is said:

咱们走吧! **Zánmen zǒu ba!** *(lit.* we [you and I] leave p) Let's go!

Note: 吧 **Ba** is a sentence particle indicating a suggestion (see 8.6).

咱们 **Zánmen** is particularly used by speakers from northern China. However, the distinction between 咱们 **zánmen** and 我们 **wǒmen** seems to be growing increasingly blurred, and 我们走吧 **wǒmen zǒu ba** 'let's go' is now common among northern as well as southern speakers.

The use of these personal pronouns is generally analogous to English. However, the neuter third person singular or plural occurs only rarely, particularly when the reference is to (an) inanimate object(s). In the sentence below, for example, there is no pronoun in the second clause:

这本小说 很长, 可是 我很喜欢。	**Zhèi běn xiǎoshuō hěn cháng, kěshì wǒ hěn xǐhuan.**	*(lit.* this mw novel very long, but I very like) This novel is very long, but I like *it* very much.

Note: The neuter third person singular or plural form must still be used in a 把 **bǎ**-structure (see last example under 20.1(2)).

In contrast, when a person is referred to, the personal pronoun must be used:

那个人很 骄傲, 可是 我很喜欢他。	**Nèi gè rén hěn jiāo'ào, kěshì wǒ hěn xǐhuan tā.**	*(lit.* that mw person very proud, but I very like him) That person is very proud but I [still] like *him* very much.

29

When an animal is referred to, the pronoun may be included or omitted. For example:

我有一只猫， 它很可爱， 我很喜欢它。	**Wǒ yǒu yī zhī māo, (tā) hěn kě'ài, wǒ hěn xǐhuan (tā).**	(*lit.* I have one mw cat, (it) very lovely, I very like (it)) I have a cat. *It* is a lovely cat. I like *it* very much.

Chinese, unlike English, does not use the third person neuter pronoun in expressions about time, distance, the weather, etc. (e.g. it's late, it's a long way); instead it employs a relevant noun.

时间不早了。	*Shíjiān* bù zǎo le.	(*lit.* time not early p) It's late.
路很近。	*Lù* hěn jìn.	(*lit.* way very near) It's quite near.
天晴了。	*Tiān* qíng le.	(*lit.* sky turn-fine p) It's cleared up.
昨天天气 很好。	Zuótiān *tiānqì* hěn hǎo.	(*lit.* yesterday weather very good) It was fine yesterday.

Note: See Chapter 16 for further discusssion of **le** at the end of a sentence.

4.2	*Possessive pronouns*

The *possessive forms* of these personal pronouns in Chinese, whether adjectives (e.g. my, your, our, etc.) or pronouns (e.g. mine, yours, ours, etc.) are all formed by adding the suffix 的 **de**:

		singular		plural	
1st person	我的 **wǒde**	my/mine	我们的 **wǒmende** 咱们的 **zánmende**	our/ours our/ours
2nd person	你的 **nǐde** 您的 **nínde** (polite)	your/yours your/yours	你们的 **nǐmende**	your/ yours
3rd person	他的 **tāde** 她的 它的	his her(s) its	他们的 **tāmende**	their/ theirs

For example:

| 我的书 | **wǒde shū** | my book(s) |
| 书是我的 | **Shū shì wǒde.** | The book(s) is/are mine. |

Note 1: 的 **De**, as part of a possessive adjective, may be omitted when the reference is to relatives or close friends, e.g.:

我妈妈	**wǒ māma**	my mother
你女朋友	**nǐ nǚ péngyou**	your girlfriend
她哥哥	**tā gēge**	her elder brother

Note 2: When a possessive adjective occurs with a numeral-measure phrase, the former precedes the latter and **de** is usually present, e.g.:

| 我的一个同事 | **wǒde yī gè tóngshì** | a colleague of mine |
| 他的两个孩子 | **tāde liǎng gè háizi** | two children of his |

| **4.3** | *Demonstrative pronouns* |

The two *demonstrative pronouns* in Chinese are 这 **zhè** 'this' and 那 **nà** 'that':

这是我的。	**Zhè shì wǒde.**	This is mine.
那是你的车票。	**Nà shì nǐde chēpiào.**	That is your train/coach ticket.
那不行。	**Nà bù xíng.**	That won't do.

这 **Zhè** and 那 **nà** can also modify nouns as *demonstrative adjectives*, but like numerals they must normally be followed by a measure. With measures, regularly 这 **zhè** becomes 这 **zhèi** and 那 **nà** becomes 那 **nèi**.

| 那个人是
我爸爸。 | **Nèi gè rén**
shì wǒ bàba. | (*lit.* that mw person be my
father) That man is my father. |
| 我要买这本
地图册。 | **Wǒ yào mǎi zhèi**
běn dìtúcè. | (*lit.* I want buy this mw atlas)
I want to buy this atlas. |

Note: Where the context is sufficient (i.e. when the noun has already been identified), the noun may be omitted:

那个是她的。	**Nèi gè shì tāde.**	That one is hers.
我喜欢这个。	**Wǒ xǐhuan zhèi gè.**	I like this one.
这位是我们 的老师。	**Zhèi wèi shì** **wǒmende lǎoshī.**	This (polite form) is our teacher.

Plurals of the demonstratives can be formed by using the measure 些 xiē (cf. 3.2 (8)): 这些 zhèi xiē 'these' and 那些 nèi xiē 'those':

这些是我们的。	**Zhèi xiē** shì wǒmende.	These are ours.
那些是你们的。	**Nèi xiē** shì nǐmende.	Those are yours.
这些箱子是我的。	**Zhèi xiē** xiāngzi shì wǒde.	These suitcases are mine.
那些衣服是他的。	**Nèi xiē** yīfu shì tāde.	Those clothes are his.
这些钱是她的。	**Zhèi xiē** qián shì tāde.	This money is hers.

When demonstratives are used with numbers, the word order is demonstrative, number, measure, noun:

这三张票是您的。	**Zhè/Zhèi sān zhāng piào** shì nínde.	These three tickets are yours (polite).
那两封信是你的。	**Nà/Nèi liǎng fēng xìn** shì nǐde.	Those two letters are yours.

If a possessive adjective is also present, it always comes first (see 5.8):

我的这三张票	**wǒde zhè/zhèi sān zhāng piào**	These three tickets of mine
你的那两封信	**nǐde nà/nèi liǎng fēng xìn**	Those two letters of yours

---

4.4 Interrogative pronouns

The main *interrogative pronouns* in Chinese are:

谁	**shéi/shuí**	who(m)
谁的	**shéide/shuíde**	whose
哪	**nǎ/něi** (+ measure word + noun)	which
哪些	**nǎ/něi + xiē** (+ noun)	which (plural)
什么	**shénme**	what

Note: 那 **nà/nèi** 'that' and 哪 **nǎ/něi** 'which' are differentiated in meaning by their tones and written forms.

When interrogative pronouns are used, the word order of the question does not change from that of statement. In other words, the inter-

rogative word comes at the point in the sentence where the answer
word is expected:

Q: 那个人是谁?
Nèi gè rén shì *shéi*?
(*lit*. that mw person be who)

Who is that person?

A: 那个人是我爸爸。
Nèi gè rén shì *wǒ bàba*.
(*lit*. that mw person be my
father)

That person is my father.

Q: (A knock on the door) 你是谁?
Nǐ shì shéi/shuí?

A: 我是你的邻居。
Wǒ shì nǐde língjū.

Note: It would be wrong to say *谁是那个人 'shéi shì nèi gè rén' in the first
example because the answer will be 那个人是我爸爸 'nèi gè rén shì wǒ bàba'
and not *我爸爸是那个人 'wǒ bàba shì nèi gè rén'. The reason is that a noun of
definite reference in Chinese will normally come first as the subject or topic of
a sentence, whether in a statement or question. Similarly, a personal pronoun
(as in the second example) is naturally of definite reference and therefore comes
first in the sentence. It would be wrong to ask *谁是你 'shéi shì nǐ' or answer *
你的邻居是我 'nǐde línjū shì wǒ'.

Q: 谁是你的中文老师?
**Shéi/shuí shì nǐde
zhōngwén lǎoshī?**
(*lit*. who be your
Chinese teacher)
Who is your Chinese
teacher?

A: 那个人/李明是我的中文老师。
**Nèi gè rén/Lǐ Míng shì
wǒde zhōngwén lǎoshī.**
(*lit*. that mw person/Li Ming
be my Chinese teacher)
That person/Li Ming is my
Chinese teacher.

Q: 谁有火柴/打火机?
Shéi yǒu huǒchái/dǎhuǒjī?
(*lit*. who have match(es)/lighter)
Who has a match/lighter?

A: 我有(火柴/打火机)。
Wǒ yǒu huǒchái/dǎhuǒjī.
(*lit*. I have match(es)/lighter)
I have (a match/lighter).

Q: 这是谁的行李?
Zhè shì shuíde xínglǐ?
(*lit*. this be whose luggage)
Whose luggage is this?

A: 这是我的(行李)。
Zhè shì wǒde xínglǐ.
(*lit*. this be my luggage)
This is mine/my luggage.

Q: 这串钥匙是谁的?
**Zhèi chuàn yàoshi shì
shuíde?**
(*lit*. this mw key(s) be whose)
Whose keys are these/Whose
is this bunch of keys?

A: (这串钥匙)是我的。
**(zhèi chuàn yàoshi
shì wǒde.**
(*lit*. this mw key(s) be mine)
They/These keys are mine/
This bunch of keys is mine.

Q: 你喜欢哪幅画？
Nǐ xǐhuan nǎ/něi fú huàr?
(*lit.* you like which mw painting)
Which painting do you like?

A: 我喜欢这幅画。
Wǒ xǐhuan zhèi fú huàr.
(*lit.* I like this mw painting)
I like this painting.

Q: 你认识哪两个人？
Nǐ rènshi nǎ/něi liǎng gè rén?
(*lit.* you know which two mw people)
Which two people do you know?

A: 我认识这两个人。
Wǒ rènshi zhè/zhèi liǎng gè rén.
(*lit.* I know this two mw people)
I know these two people.

Q: 你认识哪些字？
Nǐ rènshi nǎ/něi xiē zì?
(*lit.* you know which mw character)
Which characters do you know?

A: 我认识这些字。
Wǒ rènshi zhèi xiē zì.
(*lit.* I know these mw character)
I know these characters.

Q: 你找什么？
Nǐ zhǎo shénme?
(*lit.* you look-for what)
What are you looking for?

A: 我找我的钱包。
Wǒ zhǎo wǒde qiánbāo.
(*lit.* I look-for my purse/wallet)
I'm looking for my purse/wallet.

Q: 你喝杯什么？
Nǐ hē bēi shénme?

(*lit.* you drink mw: cup what)

What will you have to drink?

A: 我喝杯茶/咖啡/桔子水/啤酒。
Wǒ hē bēi chá/kāfēi/ júzishuǐ/píjiǔ
(*lit.* I drink mw: cup tea/ coffee/orange juice/beer)
I'll have tea/coffee/orange juice/beer.

| **4.5** | *Other pronouns* |

Other *miscellaneous pronouns* include:

大家	**dàjiā**	everybody (used before and after the verb)
人家	**rénjiā**	the other person (occurring before and after the verb)
自己	**zìjǐ**	oneself (used before and after the verb or after a personal pronoun)
谁	**shéi/shuí**	everybody/nobody (placed before the verb and *always* with 都 **dōu** 'all' or 也 **yě** 'also')

什么	**shénme**	everything/nothing (likewise placed before the verb and *always* with 都 **dōu** 'all' or 也 **yě** 'also')
大家都知道 这件事。	*Dàjiā dōu zhīdào* *zhèi jiàn shì.*	(*lit.* everybody all know this mw matter) Everybody knows this.
她认识<u>大家</u>。	**Tā rènshi** *dàjiā.*	(*lit.* she recognise everybody) She knows everybody.
<u>人家</u>不理她。	*Rénjiā* **bù lǐ tā.**	(*lit.* others not bother-with her) The others ignored her.
她不理<u>人家</u>。	**Tā bù lǐ** *rénjiā.*	(*lit.* she not bother-with others) She ignored the others.
谁都/ 也喜欢她。	*Shéi dōu/* *yě* **xǐhuan tā.**	(*lit.* everybody all/also like her) Everybody likes her.
谁都/ 也不喜欢他。	*Shéi dōu/* *yě* **bù xǐhuan tā.**	(*lit.* everybody also not like him) Nobody likes him.
她谁都/ 也不喜欢。	**Tā** *shéi dōu/* *yě* **bù xǐhuan.**	(*lit.* she everybody all/also not like) She doesn't like anybody.
她什么 都/也吃。	**Tā** *shénme* **dōu/**yě **chī.**	(*lit.* she everything all/also eat) She eats everything.
她什么 都/也不吃。	**Tā** *shénme* **dōu/**yě **bù chī.**	(*lit.* she everything all/also not eat) She doesn't eat anything.
我<u>自己</u> 不吃肉。	**wǒ** *zìjǐ* **bù** **chī ròu.**	(*lit.* I self not eat meat) I don't eat meat myself.
他老突出 <u>自己</u>。	**tā lǎo** **tūchū** *zìjǐ.*	(*lit.* he always stick-out self) He always pushes himself forward.

Note 1: 都 **Dōu** 'all' and 也 **yě** 'also' are referential adverbs used to reinforce the idea of 'everybody'. Their use is discussed in full in 14.3. A discussion of the joint occurrence of both subject and topic in a pre-verbal position (e.g. 她谁都/也不理。*Tā shéi* **dōu/**yě **bù lǐ** 'she ignores everybody') is found in 18.4 and 18.5.

Note 2: To express 'each other' or 'one another' the adverb 互相 **hùxiāng** 'mutually' is placed after the subject: e.g. 他们<u>互相</u>帮助。**Tāmen** *hùxiāng* **bāngzhù.** 'They help each other/one another.'

Note 3: We can see that 谁 **shéi/shuí** can be used either as an interrogative pronoun or to mean 'everybody/nobody'. Any possible ambiguity may be removed by the use of emphasis. Normal stress will usually encode a straightforward question whilst emphatic stress will produce a rhetorical effect, e.g.:

谁说你？ **shuí shuō nǐ?** Who is criticizing you? or Nobody is criticizing you.

你怪谁？ **Nǐ guài shuí?** Who are you blaming? or You can't blame anyone.

Note 4: 老 **Lǎo** 'always', see 10.4 Note 1.

4.6 | *Pronouns and conjunctions*

Pronouns, like nouns, may be linked by conjunctions, such as 和 **hé** (跟 **gēn**, 同 **tóng** and 与 **yǔ**) 'and' and 或 **huò** 'or' (see 1.4):

你和我	**Nǐ hé wǒ**	you and me
这个或那个	**zhèi gè huò nèi gè**	this one or that one

5 | Adjectives and attributives

5.1 | *Attributives*

Attributives are words or expressions used to qualify nouns. They may either describe or delimit them. In Chinese, all attributives precede the word they qualify. This contrasts with English where many attributives, e.g. relative clauses, prepositional and participial phrases, follow the noun.

5.2 | *Adjectives as attributives*

When *adjectives* are used as attributives in Chinese, a distinction can be made between monosyllabic adjectives and adjectives with more than one syllable.

5.2.1 | Monosyllabic adjectives

Monosyllabic adjectives are placed directly before the nouns they qualify:

旧书	*jiù* **shū**	*old* books
好朋友	*hǎo* **péngyou**	*good* friends
一条红裙子	**yī tiáo** *hóng* **qúnzi**	a *red* skirt
一个大家庭	**yī gè** *dà* **jiātíng**	a *big* family
我的一副黑眼镜	**wǒde yī fù** *hēi* **yǎnjìng**	a pair of *sunglasses* of mine

你的那个<u>小</u>背包	**nǐde nèi gè *xiǎo* bèibāo**	that small knapsack of yours
这是<u>真</u>皮。	**Zhè shì *zhēn* pí.**	This is *real* leather.
那是一个<u>新</u>手表。	**Nà shì yī gè *xīn* shǒubiǎo.**	That is a *new* watch.

Note: A monosyllabic adjective attached to a noun may often become an established word or expression and take on a distinctive meaning of its own: 大人 **dàren** 'adult' (*lit.* big person), 小费 **xiǎofèi** 'tip, gratuity' (*lit.* small fee), 公园 **gōngyuán** 'park' (*lit.* public garden), 私人 **sīrén** 'personal', 'private' (*lit.* private person), etc.

5.2.2 | Polysyllabic adjectives and **de**

If the adjective has more than one syllable, the particle 的 **de** is generally used between the adjective and the noun it qualifies:

<u>漂亮</u>的衣服	***piàoliang* de yīfu**	*beautiful* clothes
<u>年轻</u>的姑娘	***niánqīng* de gūniang**	*young* girls
一个<u>错误</u>的决定	**yī gè *cuòwù* de juédìng**	a *wrong* decision
<u>软绵绵</u>的地毯	***ruǎnmiānmiān* de dìtǎn**	*soft* carpet

The same general principle applies when a monosyllabic adjective is preceded by an adverb of degree:

<u>很新</u>的衣服	***hěn xīn* de yīfu**	very new clothes
一个<u>十分重</u>的包裹	**yī gè *shífēn zhòng* de bāoguǒ**	a very heavy parcel
一所<u>极大</u>的房子	**yī suǒ *jí dà* de fángzi**	an extremely big house

5.2.3 | Disyllabic adjectives and **de**

However, a limited number of common two-syllable adjectives are used *without* **de**. Idiomatic phrases such as 很多 **hěn duō** 'many' and 不少 **bù shǎo** 'quite a few' may be included with them:

<u>彩色</u>电视	***cǎisè* diànshì**	colour television
<u>根本</u>原则	***gēnběn* yuánzé**	fundamental principles
<u>很多</u>人	***hěn duō* rén**	a lot of people
<u>不少</u>事	***bù shǎo* shì**	quite a few matters
<u>不少</u>时间	***bù shǎo* shíjiān**	quite some time

Note 1: Other disyllabic adjectives which do not usually require **de** are: 一切 **yīqiè** 'all', 个别 **gèbié** 'specific', 新式 **xīnshì** 'new-style', 'modern', 主要 **zhǔyào** 'primary', etc.

Note 2: Disyllabic attributives without **de** may often be used with disyllabic nouns to form idiomatic expressions: 旅行支票 **lǚxíng zhīpiào** 'traveller's cheque', 圣诞礼物 **shèngdàn lǐwù** 'Christmas present', 百货商店 **bǎihuò shāngdiàn** 'department store' (*lit.* hundred-goods shop), 电视节目 **diànshì jiémù** 'television programme', etc.

5.3 | *Nominal attributives*

Nouns may also act as *nominal attributives*. Whether monosyllabic or polysyllabic, they do not generally require the particle 的 **de**. In some cases the resulting expressions have become established terms in the language, as in the first three examples below:

书架	*shū jià*	>	书架	*shūjià*	*bookshelf*
电影院	*diànyǐng yuàn*	>	电影院	*diànyǐngyuàn*	*cinema* (*lit. film* house)
时间表	*shíjiān biǎo*	>	时间表	*shíjiānbiǎo*	*timetable*
语法书	*yǔfǎ shū*				*grammar book*
电话号码	*diànhuà hàomǎ*				*telephone number*
十镑罚款	*shí bàng fákuǎn*				*ten pound fine*
两英里路	*liǎng yīnglǐ lù*				*two miles distance*

Note: Material nouns are often used as nominal attributives: 一扇铁门 yī shàn *tiě* mén 'an iron gate', 一堵砖墙 yī dǔ *zhuān* qiáng 'a brick wall', 一条金项链 yī tiáo *jīn* xiàngliàn 'a gold necklace', 一件皮夹克 yī jiàn *pí* jiākè 'a leather jacket', etc.

5.3.1 | Nominal attributives and **de**

The particle 的 **de** may be used between a nominal attributive and the noun it qualifies, but in these cases it indicates either possession or close association:

爸爸的领带	*bàba de lǐngdài*	father's tie
学校的运动场	*xuéxiào de yùndòngchǎng*	the school's sportsfield

Note: Compare this with the use of de in possessive pronouns: 我的鞋 *wǒde* xié 'my shoes', 他的/她的袜子 *tāde* wàzi 'his/her socks/stockings', etc.

5.4 | *Prepositional and postpositional phrases as attributives*

Prepositional phrases (e.g. 靠床 *kào* chuáng 'against the bed', see Chapter 19) and *postpositional phrases* (e.g. 桌子下 zhuōzi *xià* 'under the table', see Chapter 11), when used as attributives, always require **de**:

(1)   Prepositional phrases:

靠墙的桌子	*kào qiáng de zhuōzi*	the desk/table against the wall
沿路的商店	*yán lù de shāngdiàn*	the shops along the road

(2)   Postpositional phrases:

屋子里的家具	*wūzi li de jiājù*	furniture in the room
墙上的标语	*qiáng shàng de biāoyǔ*	slogans on the wall

5.5 | *Verbal phrases or clauses as attributives*

Attributives in Chinese become more complex when they contain verbs. Below are some examples of verbal phrase or clause attributives. They always require the use of the particle 的 **de**:

(1)   Verbal phrases:

卖报纸的 商店	*mài bàozhǐ de shāngdiàn*	a shop *that sells newspapers*
新来的秘书	*xīn lái de mìshū*	the secretary *who has just come*
有钱的家庭	*yǒu qián de jiātíng*	families *which have money*
要洗的衣服	*yào xǐ de yīfu*	clothes *which need washing*

(2)   Verbal clauses:

你要付的钱	*nǐ yào fù de qián*	the money *you will have to pay*
你叫的菜	*nǐ jiào de cài*	the dish(es) *you have ordered*
他们去中国 的那(一)天	*tāmen qù Zhōngguó de nèi (yī) tiān*	the day *they went to China*
革命开始的 地方	*gémìng kāishǐ de dìfang*	the place *where the revolution started*

5.6 The order of sequential attributives

Where attributives of various types (adjectival, nominal or verbal) occur in one sentence, they must follow one of the following sequences:

(1) An adjectival attributive will always precede a nominal attributive:

黑皮鞋	*hēi pí xié*	*black leather* shoes
灰色的绒大衣	*huīsè de róng dàyī*	[a] *grey felt* coat

(2) An adjectival attributive with 的 de always comes before an adjectival attributive without 的 de:

干净的小房间	*gānjìng de xiǎo fángjiān*	[a] *clean, small* room
很高的白房子	*hěn gāo de bái fángzi*	[a] *very high white* house

(3) A verbal attributive invariably precedes all other attributives:

会画画儿的新同学	*huì huà huàr de xīn tóngxué*	[a] *new* coursemate *who can draw/paint*
戴眼镜的女老师	*dài yǎnjìng de nǚ lǎoshī*	[the] *woman* teacher *who wears glasses*

5.7 Demonstrative and numeral phrases with other attributives

Demonstrative and numeral phrases precede all attributives:

这两条红裙子	*zhè liǎng tiáo hóng qúnzi*	*these two red* skirts
那些看中文杂志的人	*nà/nèi xiē kàn Zhōngwén zázhì de rén*	*those* people *who read Chinese magazines*
那只你喜欢的小花猫	*nà/nèi zhī nǐ xǐhuan de xiǎo huā māo*	*that little tabby* cat *(which) you like*

Note: The only exception is that with verbal attributives the demonstrative/numeral phrase may come after the attributive:

看中文杂志的那些人	*kàn Zhōngwén zázhì de nà/nèi xiē rén*	*those* people *who read Chinese magazines*
你喜欢的那只小花猫	*nǐ xǐhuan de nà/nèi zhī xiǎo huā māo*	*that little tabby* cat *(which) you like*

5.8 | Possessive pronoun and other attributives

A possessive pronoun will precede all qualifying phrases (e.g. demonstrative/numeral phrase and attributives):

我的三个好朋友	**wǒde sān gè hǎo péngyou**	*my three good* friends
你的那件新买的皮夹克	**nǐde nèi jiàn xīn mǎi de pí jiākè**	*that newly-bought leather* jacket *of yours*

5.9 | Ér between adjectives

When two similar adjectives qualify the same noun, they are usually joined together by the conjunction 而 ér 'as well as':

一个年轻而漂亮的姑娘	**(yī gè) niánqīng ér piàoliang de gūniang**	(a) young, beautiful girl
一间干净而整齐的房间	**(yī jiān) gānjìng ér zhěngqí de fángjiān**	(a) clean and tidy room

5.10 | Omission of the noun following an attributive

If the context makes it clear, the noun following the attributive can be omitted, though in these cases **de** must always be retained:

我喜欢那个新的。	**Wǒ xǐhuan nèi gè xīn de.**	(*lit.* I like that mw new p) I like that new one.
这是我昨天买的。	**Zhè shì wǒ zuótiān mǎi de.**	(*lit.* this be I yesterday buy p) This is what I bought yesterday.

5.11 | Attributives in word-formation

Finally, in Chinese any grammatical category or construction may be attached without 的 **de** to a following noun headword to become a word or idiom in the language:

养老金	**yǎnglǎojīn**	old-age pension (*lit.* support-old-money)
轻音乐	**qīngyīnyuè**	light music (*lit.* light-music)

旅行社	*lǚxíngshè*	travel agent (*lit.* travel-society)
双人床	*shuāngrénchuáng*	double bed (*lit.* two-people-bed)
录音机	*lùyīnjī*	tape recorder (*lit.* record-sound-machine)

Note: The italics mark out the attributives from the (non-italicised) headwords.

Part II

Verbs

 Introduction

Verbs in Chinese (as in English) may be divided into three major categories: the verb 是 **shì** 'to be', the verb 有 **yǒu** 'to have' and a broad set of verbs that may be loosely called action verbs. 是 **Shì** 'to be' is used to introduce nominal predicates. It does not occur with adjectival predicates, which come directly after the (pro)nominal subject without any copula, usually with the reinforcement of a degree adverb. Many such adjectives, if followed by the particle 了 **le**, can acquire a function similar to verbs; we have called these state verbs, since they signify state rather than action. 有 **Yǒu** 'to have', as well as indicating possession, may express existence, providing the structure for introductory phrases like 'there is/are' in English. Action verbs embrace a wide range of semantic groups including motion verbs, modal verbs, attitudinal verbs, intentional verbs, dative verbs, causative verbs, etc. Analysis of these groups enables the characterisation of many verbal constructions and their functions.

One feature common to all verbs in Chinese is that they do not conjugate for tense. The time of the action specified by the verb is normally indicated by placing a time expression before the verb or at the beginning of the sentence. Chinese verbs do have to be related to aspect, however, in that there needs to be some indication of whether the action has been completed, is ongoing, or is part of past experience. This is achieved by introducing an aspect marker 了 **le**, 过 **guo**, or 着 **zhe** as a suffix to the verb, or 在 **zài** directly before the verb. Action verbs without aspect markers usually express habitual action or intention.

Expressions indicating location, like time expressions, come before the verb. This means that the action of a verb is always expressed against a previously established setting of time and place.

Everything that comes after the verb (apart from the object) we have put in the category of complement. The various types of complement, indicating duration, frequency, result, direction, manner, consequential state, etc., follow logically from the action of the verb. One interesting feature of result and direction complements is that they can be converted into potential complements. Such potential complements have a slightly different emphasis from 能 **néng** 'to be able', which is one of a substantial number of modal verbs in Chinese.

Chinese, as a verb-oriented language, encodes most ideas in terms of verbs (instead of prepositions, abstract nouns, long attributives, etc.). It is therefore important to understand the central role of verbs in Chinese sentences and the various syntactic elements associated with them.

6 Adjectival and nominal predicates; the verb **shì**

6.1 Adjectival predicates

In this chapter we deal with predicates which describe or define the subject. In English such predicates would normally use the verb 'to be' as a *copula* or *link verb*. In Chinese they are slightly more complex, particularly in the case of adjectival predicates.

6.2 Adjectival predicates and the verb 'to be'

In an adjectival predicate the verb 'to be' is not normally used. This is a distinctive feature of Chinese:

她很高。	**Tā hěn gāo.**	(*lit.* she very tall) She is (very) tall.
这所房子的 租金很贵。	**Zhèi suǒ fángzi de** **zūjīn hěn guì.**	(*lit.* this mw house p rent very expensive) The rent of this house is (very) expensive.

6.2.1 Adjectival predicates and degree adverbs

The adjective used in such an adjectival predicate must always be modified by a *degree adverb*, most commonly 很 **hěn** 'very'. 很 **Hěn** is often unstressed, when it carries little meaning:

我很难过。	**Wǒ hěn nánguò.**	(*lit.* I very sad) I am (very) sad.
这件事 很奇怪。	**Zhèi jiàn shì** **hěn qíguài.**	(*lit.* this mw matter very strange) This matter is (very) strange.
那个人 很可靠。	**Nèi gè rén** **hěn kěkào.**	(*lit.* that mw person very reliable) That person is (very) reliable.

Other degree adverbs, unlike 很 **hěn**, are normally stressed. The most common are 真 **zhēn** 'really', 相当 **xiāngdāng** 'fairly', 非常 **fēicháng** or 十分 **shífēn** 'extremely':

那所学校 真大。	**Nèi suǒ xuéxiào** **zhēn dà.**	That school is *really* big.
那个孩子 相当聪明。	**Nèi gè háizi** ***xiāngdāng*** **cōngming.**	That child is *fairly* clever.
这个礼堂 非常宽敞。	**Zhèi gè lǐtáng** ***fēicháng* kuānchang.**	This hall is *extremely* spacious.
这条街 十分繁忙。	**Zhèi tiáo jiē** ***shífēn* fánmáng.**	This street is *extremely* busy.

Note: If a degree adverb is not used with an adjectival predicate, a contrast is implied:

这本书有用。	**Zhèi běn shū *yǒuyòng*.**	This book is useful (but that one isn't).
昨天凉快。	**Zuótiān *liángkuài*.**	Yesterday was cool (but today isn't).

6.2.2	Adjectival predicates in the negative

However, there is no need for a degree adverb when the adjectival predicate is negated by 不 **bù** 'not':

这个问题 不重要。	**Zhèi gè wèntí** **bù zhòngyào.**	(*lit.* this mw problem not important) This problem is not important.
那把椅子 不舒服。	**Nèi bǎ yǐzi** **bù shūfu.**	(*lit.* that mw chair not comfortable) That chair is not comfortable.

If both 很 **hěn** and 不 **bù** are present, the word order becomes important to the meaning:

这个问题 不很重要。	**Zhèi gè** **wèntí *bù hěn*** **zhòngyào.**	(*lit.* this mw problem not very important) This problem is not very important.
那把椅子 很不舒服。	**Nèi bǎ yǐzi** ***hěn bù* shūfu.**	(*lit.* that mw chair very not comfortable) That chair is very uncomfortable.

45

6.2.3
Adjectival predicates followed by verbs

Adjectival predicates are often followed by a verb (phrase) to indicate the area in which the quality or property expressed in the adjective applies:

这个菜 很好吃。	**Zhèi gè cài hěn hǎochī.**	(*lit.* this mw dish very good-eat) This dish is delicious.
她的英文 很难懂。	**Tāde Yīngwén hěn nán dǒng.**	(*lit.* her English very difficult- understand) Her English is difficult to understand.
中文语法 很容易学。	**Zhōngwén yǔfǎ hěn róngyì xué.**	(*lit.* Chinese grammar very easy learn) Chinese grammar is easy to learn.

Note: 好 **hǎo** 'good', as in the first example, may be followed by a number of verbs to form established words or expressions: 好听 **hǎotīng** 'pleasant to the ear', 好看 **hǎokàn** 'good-looking', 好玩 **hǎowán** 'enjoyable', etc.; 难 **nán** 'difficult' can be used similarly to convey the opposite meaning: 难吃 **nánchī** 'unpleasant to the taste', 难看 **nánkàn** 'ugly', 难听 **nántīng** 'unpleasant to the ear', etc.

6.3 | ***Non-gradable adjectives as attributives***

In the examples above, the adjectives may be described as *gradable* in that they can be modified by degree adverbs. Adjectives which have a more definite either–or quality (e.g. 男 **nán** 'male', 女 **nǚ** 'female', 真 **zhēn** 'true', 假 **jiǎ** 'false', etc.) and are therefore not so readily modified, may be called *non-gradable* adjectives. These non-gradable adjectives, when functioning as adjectival predicates, commonly require the use of the copula 是 **shì** in conjunction with the particle 的 **de**:

这是真的。	**Zhè *shì* zhēn *de*.**	(*lit.* this be true p) This is true.
他的话 是假的。	**Tāde huà *shì* jiǎ *de*.**	(*lit.* his words be false p) What he said is untrue.
这些服装 是新式的。	**Zhèi xiē fúzhuāng *shì* xīnshì *de*.**	(*lit.* these clothes be new-type p) These clothes are fashionable.

Most non-gradable adjectives exist in complementary pairs, either as antonyms (e.g. 正确 **zhèngquè** 'correct' and 错误 **cuòwù** 'false') or as positives and negatives (e.g. 正式 **zhèngshì** 'formal' and 非正式 **fēi zhèngshì** 'informal').

Note: Other common non-gradable adjectives and adjectival idioms are: 死 **sǐ** 'dead', 活 **huó** 'alive'; 雌 **cí** 'female' (animal), 雄 **xióng** 'male' (animal); 天然 **tiānrán** 'natural', 人造 **rénzào** 'man-made', 'artificial'; 有可能 **yǒu kěnéng** 'possible', 不可能 **bù kěnéng** 'impossible', etc.

6.3.1   Attributives of shape, colour or material

Terms of shape, colour or material similarly tend to indicate an absolute either–or quality or property and as adjectival predicates follow the same . . . 是 **shì** . . . 的 **de** format:

那张桌子 是圆的。	**Nèi zhāng zhuōzi** **shì yuán de.**	(*lit.* that mw table be round p) That table is round.
他的衬衫 是白的。	**Tāde chènshān** **shì bái de.**	(*lit.* his shirt/blouse be white p) His shirt/blouse is white.
这条裙子 是布的。	**Zhèi tiáo qúnzi** **shì bù de.**	(*lit.* this mw skirt be cloth p) This skirt is made of cloth.

Note 1: Other terms in this category include: (shape) 方 **fāng** 'square', 扁 **biǎn** 'flat', 长方形 **chángfāngxíng** 'oblong'; (colour) 红 **hóng** 'red', 蓝 **lán** 'blue', 黄 **huáng** 'yellow', 紫 **zǐ** 'purple', 黑 **hēi** 'black', 褐色 **hèsè**/咖啡色 **kāfēisè** 'brown', 灰色 **huīsè** 'grey'; (material) 金 **jīn** 'gold', 银 **yín** 'silver', 塑料 **sùliào** 'plastic', 尼龙 **nílóng** 'nylon', 皮 **pí** 'leather', 木 **mù** 'wood', 铁 **tiě** 'iron', 钢 **gāng** 'steel', 瓷 **cí** 'porcelain'.

Note 2: Regarding terms of colour and shape, it is possible to have different degrees of, for example, 'redness' or 'roundness'; it is therefore possible to say:

这朵花很红。	**Zhèi duǒ huā** **hěn hóng.**	This flower is very red.
那个盘子 不太圆。	**Nèi gè pánzi** **bù tài yuán.**	That plate is not quite round.

6.4   *Nominal and pronominal predicates*

Nouns and pronouns can also act as *nominal and pronominal predicates*, where they generally require the use of the copula or link verb 是 **shì** 'to be':

她是我的 笔友。	**Tā shì wǒde** **bǐyǒu.**	(*lit.* she be my pen-friend) She is my pen-friend.

这是王先生。	**Zhè *shì* Wáng xiānsheng.**	(*lit*. this be Wang mister) This is Mr Wang. (as in an introduction)
我每个月的收入是一千多镑。	**Wǒ měi gè yuè de shōurù *shì* yī qiān duō bàng.**	(*lit*. I every mw month p income be one thousand more pound) My monthly income is over a thousand pounds.
这个城市的市长是谁?	**Zhèi gè chéngshì de shìzhǎng *shì* shéi?**	(*lit*. this mw city p mayor be who) Who is the mayor of this town?
这是什么?	**Zhè *shì* shénme?**	(*lit*. this be what) What is this?
今年是猪年。	**Jīnnián *shì* zhū nián.**	(*lit*. this-year be pig year) This is the year of the pig.

Note: In the Chinese lunar calendar, the years are divided into cycles of twelve years, with each year named after a particular animal, real or imaginary: i.e. rat, ox, tiger, rabbit, dragon, snake, horse, sheep, monkey, rooster, dog, pig. Someone born in the year of the pig, for example, may say 我属猪。**Wǒ shǔ zhū** 'I belong to the pig'.

我的爱好是爬山。	**Wǒde àihào *shì* pá shān.**	(*lit*. my hobby be climbing-hills) My hobby is hill-walking/ mountain-climbing.
我(的)父亲是大夫。	**Wǒ(de) fùqīn *shì* dàifu.**	(*lit*. my father be doctor) My father is a (medical) doctor.
这儿是派出所/警察局。	**Zhèr *shì* pàichūsuǒ/ jǐngchájú.**	(*lit*. here be police-station) This is the police station.

Note 1: 派出所 **Pàichūsuǒ** (*lit*. dispatch-out-unit) and 公安局 **gōng'ānjú** (*lit*. public-security bureau) are used in mainland China for 'police station', and 警察局 **jǐngchájú** (*lit*. police bureau) in Chinese communities outside mainland China.

Note 2: It will be apparent from the above examples that 是 **shì**, in contrast with other verbs, may be followed by a noun which is of either definite or indefinite reference. Where 是 **shì** is defining something (or someone), the reference is indefinite; where it is locating something (or someone) the reference is definite. Compare:

这是一个图书馆。	**Zhè shì (yī gè) túshūguǎn.**	This is a library.
这是图书馆。	**Zhè shì túshūguǎn.**	This is the library (you're looking for).

Adjectival
and
nominal
predicates;
the verb
shì

6.4.1 | Verbs resembling shì

A number of verbs can be said to resemble the copula 是 shì:

我姓李。	**Wǒ xìng Lǐ.**	(*lit.* I surname Li) My surname is Li.
我叫爱玲。	**Wǒ jiào Àilíng.**	(*lit.* I call Ailing) My name is Ailing.
这个孩子 像他妈妈， 不像他 爸爸。	**Zhèi gè háizi** **xiàng tā māma,** **bù xiàng tā** **bàba.**	(*lit.* this mw child resemble his mother, not resemble his father) This child is like his mother, not his father.
我属龙。	**Wǒ shǔ lóng.**	(*lit.* I belong dragon) I was born in the year of the dragon. (See note under 6.4.)

6.4.2 | Nominal predicates without a copula

However, nouns indicating nationality, personal characteristics, age, or dates, price, etc., may be used as nominal predicates without a copula or link verb:

我英国人。	**Wǒ Yīngguó rén.**	(*lit.* I England person) I am from England.
我妹妹 金头发。	**Wǒ mèimei** *jīn tóufa.*	(*lit.* my younger-sister golden hair) My younger sister is a blonde.
我二十一岁。	**Wǒ èrshí yī suì.**	(*lit.* I twenty-one years-of-age) I am twenty-one.
今天星期一。	**Jīntiān xīngqī yī.**	(*lit.* today Monday) Today is Monday.
这双鞋 十二镑。	**Zhèi shuāng xié** *shí èr bàng.*	(*lit.* this pair shoes twelve pound) This pair of shoes costs twelve pounds.

6.5 | *The copula* shì *in its negative form*

In the negative form of a non-gradable adjectival predicate (6.3 and 6.3.1) or a nominal/pronominal predicate (6.4 and 6.4.1), the copula 是 shì is always present with 不 bù placed immediately before it:

他的裤子 不是黑的。	**Tāde kùzi** *bù shì* **hēi de.**	(*lit.* his trousers not be black p) His trousers are not black.
这些窗帘 不是绸的。	**Zhèi xiē chuānglián** *bù shì* **chóu de.**	(*lit.* this mw curtain not be silk p) These curtains are not made of silk.
今天不是 星期三。	**Jīntiān** *bù shì* **xīngqī sān.**	(*lit.* today not be week three) Today is not Wednesday.
他不是 美国人。	**Tā** *bù shì* **Měiguórén.**	(*lit.* he not be American) He is not American.

Note: 是 **Shì** may also be used as an *intensifier* for emphatic statements. This is discussed in detail in Chapter 22.

7 | The verb **yǒu**; comparisons

7.1 | The functions of **yǒu**

The verb 有 **yǒu** has a number of functions. Primarily it indicates possession or existence (the latter is discussed in 11.5), but it also appears in expressions of comparison.

7.1.1 | **Yǒu** indicating possession

We start here with 有 **yǒu** as a verb of possession meaning 'to have':

我有(一) 个弟弟。	**Wǒ yǒu (yī)** **gè dìdi.**	(*lit.* I have one mw younger-brother) I have a younger brother.
他有很 多钱。	**Tā yǒu hěn** **duō qián.**	(*lit.* He have very much money) He has a lot of money.
蜘蛛有 八只脚。	**Zhīzhū yǒu** **bā zhī jiǎo.**	(*lit.* spider have eight mw foot) Spiders have eight legs.
这个柜子有 五个抽屉。	**Zhèi gè guìzi** **yǒu wǔ gè** **chōuti.**	(*lit.* this mw cabinet have five mw drawer) This cabinet has five drawers.
明天我有 (一)个约会。	**Míngtiān wǒ** **yǒu (yī) gè** **yuēhuì.**	(*lit.* tomorrow I have one mw appointment) I have an appointment tomorrow.

7.1.2   **Měi** as negative of **yǒu**

有 **Yǒu** is negated by placing 没 **méi** (NOT 不 **bù**) before it:

我没有 自行车。	**Wǒ** *méi yǒu* **zìxíngchē.**	(*lit.* I not have bicycle) I haven't got a bicycle.
他们没有 电视机。	**Tāmen** *méi yǒu* **diànshìjī.**	(*lit.* they not have television-set) They don't have a television.

Note: In a negative sentence, the object of 有 **yǒu** is not normally qualified by the 'numeral 一 **yī** (+ measure word)', because in Chinese there is no need to quantify what one doesn't possess:

*我没有一辆 自行车。	**Wǒ** *méi yǒu* *yī liàng* **zìxíngchē.**	(*lit.* *I not have one mw bicycle)

没有 **Méi yǒu** may often be abbreviated to 没 **méi** in speech:

我现在 没工作。	**Wǒ xiànzài** **méi gōngzuò.**	(*lit.* I now not-have work) I haven't got a job at the moment.

7.1.3   **Yǒu** indicating change or development

有 **Yǒu** often takes modified or unmodified verbal objects to indicate change or development:

他的中文 有进步。	**Tāde Zhōngwén** *yǒu jìnbù.*	(*lit.* His Chinese have progress) He has made progress in his Chinese.
她家的生活 水平有很大 的提高。	**Tā jiā de shēnghuó** **shuǐpíng** *yǒu hěn* **dà de** *tígāo.*	(*lit.* Her family p living standard have very big p rise) The living standard of her family has greatly improved.
英国的经济 最近有一些 发展。	**Yīngguó de jīngjì** **zuìjìn** *yǒu yī xiē* *fāzhǎn.*	(*lit.* Britain p economy recently have some develop) There has been some development in Britain's economy recently.
这儿的情况 有不少变化。	**Zhèr de qíngkuàng** *yǒu bù shǎo* *biànhuà.*	(*lit.* here p situation have not-few change) There have been quite a few changes in the situation over here.

| 她的收入有<u>一些</u>增加。 | **Tāde shōurù yǒu yī xiē zēngjiā.** | (*lit.* Her income have some increase) There has been some increase in her income. |

Yǒu forming idiomatic expressions

有 **Yǒu** often takes abstract noun objects to form idiomatic expressions, which may be equivalent to English adjectives. These regularly function as gradable adjectival predicates and can be modified by adverbs of degree:

| 这本小说很<u>有意思</u>。 | **Zhèi běn xiǎoshuō hěn yǒu yìsi.** | (*lit.* this mw novel very have meaning) This novel is very interesting. |
| 那个演员<u>非常有名</u>。 | **Nèi gè yǎnyuán fēicháng yǒu míng.** | (*lit.* that mw actor/actress extremely have name) That actor/actress is extremely famous. |

These expressions must be negated by 没有 **méi(yǒu)**:

| 我今天晚上<u>没(有)</u>空。 | **Wǒ jīntiān wǎnshang méi(yǒu) kòng.** | (*lit.* I today evening not-have leisure) I am busy tonight. |
| 那个年轻人真<u>没(有)礼貌</u>。 | **Nèi gè niánqīng rén zhēn méi(yǒu) lǐmào.** | (*lit.* that mw young person really not-have politeness) That young person is really impolite. |

Note: Other commonly used idioms with 有 **yǒu** are 有钱 **yǒu qián** 'rich', 有学问 **yǒu xuéwèn** 'learned', 有经验 **yǒu jīngyàn** 'experienced'. For example:

那个商人很<u>有钱</u>。	**Nèi gè shāngrén hěn yǒu qián.**	That businessman is (very) rich.
那个教授很<u>有学问</u>。	**Nèi gè jiàoshòu hěn yǒu xuéwèn.**	That professor is very learned.
这个老人非常<u>有经验</u>。	**Zhèi gè lǎo rén fēicháng yǒu jīngyàn.**	This old man is extremely experienced.

Yǒu introducing adjectival predicates

有 **Yǒu** may also be used to introduce an adjectival predicate which incorporates a number:

这幢楼房有二十米高。	**Zhèi zhuàng lóufáng yǒu èrshí mǐ gāo.**	(*lit.* this mw storey-building have twenty metre high) This building is twenty metres high.
那条路有两百英里长。	**Nèi tiáo lù yǒu liǎng bǎi yīnglǐ cháng.**	(*lit.* that mw road have two hundred mile long) That road is two hundred miles long.

By extension 有 **yǒu** may be followed by 多 **duō** (how) and an adjective to express questions about age, time, distance, and so on:

你弟弟有多高?	**Nǐ dìdi yǒu duō gāo?**	(*lit.* you(r) younger-brother have how tall) How tall is your younger brother?
你妹妹有多大?	**Nǐ mèimei yǒu duō dà?**	(*lit.* you(r) younger-sister have how big) How old is your younger sister?
你家有多远?	**Nǐ jiā yǒu duō yuǎn?**	(*lit.* you(r) home have how far) How far is your home from here?

7.2	*Comparison*

Comparison in Chinese may be expressed in a number of ways. The most common makes use of the preposition 比 **bǐ** 'compared with', and follows the pattern X 比 **bǐ** Y + gradable adjective. (We noted in 6.2.1 that a gradable adjective unmodified by a degree adverb implies a contrast or comparison.)

我爸爸比我妈妈瘦。	**Wǒ bàba bǐ wǒ māma shòu.**	(*lit.* my father compare my mother thin) My father is thinner than my mother.
中文比英文难。	**Zhōngwén bǐ Yīngwén nán.**	(*lit.* Chinese compare English difficult) Chinese is more difficult than English.
来回票比单程票合算。	**Láihuípiào bǐ dānchéngpiào hésuàn.**	(*lit.* return-ticket compare single-journey-ticket fit-calculation) A return ticket is more economical than a single.

The adjective in a comparison cannot be modified by degree adverbs such as 很 **hěn** 'very', 非常 **fēicháng**, 十分 **shífēn** 'extremely', etc., and it would be wrong to say:

*中文比英文很难。	**Zhōngwén bǐ Yīngwén hěn nán.**	(*lit.* *Chinese compare English very difficult)

Emphatic or specific comparison

The degree of comparison may be made clear, however, either by using the adverbs 更 **gèng** or 还 **hái** meaning 'even more':

| 今天比 昨天更冷。 | **Jīntiān bǐ zuótiān gèng lěng.** | (*lit.* today compare yesterday even-more cold) Today is *even* colder than yesterday. |
| 这儿比那儿 还安静。 | **Zhèr bǐ nàr *hái* ānjìng.** | (*lit.* here compare there even-more quiet) It is *even* quieter here than there. |

or by tagging various kinds of *degree complements* to the adjectives:

中文比 英文难 得多。	**Zhōngwén bǐ Yīngwén nán de duō.**	(*lit.* Chinese compare English difficult p much) Chinese is *much* more difficult than English.
我妹妹比 我姐姐高 一点儿。	**Wǒ mèimei bǐ wǒ jiějie gāo yī diǎnr.**	(*lit.* my younger-sister compare my elder-sister tall one bit) My younger sister is *slightly/a bit* taller than my elder sister.
我哥哥 比我大 两岁。	**Wǒ gēge bǐ wǒ dà liǎng suì.**	(*lit.* my elder-brother compare me big two years-of-age) My elder brother is *two years* older than I am.

Note: For further discussion of degree complements see 13.6.

Negative comparison

A negative comparison can be expressed in two ways:

(1)   By placing 不 **bù** before 比 **bǐ** (i.e. X is not more . . . than Y):

| 今天不比 昨天冷。 | **Jīntiān *bù bǐ* zuótiān lěng.** | (*lit.* today not compare yesterday cold) Today is not colder than yesterday. |
| 这条路不 比那条近。 | **Zhèi tiáo lù *bù bǐ* nèi tiáo jìn.** | (*lit.* this mw road not compare that mw near) This is not a shorter way than that. |

(2)   By using the formulation X 没(有) **méi(yǒu)** Y 那么/这么 (**nàme/ zhème** 'so') adjective (i.e. X is not so . . . as Y):

今天的天气 没(有)昨天 (那么/这么) 暖和/凉快。	**Jīntiān de tiānqì** **méi(yǒu) zuótiān** **(nàme/zhème)** **nuǎnhuo/liángkuài.**	(*lit.* today p weather not-have yesterday (so) warm/cool) It's not so warm/cool today as it was yesterday.
我的围巾 没(有)你的 (那么/这么) 好看。	**Wǒde wéijīn** **méi(yǒu) nǐde** **(nàme/zhème)** **hǎokàn.**	(*lit.* my scarf not-have your (so) good-to-look-at) My scarf doesn't look as nice as yours

Note 1: As illustrated in the first example under (2), Chinese like English can concentrate on the contrasting attributive rather than expressing the comparison in full, i.e. it is not necessary to say 昨天的天气 zuótiān de tiānqì.

Note 2: This formulation with 有 yǒu may be used in a positive sentence when a question is asked:

这个有那个 便宜吗？	**Zhèi gè yǒu nèi** **gè piányi ma?**	(*lit.* this mw have that mw cheap p) Is this as cheap as that?
说日语有说 汉语那么 容易吗？	**Shuō Rìyǔ yǒu** **shuō Hànyǔ** **nàme róngyì ma?**	(*lit.* speak Japanese have speak Chinese so easy p) Is speaking Japanese as easy as speaking Chinese?

In fact these questions are asking about 'equivalence'; their meaning overlaps with that of the 一样 yīyàng structure (see 7.2.3).

7.2.3   Comparison: equivalence or similarity

Equivalence or similarity is conveyed by use of the adjective 一样 yīyàng 'the same' (*lit.* one kind) in the formulation X 跟 gēn Y 一样 yīyàng (i.e. X is the same as Y):

我的跟 你的一样。	**Wǒde gēn** **nǐde yīyàng.**	(*lit* my and your one-kind) Mine is the same as yours.

This structure can be extended by the addition of a further adjective:

那件行李 跟这件 一样轻。	**Nèi jiàn xínglǐ** **gēn zhèi jiàn** **yīyàng qīng.**	(*lit.* that mw luggage and this mw same light) That piece of luggage is as light as this one.
我和你 一样累。	**Wǒ hé nǐ** **yīyàng lèi.**	(*lit.* I and you same tired) I am just as tired as you are.

Note: We have seen earlier that 跟 gēn, 和 hé, 同 tóng and 与 yǔ 'and' may be used interchangeably (see 1.4).

7.3 | *Comparatives and superlatives*

Where only one item is mentioned in a comparison, a simple comparative or superlative expression like 比较 **bǐjiào** 'comparatively' or 最 **zuì** 'most' is placed before the adjective:

| 这个牌子
的蜜糖
比较便宜。 | **Zhèi gè páizi**
de mìtáng
bǐjiào piányi. | (*lit.* this mw brand p honey comparatively cheap) This brand of honey is (relatively) cheaper. |
| 那个公园
最美丽。 | **Nèi gè gōngyuán**
zuì měilì. | (*lit.* that mw park most beautiful) That park is the most beautiful [of all]. |

8 Verbs and aspect markers

8.1 | *Action, state, and dative verbs*

Having discussed 是 **shì** 'to be' and 有 **yǒu** 'to have', we will now look at action verbs, state verbs and dative verbs.

8.2 | *Action verbs*

Action verbs signify movement or action (e.g. 打 **dǎ** 'hit', 'strike', 'beat'; 跑 **pǎo** 'run'; 喝 **hē** 'drink'). Apart from being used in imperatives (see 8.6), they are generally employed for narrative purposes. One of the most prominent features of action verbs in narration is that they are almost always used in conjunction with an *aspect marker*, 了 **le**, 过 **guo** or 着 **zhe** (suffixed to the verb), or 在 **zài** (preceding the verb). However, action verbs may also occur without any marker, when they describe one of the following:

(1) *Habitual action*:

| 孩子们
天天看
电视。 | **Háizimen**
tiāntiān *kàn*
diànshì. | (*lit.* children day-day see television) The children watch television every day. |
| 马吃草。 | **Mǎ** *chī* **cǎo.** | (*lit.* horse eat grass) Horses eat grass. |

(2) *Permanent or long-term characteristics*:

| 我一九
三五年
出世。 | **Wǒ yī jiǔ**
sān wǔ nián
chūshì. | (*lit.* I one-nine-three-five year come-out-into-world) I was born in 1935. |

| 我信 | **Wǒ** *xìn* | (lit. I believe Christ-religion) |
| 基督教。 | **Jīdūjiào.** | I am a Christian. |

Note: Other religions (branches of religion): 佛教 **Fójiào** 'Buddhism', 天主教 **Tiānzhǔjiào** 'Catholicism', 伊斯兰教 **Yīsīlánjiào** 'Islam', 道教 **Dàojiào** 'Taoism', etc.

(3) *Intended action*:

我现在去	**Wǒ** *xiànzài*	(lit. I now go office)
办公室。	*qù* **bàngōngshì.**	I am going to the office now.
今天我	**Jīntiān wǒ**	(lit. today I invite-guest) It's on
请客。	*qǐngkè.*	me today.

8.3 | *Aspect markers*

The aspect markers 了 **le**, 过 **guo**, 着 **zhe** and 在 **zài**:

8.3.1 | **Le**

了 **Le** indicates the '*completion of an action*':

我写了	**Wǒ** *xiěle*	(lit. I write asp three mw letter)
三封信。	**sān fēng xìn.**	I wrote three letters.
我洗了	**Wǒ** *xǐle* (yī)	(lit. I wash asp one mw bath/
(一)个澡。	**gè zǎo.**	shower) I took a bath/shower.
我买了	**Wǒ** *mǎile*	(lit. I buy asp two mw come-return
两张来	**liǎng zhāng**	ticket) I bought two return tickets.
回票。	**láihuí piào.**	

As in these three examples, the object of a verb with 了 **le** is usually something specified or defined. If the object is a single unmodified noun, the sentence is generally felt to be incomplete:

*我吃了饭。 **Wǒ** *chīle* **fàn.** (lit. *I eat asp cooked-rice)

This problem is resolved if the object is specified or the sentence is extended:

| 我吃了 | **Wǒ** *chīle* | (lit. I eat asp two bowl rice) |
| 两碗饭。 | **liǎng wǎn fàn.** | I ate two bowls of rice. |

我吃了饭 就回家。	**Wǒ** *chīle* **fàn** *jiù huí jiā.*	(*lit.* I eat asp rice-meal then return home) I'll go home as soon as I finish the meal.

Note: For a full discussion of composite sentences like this last extended sentence, see Chapter 24.

It must be stressed that aspect markers are NOT indicators of tense. Whereas in English the form of the verb changes to indicate tense, in Chinese time expressions specify the time of the action of the verb (compare Chapter 10).

我昨天看 小说, 今天 写信, 明天 收拾房子。	**Wǒ** *zuótiān* **kàn xiǎoshuō,** *jīntiān* **xiě xìn,** *míngtiān* **shōushi fángzi.**	(*lit.* I yesterday read novel, today write letter, tomorrow tidy-up house) Yesterday I read a novel, today I'm writing letters and tomorrow I will tidy the house.

A completed action with 了 **le** may take place in the past or future.

我昨天下 了课以后 去看电影。	**Wǒ** *zuótiān* **xiàle kè yǐhòu qù kàn diànyǐng.**	(*lit.* I yesterday finish asp lesson after-that go see film) Yesterday when I'd finished class, I went to see a film.
我明天下 了课以后 去看电影。	**Wǒ** *míngtiān* **xiàle kè yǐhòu qù kàn diànyǐng.**	(*lit.* I tomorrow finish asp lesson after-that go see film) Tomorrow when I finish class, I'll go and see a film.

To express the negative of completed action, i.e. to say what did not happen in the past or has not happened, 没(有) **méi(yǒu)** is used, WITH-OUT 了 **le**:

他没(有)去 欧洲。	**Tā** *méi(yǒu)* **qù ōuzhōu.**	(*lit.* He not(-have) go Europe) He did not go to Europe.
谁没(有)听 昨天的 广播？	**Shéi** *méi(yǒu)* **tīng zuótiān de guǎngbō?**	(*lit.* who not(-have) listen yesterday p broadcast) Who didn't listen to yesterday's broadcast?

Note: However, 不 **bù** is used for a habitual action, whether in the past, present or future:

他以前 不抽烟。	**Tā** *yǐqián* **bù chōuyān.**	(*lit.* He before not inhale-smoke) He did not smoke before.

| 我一向不喝酒, 现在不喝, 将来也不喝。 | **Wǒ yīxiàng bù hē jiǔ, xiànzài bù hē, jiānglái yě bù hē.** | (lit. I up-to-now not drink wine, now not drink, future also not drink) I've never drunk before, I don't drink now, and I won't drink in the future. |
| 这个人从来不说脏话。 | **Zhèi gè rén cónglái bù shuō zānghuà.** | (lit. this mw person from-the-start not speak dirty words) This man has never used bad language. |

8.3.2　Guo

过 **Guo** denotes that an action is a *'past experience'*:

| 我看过京剧。 | **Wǒ kànguo Jīngjù.** | (*lit.* I see asp Beijing-drama) I have seen Peking opera. (I therefore know what it is.) |
| 我喝过茅台(酒)。 | **Wǒ hēguo máotái(jiǔ).** | (*lit.* I drink asp Maotai (wine/spirit)) I have tried Maotai. (I therefore know what it tastes like.) |

To illustrate the difference between 了 **le** and 过 **guo**, consider the following:

我们吃过北京烤鸭。	**Wǒmen chīguo Běijīng kǎoyā.**	(*lit.* we eat asp Beijing roast-duck) We have tried Beijing duck before.
那天我们吃了北京烤鸭。	**Nèi tiān wǒmen chīle Běijīng kǎoyā.**	(*lit.* that day we eat asp Beijing roast-duck) We had Beijing duck that day.
他们今年去过台湾。	**Tāmen jīnnián qùguo Táiwān.**	(*lit.* they this-year go asp Taiwan) They went to Taiwan this year (but they are back now).
他们今年去了台湾。	**Tāmen jīnnián qùle Táiwān.**	(*lit.* they this-year go asp Taiwan) They went to Taiwan this year (and they are still there).

The sentence 他们今年去过台湾。 **Tāmen jīnnián qùguo Táiwān** shows that 过 **guo** can be used to indicate experience within a defined period of time, 今年 **jīnnián** 'this year' (as well as experience up to the present). The defined period can of course be any period including the immediate past. Hence the colloquial enquiry 你吃过饭没有 **Nǐ chīguo fàn méiyǒu** 'Have you eaten?' is acceptable because the speaker has subconsciously in mind the immediate meal-time.

没(有) **Méi(yǒu)** also functions as the negative in a past experience sentence, but in this construction 过 **guo** is retained:

他没(有)	**Tā méi(yǒu)**	(*lit.* he not go asp Africa)
去过非洲。	**qùguo Fēizhōu.**	He has never been to Africa.
谁没(有)	**Shéi méi(yǒu)**	(*lit.* who not(-have) drink asp
喝过茅台？	**hēguo máotái?**	Maotai) Who has not tried Maotai?

8.3.3 Zài

在 **Zài**, which is placed before the verb, indicates an '*action in progress*':

交响乐团	**Jiāoxiǎng yuè**	(*lit.* join-sound music-group asp:
在演奏	**tuán zài yǎnzòu**	in-the-process-of play Beethoven p
贝多芬的	**Bèiduōfēn**	music-song) The symphony orchestra
乐曲。	**de yuèqǔ.**	is playing Beethoven's music.
姐姐在念	**Jiějie zài niàn**	(*lit.* elder-sister asp: in-the-process-
大学。	**dàxué.**	of read university) (My) elder sister
		is studying at the university.

Note: The use of 在 **zài** in this construction appears to derive from its function as a preposition (coverb). The fact that the sentences 他在学习。 **tā zài xuéxí** and 他在那儿学习。 **tā zài nàr xuéxí** can be seen to be identical in meaning 'He is (there) studying' would seem to confirm this point. The 那儿 **nàr** in the second sentence, in fact, provides no precise indication of place.

正 **Zhèng** 'just' is regularly used with 在 **zài** and makes the sentence slightly more emphatic:

他们正在	**Tāmen**	(*lit.* they just asp: in-the-process-of
打乒乓球。	**zhèng zài dǎ**	beat pingpong-ball) They are just
	pīngpāngqiú.	playing pingpong/table tennis.

The sentence particle 呢 **ne** may be added to 'action-in-progress' sentences to introduce a tone of mild assertion:

她(正)在收	**Tā (zhèng)**	(*lit.* she (just) asp: in-the-process-of
拾客厅呢。	**zài shōushi**	tidy-up lounge p) She is just tidying
	kètīng ne.	up the lounge.

Note: It is possible to express action in progress without 在 **zài**, employing 正 **zhèng** and 呢 **ne**:

| 他们正 | **Tāmen zhèng** | (*lit.* they just rest p) |
| 休息呢。 | **xiūxi ne.** | They are just having a rest. |

在 **Zài** can refer to defined periods of time other than the immediate present:

你近来在 做什么？	**Nǐ jìnlái zài zuò shénme?**	(*lit.* you recently asp: in-the-process-of do what) What have you been doing recently?
他去年在 学骑马。	**Tā qùnián zài xué qí mǎ.**	(*lit.* He last-year asp: in-the-process-of learn ride-horse) He was learning to ride (a horse) last year.

With a frequency adverb, it can also express continuing or persistent 'action in progress':

他们天天在 吵架。	**Tāmen *tiāntiān zài* chǎojià.**	(*lit.* they day-day asp: in-the-process-of quarrel) They are quarrelling every day.
他以前 每天晚上 都在喝酒。	**Tā yǐqián *měi tiān wǎnshang* dōu zài hē jiǔ.**	(*lit.* He before every-day evening all in-the-process-of drink wine) He used to be drinking every night.

In negative 'action-in-progress' sentences, which rarely occur, the negator 不 **bù** comes before 在 **zài**:

我不在跟 你说，我在 跟她说。	**Wǒ bù zài gēn nǐ shuō, wǒ zài gēn tā shuō.**	(*lit.* I not asp: in-the-process-of with you talk, I asp: in-the-process-of with her talk) I am not talking to you; I am talking to her.

8.3.4 | Zhe

着 **Zhe** implies either that the action is an '*accompaniment to another action*':

老师笑着说， '谢谢！'	**Lǎoshī *xiàozhe* shuō, 'Xièxie!'**	(*lit.* teacher smile asp say: thank-thank) The teacher smiling/with a smile said, 'Thanks!'
他们站着 聊天。	**Tāmen *zhànzhe* liáotiān.**	(*lit.* they stand asp chat) They stood chatting.

or a '*state resulting from an action*':

妹妹穿着 一条白裙子。	**Mèimei *chuānzhe* yī tiáo bái qúnzi.**	(*lit.* younger-sister wear asp one mw white skirt) (The) younger sister is wearing a white skirt.

61

门关着。	**Mén guānzhe.**	(*lit.* door closed asp) The door is closed.
窗开着。	**Chuāng kāizhe.**	(*lit.* window open asp) The window is open.
门上贴着 一幅对联。	**Mén shang tiēzhe yī fù duìlián.**	(*lit.* door-on paste asp one mw couplet) On the door was posted/pasted a couplet.

Note: Most verbs expressing the wearing of articles of clothing may be suffixed with 着 **zhe**: 穿着皮鞋/袜子 **chuānzhe píxíe/wàzi** 'wearing leather shoes/socks', 戴着帽子/手套 **dàizhe màozi/shǒutào** 'wearing a hat/gloves', 打着领带 **dǎzhe lǐngdài** 'wearing a tie', 围着围巾 **wéizhe wéijīn** 'wearing a scarf', etc.

(正)在 (**Zhèng**) **zài** and 着 **zhe** have similar meanings, but the following sentences illustrate the difference between them:

| 她(正)在穿 大衣。 | **Tā (zhèng)zài chuān dàyī.** | (*lit.* she right-now put-on big-coat) She is putting on an overcoat. |
| 她穿着 大衣。 | **Tā chuānzhe dàyī.** | (*lit.* she wear asp big-coat) She is wearing an overcoat. |

Note: There is some similarity between the use of 在 **zài** and 着 **zhe** when a verb-**zhe** phrase is modified by an adverbial expression:

| 她们高高兴兴 地唱着歌。 | **Tāmen gāogaoxìngxing de chàngzhe gē.** | (*lit.* they high-spirited p sing asp song) |
| 她们高高兴兴 地在唱歌。 | **Tāmen gāogaoxìngxing de zài chànggē.** | (*lit.* they high-spirited p asp: in-the-process-of sing-song) |

Both the above sentences mean 'they are/were singing happily'. If there is any distinction, the first emphasises a persistent state while the second implies an ongoing action.

It is also possible for 着 **zhe** to be used in action-in-progress sentences:

| 他们(正)在 讨论着那个 问题。 | **Tāmen (zhèng) zài tǎolùnzhe nèi gè wèntí.** | (*lit.* they just asp: in-the-process-of discuss asp that mw question) They are just discussing that question. |

8.4 | State verb

The aspect marker 了 **le** may be used with adjectival predicates (see Chapter 6) to create *state verbs*. Whereas adjectives indicate existing or permanent properties, state verbs express changed or changing features. Compare the following pairs:

State verb	Adjective
我重了两公斤。	这个箱子真重。
Wǒ *zhòngle* liǎng gōngjīn.	**Zhèi gè xiāngzi zhēn *zhòng*.**
(*lit.* I heavy asp two kilo)	(*lit.* this mw box/suitcase really heavy)
I have put on two kilos (of weight).	This box/suitcase is really heavy.
天黑了。 **Tiān *hēile*.**	天很黑。 **Tiān hěn *hēi*.**
(*lit.* sky black asp/p)	(*lit.* sky very black)
It has gone dark.	It is (very) dark.
你胖了。 **Nǐ *pàngle*.**	她很胖。 **Tā hěn *pàng*.**
(*lit.* you fat asp/p)	(*lit.* she very fat)
You've put on weight.	She is very fat.

Note 1: This use of **le** at the end of a sentence is linked with the function of 了 **le** as sentence particle (see Chapter 16).

Note 2: To say 你胖了 **nǐ pàngle** in a Chinese context is a compliment since it implies that the person you are addressing looks to be in good health.

8.5	*Dative verbs*

There are a few *dative verbs* which take two objects in the order *indirect object* followed by *direct object*.

姐姐给妹妹 一盒糖。	**Jiějie *gěi* mèimei yī hé táng.**	(The) elder sister gave (her) younger sister a box of sweets.
他送我 一支钢笔。	**Tā *sòng* wǒ yī zhī gāngbǐ.**	He gave me a pen [as a gift].
我还他 两镑钱。	**Wǒ *huán* tā liǎng bàng qián.**	I gave him back [his] two pounds.

Note: As we can see from the examples above and also those given below, aspect marker 了 **le** can generally be omitted with dative verbs indicating completed actions. But see also 8.5.2.

Certain action verbs with 给 **gěi** 'to give' as a suffix follow the same pattern:

她交给我 一篇作文。	**Tā *jiāo gěi* wǒ yī piān zuòwén.**	She handed in a composition to me.

| 我递给他
两封信。 | **Wǒ dì gěi tā
liǎng fēng xìn.** | I passed him two letters. |
| 他们带给
我一束花。 | **Tāmen dài gěi
wǒ yī shù huā.** | They brought me a bouquet
of flowers. |

This dative construction may be reversed with the subject of the verb becoming the recipient:

| 我收到她
一封信。 | **Wǒ shōudào tā
yī fēng xìn.** | (*lit.* I receive her one mw letter)
I received a letter from her. |
| 我得到他们
很多帮助。 | **Wǒ dédào tāmen
hěnduō bāngzhù.** | (*lit.* I get them very much help)
I got a lot of help from them. |

8.5.1 | Dative verbs relating to spoken activity

Some verbs relating to spoken activity may also be used in a dative construction:

他们叫我老李。	**Tāmen jiào wǒ Lǎo Lǐ.**	They call me Old Li.
他告诉我一件事。	**Tā gàosù wǒ yī jiàn shì.**	He told me something.
老师问我 一个问题。	**Lǎoshī wèn wǒ yī gè wèntí.**	The teacher asked me a question.

Note: An idiom with 问 **wèn** in the dative construction is 我爸爸问你好。
Wǒ bàba wèn nǐ hǎo. 'My father sends you his regards.'

8.5.2 | Dative verbs and aspect markers

The aspect markers 了 **le**, 过 **guo** and occasionally (正)在 (**zhèng**) **zài** may occur with dative verbs but not 着 **zhe**.

他借过你 钱没有？	**Tā jièguo nǐ qián méiyǒu?**	(*lit.* He borrow asp you money not-have) Has he ever borrowed money from you?
他们送了我 一个景泰蓝 花瓶。	**Tāmen sòngle wǒ yī gè jǐngtàilán huāpíng.**	(*lit.* they give asp me one mw cloisonné vase) They gave me a cloisonné vase.
她(正)在教 我们英语。	**Tā (zhèng) zài jiāo wǒmen Yīngyǔ.**	(*lit.* she (just) asp: in-the- process-of teach us English) She is teaching us English now.

Note: For a further discussion of dative constructions, see 21.4.

8.6 | Causative verbs

There are a number of causative verbs like 催 **cuī** 'urge' 叫 **jiào** 'tell',
命令 **mìnglìng** 'order', 带领 **dàilǐng** 'guide', 'lead', etc. in the language.
These verbs take objects which are usually human or animate beings
and can therefore engender further actions on their own under the
verbal or physical instigation or manoeuvre initiated by the subject (for
details, see 21.5):

哥哥催我 去报名。	**Gēge cuī wǒ qù bàomíng.**	(lit. elder brother urge me go register/put one's name down) (My) elder brother urged me to go and register/put my name down.
她要我 帮助她。	**Tā yào wǒ bāngzhù tā.**	(lit. she want me help her) She wants/wanted me to help her.
学校要求我 们穿校服。	**Xuéxiào yāoqiú wǒmen chuān xiàofú.**	(lit. school require us wear school uniform) The school requires us to wear school uniform.
姐姐拉/推 我上了车。	**Jiějie lā/tuī wǒ shàngle chē.**	(lit. elder sister pull/push me get on asp bus/train) (My) elder sister pulled/pushed me on to the bus/train.

We can see from these examples that causative verbs themselves do not
normally incorporate aspect markers whether they indicate past,
progressive, completed or habitual action; but if the second verb in the
construction indicates completed action, it can take the aspect
marker 了 **le**.

Note also that in some cases an action verb may be used as either a
dative or a causative verb:

他们帮(了) 我很多忙。	**Tāmen bāng(le) wǒ hěnduō máng.** (dative verb)	(lit. they help (asp) me a lot busy-ness) They gave me a lot of help.
他们帮我 办了很多 事儿。	**Tāmen bāng wǒ bànle hěnduō shìr.** (causative verb)	(lit. they help me do asp a lot things) They helped me deal with a lot of things.
老师教 (了)我们 一首歌。	**Lǎoshī jiāo(le) wǒmen yī shǒu gē.** (dative verb)	(lit. teacher teach (asp) us one mw song) The teacher taught us a song.

| 老师教
我们唱了
一首歌。 | **Lǎoshī jiāo wǒmen chàngle yī shǒu gē.** (causative verb) | (lit. teacher teach us sing asp one mw song) The teacher taught us to sing a song. |

8.7　Imperatives

Action verbs, dative verbs and causative verbs may also be used in *imperatives*. In these sentences the subject (apart from 咱们 **zánmen** 'we' inclusive or 我们 **wǒmen** 'we') is generally omitted, and the particle 吧 **ba** is often added at the end to connote suggestion:

吃(一)点 儿乳酪吧。	**Chī (yī) diǎnr rǔlào ba.** (action verb)	(*lit.* eat (a) little cheese p) Have a bit of cheese.
咱们打 (一)场 篮球吧。	**Zánmen dǎ (yī) chǎng lánqiú ba.** (action verb)	(*lit.* we hit (a) game basketball p) Let's have a game of basketball.
给我一杯 桔子水吧。	**Gěi wǒ yī bēi júzishuǐ ba.** (dative verb)	(*lit.* give me one glass orange-juice p) Give me a glass of orange juice.
送他一瓶 酒吧。	**Sòng tā yī píng jiǔ ba.** (dative verb)	(*lit.* give-as-a-gift him one bottle wine/spirit p) Give him a bottle of wine/spirits.
教我们打 太极拳吧。	**Jiāo wǒmen dǎ tàijíquán ba.** (causative verb)	(*lit.* teach us hit shadow-boxing p) Teach us (to do) shadow boxing.
提醒他去 登记吧。	**Tíxǐng tā qù dēngjì ba.** (causative verb)	(lit. remind him go register p) Remind him to go and register.

Without the particle 吧 **ba**, imperatives are more like commands:

过来!	**Guò lái!**	(*lit.* across come) Come (over) here!
站起来!	**Zhàn qǐ lái!**	(*lit.* stand up-come) Stand up!
别撒谎!	**Bié sā huǎng!**	(lit. don't tell lie) Don't lie/tell lies.
别乱来!	**Bié luànlái!**	(lit. don't confusion come) Don't do/touch it [because I know you'll make a mess of it].

Note: For negative commands, see 15.2 (6).

8.7.1 | Polite requests

Polite requests may be expressed by using 请 **qǐng** 'please' at the beginning of the imperative with or without the second person pronoun and the particle 吧 **ba** (see 21.5.1):

请(你)说 英文(吧)。	**Qǐng (nǐ) shuō Yīngwén (ba).**	(*lit.* please (you) speak English (p)) Please speak English.
请跟我来。	**Qǐng gēn wǒ lái.**	(*lit.* please follow me come) Please follow me.
请(你)原谅。	**Qǐng (nǐ) yuánliàng.**	(*lit.* please (you) excuse) Please forgive me.
请坐!	**qǐng zuò!**	(lit. please sit) Please sit down.

8.7.2 | Imperatives and aspect markers

The aspect marker 着 **zhe** (not 了 **le**, 过 **guo** or 在 **zài**) may be used in imperatives to imply that the action is expected to be continued in some way. In these cases the verb is generally monosyllabic:

放着吧。/ 留着吧。	**Fàngzhe ba/ Liúzhe ba.**	(*lit.* put asp p) Keep it.
带着吧。	**Dàizhe ba.**	(*lit.* carry asp p) Bring [it] with you.
请等着。	**Qǐng děngzhe.**	(*lit.* please wait asp) Please wait.

9 Motion verbs and direction indicators

9.1 | *Motion verbs and simple direction indicators*

There are a number of common *motion verbs* in Chinese, which express not only motion but also direction. They may be used *transitively* or *intransitively* and they fall naturally into two groups:

(1) The first group consists of the two basic verbs 来 **lái** 'come' and 去 **qù** 'go':

我来。	**Wǒ lái.**	I'll come.
他们不来。	**Tāmen bù lái.**	They won't come.
我不去。	**Wǒ bù qù.**	I won't go.
他们去。	**Tāmen qù.**	They'll go.

Used transitively, these can take location objects:

| 她来我这儿。 | **Tā *lái wǒ zhèr*.** | She'll come to my place. |
| 我们去北京。 | **Wǒmen *qù Běijīng*.** | We are going to Beijing. |

(2) The second group comprises a number of verbs which regularly precede 来 lái and 去 qù to express movement in particular directions. Linked with 来 lái they indicate movement towards the speaker, and with 去 qù movement away from the speaker:

(a) 上 shàng 'upwards':

| 她上来了。 | **Tā *shàng lái* le.** | She came up. |
| 他上去了。 | **Tā *shàng qù* le.** | He went up. |

If used transitively, the location object is always placed between the verb and 来 lái or 去 qù:

| 她上楼来了。 | **Tā *shàng* lóu *lái* le.** | She came upstairs. |
| 他上楼去了。 | **Tā *shàng* lóu *qù* le.** | He went upstairs. |

Note: The particle 了 le which comes at the end of these sentences has the simultaneous functions of aspect marker and sentence particle (see 16.2.2).

(b) 下 xià 'downwards':

他们下来了。	**Tāmen *xià lái* le.**	They came down.
他们下去了。	**Tāmen *xià qù* le.**	They went down.
他们下楼来了。	**Tāmen *xià* lóu *lái* le.**	They came downstairs.
他们下楼去了。	**Tāmen *xià* lóu *qù* le.**	They went downstairs.

(c) 过 guò 'across or over a distance':

请过来。	**Qǐng *guò lái*.**	Please come over (here).
请过去。	**Qǐng *guò qù*.**	Please go over (there).
汽车过桥来了。	**Qìchē *guò* qiáo *lái* le.**	The car has come over the bridge.

| 船过河 去了。 | **Chuán** *guò* **hé** *qù* **le.** | The boat has gone across to the other side of the river. |

(d) 回 **huí** 'returning to a place':

妈妈回来了。	**Māma** *huí lái* **le.**	Mother has come back.
爷爷回去了。	**Yéye** *huí qù* **le.**	Grandfather has gone back.
爸爸回家 来了。	**Bàba** *huí* jiā *lái* **le.**	Father has come home.
大使回伦敦 去了。	**Dàshǐ** *huí* Lúndūn *qù* **le.**	The ambassador has gone back to London.

(e) 进 **jìn** 'entering':

请进来。	**Qǐng** *jìn lái.*	Please come in.
请进去。	**Qǐng** *jìn qù.*	Please go in.
客人进 屋子来了。	**Kèren** *jìn* wūzi *lái* **le.**	The guest(s) came into the room.
奶奶进 城去了。	**Nǎinai** *jìn* chéng *qù* **le.**	Grandmother has gone to town.

(f) 出 **chū** 'exiting':

| 女主人 出来了。 | **Nǚ zhǔrén** *chū lái* **le.** | The hostess came out. |
| 老板出去了。 | **Lǎobǎn** *chū qù* **le.** | The boss has gone out. |

Note: 出 **chū** is seldom used transitively with 来 **lái** or 去 **qù**, but there are established phrases such as:

| 她出门去了。 | **Tā** *chū* mén *qù* **le.** | (*lit.* She out door go p) She is away. |

(g) 起 **qǐ** 'directly upwards':

| 弟弟起来了。 | **Dìdi** *qǐ lái* **le.** | My younger brother has got up. |

Note: 起 **Qǐ** does not occur with 去 **qù** in spoken Chinese. It is also rarely used transitively with an object.

(h) 到 **dào** 'arriving':

| 春天到来了。 | **Chūntiān** *dàolái* **le.** | Spring has arrived. |

校长到我 家来了。	**Xiàozhǎng** **dào wǒ jiā lái le.**	The headmaster came to my house.
姐姐到 剧院去了。	**Jiějie dào** **jùyuàn qù le.**	(My) elder sister went to the theatre.

Note: 到 Dào is not used with 去 qù on its own, but it can occur with 去 qù with a location object. (See 19.1.1 (2) where 到 dào is classified as a coverb.)

9.2 Motion verbs and compound direction indicators

These motion verbs not only function as independent verbal expressions, but also serve as *direction indicators* for other *action verbs*. Again, 来 lái or 去 qù imply motion towards or away from the speaker, and their partner verbs 上 shàng, 下 xià, 过 guò, 回 huí, 进 jìn, 出 chū and 起 qǐ express more precise directions.

公共汽车 开过来了。	**Gōnggòng qìchē** **kāi guòlái le.**	(*lit.* public car drive across come p) The bus drove up.
警察 跑过去了。	**Jǐngchá pǎo** **guòqù le.**	(*lit.* policeman/policewoman run across go p) The policeman/ policewoman hurried across (away from the speaker).
海鸥 飞回来了。	**Hǎi'ōu** **fēi huílái le.**	(*lit.* gull fly back p) The gulls flew back (to where the speaker is).

If the action verb is used transitively, the object may be placed either after the whole verb phrase or before 来 lái or 去 qù:

他们带来了 一包烟。 or, 他们带了 一包烟来。	**Tāmen dài lái le** **yī bāo yān.** **Tāmen dài le yī bāo** **yān lái.**	They have brought a packet of cigarettes.
他拿出来一支烟。 or, 他拿出一支烟来。	**Tā ná chūlái yī zhī yān.** **Tā ná chū yī zhī yān lái.**	He took out a cigarette.

However, if the object is a location, it must go between the first part of the direction indicator and 来 lái or 去 qù:

她跑上楼去了。 NOT, *她跑上去楼了。	**Tā pǎo shàng lóu qù le.** **Tā pǎo shàngqù lóu le.**	She ran upstairs.

Further examples:

(1)   intransitive:

太阳正在升起来。	**Tàiyáng zhèngzài** *shēng qǐlái.*	The sun is rising.
客人们都坐下来了。	**Kèrenmen dōu** *zuò xiàlái* le.	The guests all sat down.
医生走过来了。	**Yīshēng** *zǒu* *guòlái* le.	The doctor came over.
运动员跑出来了。	**Yùndòngyuán** *pǎo chūlái* le.	The athlete ran out (towards the speaker).
小猫爬上去了。	**Xiǎo māo** *pá shàngqù* le.	The kitten has climbed up (away from the speaker).
汽车开过去了。	**Qìchē** *kāi* *guòqù* le.	The car has gone past.

(2)   transitive:

妈妈买回一条鱼来。	**Māma** *mǎi huí* *yī tiáo yú lái.*	Mum has bought a fish. (*lit.* bought and come back with a fish)
邮递员递过几封信来。	**Yóudìyuán** *dì guò* *jǐ fēng xìn lái.*	The postman handed over a few letters.
爸爸跳下床来。	**Bàba** *tiào xià* *chuáng lái.*	Father jumped out of bed.
姐姐走进商店去了。	**Jiějie** *zǒu jìn* *shāngdiàn qù* le.	(The) elder sister walked into a shop.
经理跑回公司去了。	**Jīnglǐ** *pǎo huí* *gōngsī qù* le.	The manager has gone (or hurried) back to the company.
行人横过马路去了。	**Xíngrén** *héng* *guò mǎlù qù* le.	The pedestrian has crossed the road (to the other side).
护士走出救护车来。	**Hùshi** *zǒu chū* *jiùhùchē lái.*	The nurse came out of the ambulance.
气球飘上天空去了。	**Qìqiú** *piāo shàng* *tiānkōng qù* le.	The balloon floated up into the sky.
爷爷赶回家来了。	**Yéye** *gǎn huí* *jiā lái* le.	Grandfather came hurrying home.

鸭子游到 对岸<u>去</u>了。	**Yāzi yóu dào** **duì'àn qù le.**	The duck(s) swam to the opposite bank.

Motion verbs with metaphorical meaning

Motion verb expressions may carry meanings beyond simply physical movement. For example:

(1) The motion verb 过去 **guò qù** may indicate the passsage of time:

冬天<u>过去</u>了。	**Dōngtiān** **guò qù le.**	Winter has passed.

(2) The direction indicators 起来 **qǐlái**, 下来 **xiàlái** and 下去 **xiàqù**, which can be used with both state and action verbs, may convey various meanings:

(a) 起来 **qǐlái** (i) mentioning or recollecting something:

她提起这 件事<u>来</u>。	**Tā tí qǐ zhèi** **jiàn shì lái.**	She brought this matter up.
她想起那 件事<u>来</u>。	**Tā xiǎng qǐ** **nèi jiàn shì lái.**	She recalled that incident.

(b) 起来 **qǐlái** (ii) initiating an action or a state:

他<u>唱起歌来</u>。	**Tā chàng qǐ** **gē lái.**	He started singing.
孩子<u>哭起来</u>了。	**Háizi kū qǐlái le.**	The child started to cry.
天气暖和 <u>起来</u>了。	**Tiānqì nuǎnhuo** **qǐlái le.**	The weather is getting warmer.

(c) 下来 **xiàlái** gradual diminishing of an action or state:

汽车停 <u>下来</u>了。	**Qìchē tíng** **xiàlái le.**	The car has gradually come to a stop.
大家都 <u>静下来</u>了。	**Dàjiā dōu** **jìng xiàlái le.**	Everybody became quiet.

(d) 下去 **xiàqù** continuation or resumption of an action:

请<u>说下去</u>。	**Qǐng shuō** **xiàqù.**	Please go on (with what you were saying).
坚持<u>下去</u>。	**Jiānchí xiàqù!**	Stick it out/keep at it.

9.4 | *Direction indicators with specific meanings*

上 shàng, 下 xià, 出 chū and 过 guò may occur alone with action verbs, i.e. without 来 lái or 去 qù. They then have specific meanings, depending on the verbs they are associated with. Some of the most common usages are:

(1) 上 shàng

    (a)   putting on the body or the surface of something:

他穿上一件蓝衬衫。	**Tā *chuān shàng* yī jiàn lán chènshān.**	He put on a blue shirt/blouse.
老教授戴上他的眼镜。	**Lǎo jiàoshòu *dài shàng* tāde yǎnjìng.**	The old professor put on his glasses.
她贴上两张邮票。	**Tā *tiē shàng* liǎng zhāng yóupiào.**	She stuck two stamps on [the envelope].

    (b)   closing something:

她闭上了眼睛。	**Tā *bì shàng* le yǎnjing.**	She closed her eyes.
他关上了窗户。	**Tā *guān shàng* le chuānghu.**	He closed the window.

    (c)   implying success:

他考上大学了。	**Tā *kǎo shàng* dàxué le.**	He has passed the examination for university.

    (d)   making an addition:

请加上三个。	**Qǐng *jiā shàng* sān gè.**	Please add three more.
算上我。	**Suàn shàng wǒ.**	Count me in.

(2) 下 xià

    (a)   removing, detaching:

她脱下毛衣。	**Tā *tuō xià* máoyī.**	She took off her sweater.
他摘下一朵花儿。	**Tā *zhāi xià* yī duǒ huār.**	He plucked a flower.

(b)   noting down:

| 他记下了 这句话。 | **Tā** *jì xià* **le zhèi jù huà.** | He made a note of these words. |

(3)   出 **chū** revealing:

| 他说出了 这件事。 | **Tā** *shuō chū* **le zhèi jiàn shì.** | He revealed this matter. |
| 他想出了 一个好办法。 | **Tā** *xiǎng chū* **le yī gè hǎo bànfǎ.** | He came up with a good plan. |

(4)   过 **guò** doing in excess:

| 他坐过站了。 | **Tā** *zuò guò* **zhàn le.** | He went past the stop/station. |

10   Verbs and time

10.1   *Time expressions*

We have seen in Chapter 8 the importance of time expressions in the Chinese sentence, in that they provide a time reference or context for the action of the verb, which does not change tense. The following sentences illustrate the point:

我昨天 进城去。	**Wǒ** *zuótiān* **jìn chéng qù.**	(*lit.* I yesterday into city go) I went to town *yesterday*.
我明天 进城去。	**Wǒ** *míngtiān* **jìn chéng qù.**	(*lit.* I tomorrow into city go) I'll go to town *tomorrow*.
我常常 进城去。	**Wǒ** *chángcháng* **jìn chéng qù.**	(*lit.* I often into city go) I *often* go to town.

Because of their significance, time expressions invariably occur in an early position before the verb, often at the beginning of the sentence. In the mind of the Chinese speaker, the time reference has to be made clear before the action is stated. This means that the word order of a Chinese sentence is likely to contrast with its English translation, which will almost certainly have the time reference towards the end of the sentence:

| 星期四见。 | **Xīngqī** *sì* **jiàn.** | (*lit.* Thursday see) See [you] on Thursday. |
| 我们明天 下午去 东京。 | **Wǒmen** *míngtiān xiàwǔ* **qù Dōngjīng.** | (*lit.* we tomorrow afternoon go Tokyo) We are going to Tokyo tomorrow afternoon. |

Time expressions indicating a *point of time* for an action can be placed
either in front of the subject or after it:

明年我上 北京去。	**Míngnián wǒ** **shàng Běijīng qù.**	(*lit.* next-year I up-to Beijing go) I am going to Beijing next year.

or,

我明年上 北京去。	**Wǒ míngnián** **shàng Běijīng qù.**	(*lit.* I next-year up-to Beijing go) I am going to Beijing next year.

If the time expression is more specific, it is likely to come after the
subject:

我早上 七点(钟) 起床。	**Wǒ zǎoshàng** **qī diǎn (zhōng)** **qǐ chuáng.**	(*lit.* I morning seven hour (clock) get-up bed) I get up at seven in the morning.

Note: The following are examples of some of the most common point-of-time
expressions, which normally appear before the verb:

Year

去年 qùnián 'last year'; 今年 jīnnián 'this year'; 明年 míngnián 'next year';
前年 qiánnián 'the year before last'; 三年前 sān nián qián 'three years ago';
一年后 yī nián hòu 'a year later'; 一九九五年 yī jiǔ jiǔ wǔ nián '(in) 1995'.

我今年十九岁。	**Wǒ jīnnián shíjiǔ suì.**	I'm nineteen *this year*.
我爷爷三年前 去世了。	**Wǒ yéye sān nián qián** **qùshì le.**	My grandpa died *three* *years ago*.
她一九九五年毕业。	**Tā yī jiǔ jiǔ wǔ nián bìyè.**	She graduated *in 1995*.

Season

春天 chūntiān 'spring'; 夏天 xiàtiān 'summer'; 秋天 qiūtiān 'autumn'; 冬天
dōngtiān 'winter'; 去年春天 qùnián chūntiān 'spring last year'.

去年春天我去中国。	**Qùnián chūntiān** **wǒ qù Zhōngguó.**	I went to China *in the* *spring of last year*.

Month

The months in Chinese are formed simply by placing the cardinal numbers
one to twelve before 月 yuè 'month'/'moon': 一月 yīyuè (also 正月 zhēngyuè)
'January'; 二月 èryuè 'February'; 三月 sānyuè 'March'; etc.

我父母三月来。	**Wǒ fùmǔ sānyuè lái.**	My parents are coming *in March*.

For days of the month 号 hào, or more formally 日 rì, follows the number: 十月二号/日 shíyuè èr hào/rì '2nd October'.

他们十月二号 来我家。	**Tāmen** shíyuè èr **hào lái wǒ jiā.**	They will come to my place *on the second of October.*

Other expressions include: 上个月 shàng gè yuè 'last month'; 这个月 zhèi gè yuè 'this month'; 下个月 xià gè yuè 'next month'; 两个月前 liǎng gè yuè qián 'two months ago'; 三个月后 sān gè yuè hòu 'three months later/in three months'; 去年一月 qùnián yīyuè 'in January last year'; 今年二月 jīnnián èryuè 'in February this year'; 明年三月 míngnián sānyuè 'in March next year'.

我上个月买了 一辆新汽车。	**Wǒ** shàng gè yuè **mǎi le yī liàng xīn qìchē.**	I bought a new car *last month.*
他三个月后 结婚。	**Tā** sān gè yuè hòu **jiéhūn.**	He's getting married *in three months' time.*
我今年二月 离开这儿。	**Wǒ** jīnnián èryuè **líkāi zhèr.**	I'll leave this place *in February this year.*

Week

上(个)星期 Shàng (gè) xīngqī 'last week'; 这(个)星期 zhèi (gè) xīngqī 'this week'; 下(个)星期 xià (gè) xīngqī 'next week'; 两(个)星期(以)前 liǎng (gè) xīngqī (yǐ)qián 'two weeks ago'; 三(个)星期(以)后 sān (gè) xīngqī (yǐ)hòu 'three weeks later/in three weeks'.

我们下(个)星期 考试。	**Wǒmen** xià (gè) **xīngqī kǎoshì.**	We'll have an examination *next week.*
张太太两(个)星期 (以)前来过这儿。	**Zhāng tàitai** liǎng **(gè) xīngqī (yǐ)qián láiguo zhèr.**	Mrs Zhang was here *two weeks ago.*

Days

For days of the week apart from Sunday the cardinal numbers one to six are placed after 星期 xīngqī or 礼拜 lǐbài 'week', and for Sunday either 天 tiān or 日 rì is used instead of a number: 星期一 xīngqī yī 'Monday'; 星期二 xīngqī èr 'Tuesday'; 星期三 xīngqī sān 'Wednesday'; 星期日 xīngqī rì/星期天 xīngqī tiān 'Sunday'; 上(个)星期一 shàng (gè) xīngqī yī 'last Monday' (*lit.* Monday last week); 这个星期二 zhèi gè xīngqī èr 'this Tuesday'; 下星期三 xià xīngqī sān 'next Wednesday' (*lit.* Wednesday next week).

我们星期三 开会。	**Wǒmen** xīngqī sān **kāihuì.**	We are holding a meeting *on Wednesday.*

Other expressions for days include: 昨天 zuótiān 'yesterday'; 前天 qiántiān 'the day before yesterday'; 今天 jīntiān 'today'; 明天 míngtiān 'tomorrow'; 后天 hòutiān 'the day after tomorrow'; 八天(以)前 bā tiān (yǐ)qián 'eight days ago'; 九天(以)后 jiǔ tiān (yǐ)hòu 'nine days later/in nine days'.

她前天回家。	**Tā *qiántiān* huí jiā.**	She came back *the day before yesterday.*
我后天休息。	**Wǒ *hòutiān* xiūxi.**	I'll take a day off *the day after tomorrow.*

Time of day

早上 **Zǎoshàng** '(in) the morning'; 上午 **shàngwǔ** '(in) the morning (i.e. fore-noon)'; 下午 **xiàwǔ** '(in) the afternoon'; 中午 **zhōngwǔ** '(at) noon'; 晚上 **wǎnshang** '(in) the evening'; 夜里 **yèlǐ** '(at) night'; 半夜 **bànyè** 'midnight/in the middle of the night'.

早上天气 不错。	***Zǎoshang* tiānqì bù cuò.**	The weather wasn't bad *in the morning.*
下午天气 变了。	***Xiàwǔ* tiānqì biàn le.**	The weather changed *in the afternoon.*
她半夜醒来。	**Tā *bànyè* xǐng lái.**	She woke up *in the middle of the night.*

两点(钟) **Liǎng diǎn (zhōng)** 'two o'clock'; 两点半 **liǎng diǎn bàn** 'half past two'; 两点一刻 **liǎng diǎn yī kè** 'a quarter past two'; 两点三刻 **liǎng diǎn sān kè** (*lit.* two hour three quarters) 'a quarter to three'; 一点零五分 **yī diǎn líng wǔ fēn** 'five minutes past one'; 四点二十五分 **sì diǎn èrshí wǔ fēn** 'twenty-five minutes past four'; 一点差五分 **yī diǎn chà wǔ fēn** 'five minutes to one'; 早上九点(钟) **zǎoshang jiǔ diǎn (zhōng)** 'nine o'clock in the morning'.

我两点半 下班。	**Wǒ *liǎng diǎn bàn* xiàbān.**	I came off work *at half past two.*
他们一点差 五分吃午饭。	**Tāmen *yī diǎn chà wǔ fēn* chī wǔfàn.**	They have lunch *at five to one.*
我们早上 九点(钟)出发。	**Wǒmen *zǎoshang jiǔ diǎn (zhōng)* chūfā.**	We'll set out *at nine in the morning.*

General

上(一)次 **Shàng (yī) cì** 'last time'; 下(一)次 **xià (yī) cì** 'next time'; (在)四点与 四点半之间 **(zài) sì diǎn yǔ sì diǎn bàn zhījiān** '*between* four and four thirty'; (在)假期里 **(zài) jiàqī li** '*during* the holidays'; 周末 **zhōumò** '(over) the week-end'; 四天内 **sì tiān nèi** '*within* four days'.

我下次再来 看你。	**Wǒ *xià cì* zài lái kàn nǐ.**	I'll come and see you again *next time.*
假期里我 去旅行。	***Jiàqī li* wǒ qù lǚxíng.**	I went travelling *during the holidays.*

10.2.1	Detailed time expressions

In detailed time expressions giving years, months, dates, etc., the larger al-ways precede the smaller. For example, 2.35 p.m. on 31 August, 1995 is:

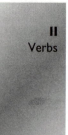

一九九五年八月	yī jiǔ jiǔ wǔ nián bā	(lit. 1995 year 8 month
三十一号下午	yuè sānshí yī hào xiàwǔ	31 day afternoon
两点三十五分	liǎng diǎn sānshí wǔ fēn	2 hour 35 minute)

Note 1: Lengthy expressions of time and date are more likely to be placed at the beginning of a sentence before the subject.

Note 2: The descending order of scale for these time expressions is similar to that for location expressions, e.g. addresses (see Chapter 1).

10.3 Point-of-time expressions incorporating verbal phrases

More complex point-of-time expressions in the form of verb phrases also go before the main verb. In these phrases the verb is followed by ... 的时候 ... de shíhou or shí 'when/while', 以后 yǐhòu or 之后 zhīhòu 'after', or 以前 yǐqián or 之前 zhīqián 'before':

我们上课 (的)时(候), 老师说...	Wǒmen shàngkè (de) shí(hou), lǎoshī shuō...	(lit. we have-class p time, teacher say) When we were in class, the teacher said...
我下了班 以后就去 踢足球了。	Wǒ xià le bān yǐhòu jiù qù tī zúqiú le.	(lit. I finish asp work-shift after immediately go kick football p) After I came off work, I went to play football.
回家以前 她来找我。	Huí jiā yǐqián tā lái zhǎo wǒ.	(lit. return home before she come look-for me) Before she went home, she came to see me.

The last two examples illustrate that if the time phrase and the main verb have the same subject, the subject may go before either verb.

Note 1: The adverb 就 jiù 'then' is regularly found in the second clause of such sentences. It is placed immediately before the verb (and after the subject, if there is one). (See Chapter 24.)

Note 2: These time expressions may be preceded by the preposition 在 zài 'in/during'. Expressions with (的)时(候) (de) shí(hou) may also be linked with the preposition 当 dāng 'when' if a subject is present:

在洗澡以前	zài xǐzǎo yǐqián	before having a bath
当我起床(的)时(候)	dāng wǒ qǐchuáng (de) shí(hou)	while I was getting up
NOT: *当起床(的)时(候)	dāng qǐchuáng (de) shí(hou)	

Note 3: Other complex point-of-time expressions are:

在中国逗留期间	**zài Zhōngguó dòuliú** *qījiān*	*while* staying in China
在英国访问期间	**zài Yīngguó fǎngwèn** *qījiān*	*while* visiting England
我在中国逗留 期间病了。	**Wǒ zài Zhōngguó dòuliú** *qījiān* **bìng le.**	I fell ill *during my stay in China.*

10.4 | *Imprecise points of time*

Adverbs expressing *imprecise points of time* are generally placed after
the subject:

他已经毕业了。	**Tā** *yǐjing* **bìyè le.**	He has *already* graduated.
救火车立刻 到了。	**Jiùhuǒchē** *lìkè* **dào le.**	The fire engine arrived *at once.*
她先喝汤。	**Tā** *xiān* **hē tāng.**	She drank the soup *first.*

One cannot say:

*已经他毕业了。	*Yǐjing* **tā bìyè le.**	
*立刻救火车到了。	*Lìkè* **jiùhuǒchē dào le.**	

Note 1: Common adverbs of this kind include: 马上 **mǎshàng** 'immediately';
常常 **chángcháng** 'often'; 总/老 **zǒng/lǎo** 'always'; 从(来)不 **cóng(lái) bù** 'never';
一直(都) **yīzhí (dōu)** 'all along'.

我马上就来。	**Wǒ** *mǎshàng* **jiù lái.**	I'll be with you *immediately.*
他老提起 这回事。	**Tā** *lǎo* **tí qǐ** **zhèi huí shì.**	He's *always* bringing up this matter.
我从来不抽烟。	**Wǒ** *cónglái bù* **chōuyān.**	I have *never* smoked.
他一直都 在帮助我。	**Tā** *yīzhí dōu* **zài bāngzhù wǒ.**	He's been helping me *all along.*

Note 2: There are however some adverbs which can occur both before and
after the subject: 将来/以后 **jiānglái/yǐhòu** 'in future'; 现在 **xiànzài** 'now'; 过去
guòqù 'in the past'; 起初 **qǐchū** 'at first'; 首先 **shǒuxiān** 'first of all'; 以前 **yǐqián**
'formerly'; 后来 **hòulái** 'later/afterwards'; 接着 **jiēzhe** 'next'; 最后 **zuìhòu** 'finally/
in the end'; 最近 **zuìjìn** 'lately'; 近来 **jìnlái** 'recently/lately'.

我现在去银行。	**Wǒ** *xiànzài* **qù yínháng.**	I'm going to the bank *now.*
起初我不相信他。	*Qǐchū* **wǒ bù xiāngxìn tā.**	*At first* I didn't believe him.

我后来去 澳大利亚了。	**Wǒ hòulái qù Àodàlìyà le.**	I went to Australia *later on*.
最后她同意了。	**Zuìhòu tā tóngyì le.**	She *finally* agreed [to it].
你近来怎么样？	**Nǐ jìnlái zěnme yàng?**	How have you been *lately*?

10.5 Indefinite points of time

Phrases indicating *indefinite points of time* (often with 有 **yǒu**) are invariably placed at the beginning of a sentence, as they set the time for a narrative:

| 一天我去他家。 | **Yī tiān wǒ qù tā jiā.** | One day I went to his place. |
| 有一年那儿
下大雪。 | **Yǒu yī nián nàr
xià dà xuě.** | One year that place had a heavy snowfall. |

Note: Many expressions of this type can be formulated. For example, (有)一个星期天 (**yǒu**) **yī gè xīngqī tiān** 'one Sunday'; (有)一个星期天晚上 (**yǒu**) **yī gè xīngqī tiān wǎnshang** 'one Sunday evening'.

| 有(一)个星期天
我们去爬山。 | **Yǒu (yī) gè xīngqī tiān
wǒmen qù pá shān.** | One Sunday we went mountain-climbing. |

10.6 Frequency expressions with **měi**

Frequency expressions with 每 **měi** 'every' may be placed before or after the subject. They are usually followed by the adverb 都 **dōu** 'all':

我每天都 锻炼身体。	**Wǒ měi tiān dōu duànliàn shēntǐ.**	(*lit.* I every day all temper body) I do physical exercises/I work out every day.
他每次都 马上回信。	**Tā měi cì dōu mǎshàng huí xìn.**	(*lit.* He every time all immediately reply-to letter) He replies immediately to letters every time.
每个星期六 早上我都去 市场买东西。	**Měi (gè) xīngqī liù zǎoshang wǒ dōu qù shìchǎng mǎi dōngxi.**	(*lit.* every mw Saturday morning I all go market buy things) I go shopping in the market every Saturday morning.

10.7 *Time expressions in existence sentences*

Time expressions may also introduce existence sentences with 有 **yǒu** 'there is/are' in the pattern: time expression + 有 **yǒu** + (qualifier) + noun. In contrast, parallel English sentences usually begin with 'there is/are'.

今(天)晚(上) 有一个 音乐会。	*Jīn(tiān)* *wǎn(shang) yǒu* *yī gè yīnyuèhuì.*	(*lit.* today evening there-is one mw concert) There will be a concert this evening.
下星期六 也有篮球/ 羽毛球 比赛吗?	*Xià xīngqī liù* *yě yǒu lánqiú/* *yǔmáoqiú* *bǐsài ma?*	(*lit.* next Saturday also there-is basketball/badminton contest p) Is there a basketball/badminton match next Saturday too?
明天没(有) 公共汽车 到城里去。	*Míngtiān méi(yǒu)* *gōnggòng qìchē* *dào chéng li qù.*	(*lit.* tomorrow there-isn't public car to town-in go) There aren't any buses to town tomorrow.

Note: For similar use of location phrases, see 11.5.

10.7.1 Time expressions in emergence or disappearance sentences

Time expressions can also introduce emergence or disappearance sentences in which the verb is marked by the aspect marker 了 **le**:

| 刚刚走了
一辆火车。 | *Gānggāng zǒule*
yī liàng huǒchē. | (*lit.* just-now leave asp one mw train) A train left just now. |
| 马上来了
一辆救护车。 | *Mǎshàng láile yī*
liàng jiùhùchē. | (*lit.* immediately come asp one mw ambulance) An ambulance arrived immediately. |

Note: Location phrases occur in a similar construction. See 11.6.

11 **Verbs and location**

11.1 *Location expressions*

Like the time expressions described in Chapter 10, *location phrases*, which identify the locus of an action or event, always precede the verb. Place and time have to be made clear before the verb is expressed to establish the context for the action.

| 他们在西安工作。 | **Tāmen zài Xī'ān gōngzuò.** | They are working *in* Xi'an. |
| 请在这儿等我。 | **Qǐng zài zhèr děng wǒ.** | Please wait for me *here*. |

Where a location phrase and a time phrase are both present, the time phrase normally precedes the location phrase; it may come right at the beginning of the sentence, that is, before the subject:

| 他们昨天在图书馆学习。 | **Tāmen zuótiān zài túshūguǎn xuéxí.** | (*lit.* they yesterday at library study) They were studying at the library yesterday. |
| 去年我在香港做生意。 | **Qùnián wǒ zài Xiānggǎng zuò shēngyi.** | (*lit.* last-year I at Hong Kong do business) Last year I was doing business in Hong Kong. |

As illustrated in the above examples, *location phrases* may take the form of 在 zài 'in, at' with a simple *location pronoun* (这儿 zhèr 'here', 那儿 nàr 'there' or 哪儿 nǎr 'where') or with a place name or *location noun* (西安 Xī'ān, 香港 Xiānggǎng 'Hong Kong', 图书馆 túshūguǎn 'library').

11.2 **Zài** *and postpositional phrases*

Another, perhaps more common form of location phrase uses 在 zài with what we will call a *postpositional phrase*, which consists of a noun followed by a *postposition*.

Postposition			Postpositional phrase		
里	**li**	in(side)	屋子里	**wūzi li**	in the room
外	**wài**	out(side)	城外	**chéng wài**	outside the town
上	**shang**	on, above, over	桌子上	**zhuōzi shang**	on the table
下	**xià**	under, below	树下	**shù xià**	under the tree
前	**qián**	in front of	门前	**mén qián**	in front of the door

Postposition			Postpositional phrase		
后	hòu	at the back of/behind	沙发后	shāfā hòu	behind the sofa
边/旁边	biān/pángbiān	by the side of	路边	lù biān	by the side of the road
中/中间	zhōng/zhōngjiān	in the middle of	大厅中间	dàtīng zhōngjiān	in the middle of the hall
对面	duìmiàn	opposite	学校对面	xuéxiào duìmiàn	opposite the school
那儿/这儿	nàr/zhèr	At a place (where sb or sth is)	律师那儿	lùshī nàr	at the lawyer's place

Note 1: Other postpositions include: 底下 dǐxia 'underneath', 之间 zhījiān 'between', 'among', 四周 sìzhōu 'around', 附近 fùjìn 'nearby', 隔壁 gébì 'next door to', etc.

Note 2: Inevitably there are some idiomatic differences between Chinese postpositions and English prepositions, e.g. 钥匙在门上 yàoshi zài mén shang (*lit.* key be-at door-on) 'the key is in the door'; 报上 bào shang (*lit.* newspaper-on) 'in the newspaper'; 太阳下散步 tàiyáng xià sànbù (*lit.* sun under stroll) 'stroll in the sun'.

11.2.1 Disyllabic postpositions

里 Li, 外 wài, 上 shang, 下 xià, 前 qián and 后 hòu take the suffixes -面 -miàn/-mian, -边 -biān/-bian or more colloquially -头 -tou to form disyllabic postpositions.

-面	-miàn/-mian	-边	-bian	-头	-tou	
里面	lǐmiàn	里边	lǐbian	里头	lǐtou	in(side)
外面	wàimiàn	外边	wàibian	外头	wàitou	out(side)
上面	shàngmian	上边	shàngbian	上头	shàngtou	on, above, over
下面	xiàmian	下边	xiàbian	下头	xiàtou	under, below
前面	qiánmian	前边	qiánbian	前头	qiántou	in front (of)
后面	hòumian	后边	hòubian	后头	hòutou	at the back (of)

Note: Other disyllabic postpositions with -面 -miàn or -边 -bian are:

左面/左边	**zuǒmiàn/zuǒbian**	to the left (of)
右面/右边	**yòumiàn/yòubian**	to the right (of)
东面/东边	**dōngmiàn/dōngbian**	to the east (of)
南面/南边	**nánmiàn/nánbian**	to the south (of)
西面/西边	**xīmiàn/xībian**	to the west (of)
北面/北边	**běimiàn/běibian**	to the north (of)

Such disyllabic postpositions usually follow disyllabic nouns to maintain a matching rhythm:

窗户前面/前边	**chuānghu qiánmian/qiánbian**	in front of the window
大门后面/后边	**dàmén hòumian/hòubian**	behind the door/gate
马路旁边	**mǎlù pángbiān**	by the side of the road
花园中间	**huāyuán zhōngjiān**	in the middle of the garden

There is also a tendency to match monosyllabic elements, and the above examples could be reformulated as:

窗前	**chuāng qián**
门后	**mén hòu**
路旁/路边	**lù páng** (written)/**lù bian** (colloq.)
园中	**yuán zhōng** (written)

The general rule to remember is that a disyllabic noun can be followed by either a disyllabic or monosyllabic postposition whereas a monosyllabic noun is only followed by a monosyllabic postposition, e.g.:

朋友之间/朋友间	**péngyou zhījiān/péngyou jiān**	amongst/between friends
海滩上面/海滩上	**hǎitān shàngmian/hǎitān shàng**	on the beach
屋子里面/屋子里/屋里/*屋里面	**wūzi lǐmiàn/wūzi lǐ/wūlǐ/wū lǐmiàn**	in the room
大海上面/大海上/海上/*海上面	**dàhǎi shàngmian/dàhǎi shàng/hǎi shàng/hǎi shàngmian**	on the sea

| 11.2.2 | Disyllabic postpositions as location pronouns |

Disyllabic postpositions can also act as location pronouns and form location phrases with 在 zài:

在后边	**zài hòubian**	at the back
在里头	**zài lǐtou**	inside
在上面	**zài shàngmian**	on top

| 11.3 | *Simple location sentences* |

Simple location sentences are formed by using the verb 在 zài 'to be in/at' followed by a location noun or pronoun, or a postpositional phrase:

厕所在二楼。	**Cèsuǒ *zài* èr lóu.**	The toilet is on the first floor.
你的座位在第三排。	**Nǐ de zuòwèi *zài* dì sān pái.**	Your seat is in the third row.
最近的邮筒在哪儿?	**Zuì jìn de yóutǒng *zài* nǎr?**	Where is the nearest pillar-box?
孩子都在外头。	**Háizi dōu *zài* wàitou.**	The children are all outside.
书房在中间。	**Shūfáng *zài* zhōngjiān.**	The study is in the middle.
她在花园里。	**Tā *zài* huāyuán li.**	She is in the garden.
书在书架上。	**Shū *zài* shūjià shang.**	The book is on the bookshelf.
我家在海德公园附近。	**Wǒ jiā *zài* Hǎidé gōngyuán fùjìn.**	My home is near Hyde Park.

Postpositions should not be attached to place names:

| 她在中国。
NOT: *她在中国里。 | **Tā zài Zhōngguó.**
Tā zài Zhōngguó li. | She is in China. |
| 我朋友在北京。
NOT: *我朋友在北京里。 | **Wǒ péngyou zài Běijīng.**
Wǒ péngyou zài Běijīng li. | My friend is in Beijing. |

With nouns indicating location, rather than objects, the postposition 里 li 'in' is optional:

我在图书馆。   **Wǒ zài túshūguǎn.**   I was in the library.
or, 我在图书馆里。 **Wǒ zài túshūguǎn li.**

Note: It must be made clear that 在 **zài** has two functions: (1) location verb 'to be in/at' and (2) a location preposition (coverb) 'in'/'at' (see 11.4 below).

11.4   *Location phrases modifying main verbs*

As illustrated by the first set of simple sentences in 11.1, in a location phrase used adverbially to modify the main verb of the sentence, 在 **zài** functions as a preposition (or coverb) meaning 'in' or 'at'. (For further discussion of 在 **zài** and other similar prepositions, see Chapter 19 on coverbs.)

他在花园里割草。	**Tā** *zài huāyuán li* **gē cǎo.**	(*lit.* He at garden in cut grass) He is cutting the grass *in the garden*.
我们在海滩上晒太阳。	**Wǒmen** *zài hǎitān shang* **shài tàiyáng.**	(*lit.* we at beach on bask sun) We were sunbathing *on the beach*.
他们在客厅里听音乐。	**Tāmen** *zài kètīng li* **tīng yīnyuè.**	(*lit.* they at lounge in listen music) They listened to music *in the lounge*.
妈妈在市场买菜。	**Māma** *zài shìchǎng* **mǎi cài.**	(*lit.* mother at market buy food) Mum is buying food *at the market*.
你在大学学什么科目？	**Nǐ** *zài dàxué* **xué shénme kēmù?**	(*lit.* you at university study what subject) What subject are you studying *at the university*?
我在银行开了一个账户。	**Wǒ** *zài yínháng* **kāi le yī gè zhànghù.**	(*lit.* I at bank open asp one mw account) I have opened an account *at the bank*.
姐姐在外面晾衣服。	**Jiějie** *zài wàimiàn* **liàng yīfu.**	(*lit.* elder-sister at outside take-out-to-dry clothes) My elder sister was hanging *out* clothes to dry (*outside*).
她在草地上躺着。	**Tā** *zài cǎodì shang* **tǎngzhe.**	(*lit.* she at grass-land on lie asp) She was lying *on the grass*.

In the last example, 躺 **tǎng** must have the aspect marker 着 **zhe** (which almost functions as a rhythm filler), since the verb that comes at the end of a statement must have more than one syllable:

她在草地上休息/ 打滚/晒太阳。	**Tā zài cǎodì shang xiūxi/dǎgǔn/ shài tàiyáng.**	She rested/rolled/sunned herself on the grass.
NOT: *她在草地 上躺/坐/站。	**Tā zài cǎodì shang tǎng/zuò/zhàn.**	She lay/sat/stood on the grass.

Note: The verb 住 zhù 'live/lodge' is the main exception to this rule.

However, when the location phrase with 在 zài comes at the end of
the sentence, the structure is only acceptable with verbs like 躺 tǎng
'lie', 坐 zuò 'sit', 站 zhàn 'stand', 蹲 dūn 'crouch', 停 tíng 'stop/park/
alight' 降落 jiàngluò 'land/descend', etc., where the action terminates
on arrival at the location. (For more about 在 zài phrases see 13.5):

她躺/坐/蹲/ 站在草地上。	**Tā tǎng/zuò/dūn/zhàn zài cǎodì shang.**	She lay/sat/crouched/ stood on the grass.
*她唱/吃在 草地上。	**Tā chàng/chī zài cǎodì shang.**	She sang/ate on the grass.
*她休息/打滚/晒 太阳在草地上。	**Tā xiūxi/dǎgǔn/shài tàiyáng zài cǎodì shang.**	She rested/rolled/ sunned herself on the grass.

11.5 *Location phrases in existence sentences*

Sentences expressing the *existence* of someone or something in a particular locality usually have a phrase indicating location plus the verb
有 yǒu 'there is/are' as follows: phrase indicating location + 有 yǒu
+ (qualifier) + noun(s).

This construction is similar to the time expression existence sentences discussed in 10.7. Again, there is a contrast with English in
which parallel sentences usually begin with 'There is/are . . .':

镜子旁边有 一盆花儿。	**Jìngzi pángbiān yǒu yī pén huār.**	(*lit.* mirror beside have one mw pot flower) There is a pot of flowers beside the mirror.
松树底下有 一只兔子。	**Sōngshù dǐxia yǒu yī zhī tùzi.**	(*lit.* pine-tree under there-is one mw hare [or rabbit]) There is a hare under the pine tree.
舞台上只有 两个演员。	**Wǔtái shang zhǐ yǒu liǎng gè yǎnyuán.**	(*lit.* stage on only there-are two mw actor) There are only two actors on the stage.

这儿附近有 洗衣店吗?	**Zhèr fùjìn yǒu** **xǐyīdiàn ma?**	(*lit.* here nearby there-is laundry p) Is there a laundry near here?
哪儿有 厕所?	**Nǎr yǒu** **cèsuǒ?**	(*lit.* where there-is toilet) Where is there a toilet?
里边有人。	**Lǐbian yǒu rén.**	(*lit.* inside there-are people) There is somebody inside.

Note: We have already pointed out (see Chapter 1) that the subject of a verb tends to be of definite reference. The last two examples could therefore be rephrased as:

厕所在哪儿?	**Cèsuǒ zài nǎr?**	Where is *the* toilet?
人在里边。	**Rén zài lǐbian.**	*The* person/people (or, colloquially, 's/he'/'they') is/are inside.

As illustrated by the above examples, the noun following 有 yǒu is always of indefinite reference. It would not be natural to say:

*动物园 里有那 头熊猫。	**Dòngwùyuán** **li yǒu nèi tóu** **xióngmāo.**	(*lit.* zoo in there-is that mw panda) There is that panda in the zoo.

11.5.1 | **Shì** in existence sentences

The verb 是 shì may also be used in existence sentences which start with a phrase indicating location. The function of 是 shì in these sentences is more complex than that of 有 yǒu. When the emphasis is on 'defining' what exists at a location, 是 shì is followed by a noun of indefinite reference:

剧场隔壁 是一个 展览馆。	**Jùchǎng gébì** **shì yī gè** **zhǎnlǎnguǎn.**	(*lit.* theatre next-door be one mw exhibition-hall) Next door to the theatre is *an* exhibition hall.

When the emphasis is on 'locating' where something is, the noun after 是 shì is of definite reference:

客厅对面 是卧室。	**Kètīng duìmiàn** **shì wòshì.**	(*lit.* guest-hall opposite be bedroom) Opposite the sitting- room is *the* bedroom.

Note: See also the last note under 6.4.

是 **Shì** can also be modified by 都 **dōu** or 全 **quán** 'all' to mean that a location is filled or covered with identified objects or people:

冰箱里边 都是水果。	**Bīngxiāng lǐbian** ***dōu shì shuǐguǒ.***	(*lit.* ice-box inside all be fruit) Inside the fridge there was nothing but fruit.
地上 全是水。	**Dì shang** ***quán shì shuǐ.***	(*lit.* floor/ground on all be water) There is water all over the floor/ground.

│ 11.5.2 │ **Zhe** in existence sentences

Like 有 **yǒu** and 是 **shì**, action verbs suffixed with the aspect marker 着 **zhe** may be used in location-related existence sentences. As in 8.3.4, these verbs indicate a 'state resulting from an action':

墙上挂着 一幅画。	**Qiáng shang** ***guàzhe yī fú huà.***	(*lit.* wall on hang asp one mw painting) There is a painting hanging on the wall.
桌子上 放着两 杯茶。	**Zhuōzi shang** ***fàngzhe liǎng*** **bēi chá.**	(*lit.* table on put asp two mw:cup tea) There are two cups of tea (placed) on the table.
房子里 住着不 少人。	**Fángzi li *zhùzhe*** **bù shǎo rén.**	(*lit.* house in live asp not few person) There are quite a lot of people living in the house.
戏院入口 处排着 一队人。	**Xìyuàn** **rùkǒuchù *páizhe*** **yī duì rén.**	(*lit.* theatre entrance queue asp one mw:queue people) There was a line of people queuing at the entrance to the theatre.

Note: Some nouns (e.g. 入口处 **rùkǒuchù** 'entrance') which themselves indicate some form of location are commonly used without a postposition.

If the action verb denotes persistent activity, (正)在 **(zhèng)zài** is used instead of 着 **zhe**:

体育馆里 (正)在进行 体操比赛。	**Tǐyùguǎn li** ***(zhèng)zài*** ***jìnxíng tǐcāo*** **bǐsài.**	(*lit.* gymnasium in (just) asp: in-the-process-of conduct gymnastics competition) A gymnastics contest is going on in the gymnasium.
广场上 (正)在举办 工艺品 展览。	**Guǎngchǎng** **shang *(zhèng)zài*** ***jǔbàn gōngyìpǐn*** **zhǎnlǎn.**	(*lit.* square on (just) asp: in-the-process-of hold handicraft exhibition) A handicraft exhibition is being held in the square.

Le *in emergence or disappearance sentences*

In the same way, a phrase indicating location may be followed by a verb with the aspect marker 了 **le** to express the *emergence* or *disappearance* of something or somebody at or from that location. The pattern is: phrase indicating location + action verb + 了 **le** + (qualifier) + noun(s).
For example:

我家来了 很多客人。	**Wǒ jiā láile hěn duō kèren.**	(*lit.* my house come asp very many guest) Many guests came to/turned up at my place.
图书馆 丢了不 少书。	**Túshūguǎn diūle bù shǎo shū.**	(*lit.* library lost asp not few book) The library has lost quite a few books.

Note: Compare the similar structure for time expressions (10.7.1).

| 11.7 | *Order of sequence of time and location phrases*

Where a location phrase and a time phrase occur in an existence or an emergence/disappearance sentence, either phrase may come first. (This differs from the adverbial use of location and time phrases, discussed in 11.1 in which the time expression must come first.) For instance:

昨天晚上 城里有一个 示威游行。	*Zuótiān wǎnshang chéng li yǒu yī gè shìwēi yóuxíng.*	(*lit.* yesterday evening town-in there-was one mw demonstration parade)
or, 城里 昨天晚上 有一个示威 游行。	*Chéng li zuótiān wǎnshang yǒu yī gè shìwēi yóuxíng.*	(*lit.* town in yesterday evening there-was one mw demonstration parade) There was a demonstration in (the) town yesterday evening.

12 Verbs: duration and frequency

| 12.1 | *Duration expressions*

Unlike defined point-of-time expressions, duration and frequency expressions usually come after the verb. As observed above, in a Chinese sentence, setting in time and space is established before the action of the verb is expressed; duration and frequency on the other hand, as consequences of the verb, are delineated after the action of the verb has been described.

Duration expressions naturally take the form of a numeral followed by a time word. In some cases the time word requires a measure (e.g. 月 **yuè** 'month', 钟头 **zhōngtóu** 'hour', 礼拜 **lǐbài** 'week', which take 个 **gè**). In other cases the time word is itself a measure word, and numerals may therefore be placed immediately before it (e.g. 一年 **yī nián** 'one year', 四天 **sì tiān** 'four days'). With 小时 **xiǎoshí** 'hour' and 星期 **xīngqī** 'week' the measure 个 **gè** is optional. Another more general duration expression is 很久/很长时间 **hěn jiǔ/hěn cháng shíjiān** 'a long time'.

Note: Since numerals up to twelve are used with 月 **yuè** to denote the calendar months (see Chapter 10 above), care must be taken to distinguish, for example 三月 **sān yuè** 'March' and 三个月 **sān gè yuè** 'three months'.

我在英国住了两年。	**Wǒ zài Yīngguó zhùle liǎng nián.**	(*lit.* I at Britain live asp two year) I lived in Britain for two years.
我准备在英国呆/待六个月。	**Wǒ zhǔnbèi zài Yīngguó dāi liù gè yuè.**	(*lit.* I prepare at Britain stay six mw month) I am preparing/intend to stay in Britain for six months.
我睡了八个小时/钟头。	**Wǒ shuìle bā gè xiǎoshí/zhōngtóu.**	(*lit.* I sleep asp eight mw hour) I slept for eight hours.
我们谈了很久。	**Wǒmen tánle hěn jiǔ.**	(*lit.* we talk asp very long) We talked for a long time.

12.1.1	Duration expressions and noun objects

If the verb in the sentence has a noun object as well as a duration phrase, the duration phrase is placed between the verb and the noun:

我学过四个多月中文。	**Wǒ xuéguo sì gè duō yuè Zhōngwén.**	(*lit.* I study asp four mw more month Chinese) I studied Chinese for more than four months (at one stage).
我打了半个钟头羽毛球。	**Wǒ dǎle bàn gè zhōngtóu yǔmáoqiú.**	(*lit.* I hit asp half mw hour badminton) I played badminton for half an hour.

The duration phrase may also be regarded as attributive and used with or without 的 **de**:

我学过四个 多月的中文。	**Wǒ xuéguo sì gè duō yuè de Zhōngwén.**	(*lit.* I study asp four mw month p Chinese) I studied Chinese for four months (at one stage).
我明天下午 要讲两个钟 头的课。	**Wǒ míngtiān xiàwǔ yào jiǎng liǎng gè zhōngtóu de kè.**	(*lit.* I tomorrow afternoon will talk two mw hour p lesson) I am going to lecture for two hours tomorrow afternoon.

This is the case whether the sentence is a simple or causative construction:

钢琴老师 要求我每天 练三个小时 (的)琴。	**Gāngqín lǎoshī yāoqiú wǒ měitiān liàn sān gè xiǎoshí (de) qín.**	(*lit.* piano teacher require me every day practise three mw hour de piano) The piano teacher told me to practise the piano three hours a day.
法官判 小偷坐 一年牢。	**Fǎguān pàn xiǎotōu zuò yī nián láo.**	(*lit.* judge sentence thief sit one year prison) The judge sentenced the thief to one year in prison.

12.1.2 Repetition of the verb in a noun-object-duration structure

An alternative pattern when a noun object is present is to repeat the verb after the object and then place the duration phrase after the repeated verb:

我学中文 学了四年。	**Wǒ xué Zhōngwén xuéle sì nián.**	(*lit.* I study Chinese study asp four year) I studied Chinese for four years.
他们聊天 聊了一个 晚上。	**Tāmen liáotiān liáole yī gè wǎnshang.**	(*lit.* they chat chat asp one mw evening) They chatted the whole evening.

In this construction the repeated verb is usually one of completed action with aspect marker 了 le.

12.1.3 Duration expressions and pronoun objects

When there is a pronoun object, the duration phrase always follows the pronoun:

我等了他半 个多钟头。	**Wǒ děngle tā bàn gè duō zhōngtóu.**	(*lit.* I wait asp him half mw more hour) I waited for him for over half an hour.

12.1.4 Duration expressions in dative construction

In a dative construction, where both direct and indirect objects are present, the duration phrase comes after the indirect object and precedes the direct object as an attributive (see 12.1.1):

老师教了我 两个小时 (的)中文。	**Lǎoshī jiāo le wǒ liǎng gè xiǎoshí (de) zhōngwén.**	(*lit.* teacher teach asp me two mw hour de Chinese) The teacher taught me two hours of Chinese.
她欠了银行 半年(的)债。	**Tā qiàn le yínháng bàn nián (de) zhài.**	(*lit.* she owe asp bank half year de debt) She was in debt to the bank for six months.

12.1.5 Duration expressions and definite reference

If the duration expression alludes to a period of time in the past within which something has or has not happened, it then takes on definite reference and is placed, like other time expressions, before the verb. Duration expressions of this type are often followed by 里/内 **li/nèi** 'within (the last) . . .' or 以来 (**yǐ**)**lái** 'since . . .':

我三个月 内/里看了 五次电影。	**Wǒ *sān gè yuè* *nèi/li* kànle wǔ cì diànyǐng.**	(*lit.* I three mw month within see asp five times film) I have been to the cinema five times *in the past three months*.
我半年 没去看 电影了。	**Wǒ *bàn nián* méi qù kàn diànyǐng le.**	(*lit.* I half year not go see film p) I have not been to see a film *for the last six months*.
我一年 (以)来都 在实验室 工作。	**Wǒ *yī nián* *(yǐ)lái* dōu zài shíyànshì gōngzuò.**	(*lit.* I one year so-far all at laboratory work) I have been working in the laboratory *for the whole of the past year*.
我圣诞节 以来都没 上过班。	**Wǒ *Shèngdànjié yǐlái* dōu méi shàngguo bān.**	(*lit.* I Christmas so-far all not go-on asp shift) I have not been back to work ever *since Christmas*.
我这三年 来都没见 过我的 表弟。	**Wǒ *zhèi sān nián lái* dōu méi jiànguo wǒde biǎo dì.**	(*lit.* I this three year within all not see asp my cousin) I haven't seen my cousin *for the last three years*.

Note: In Chinese, terms for cousins, like other family relationships, are very precise. On the mother's side they are 表哥 **biǎo gē**, 表弟 **biǎo dì**, 表姐 **biǎo jiě**, 表妹 **biǎo mèi**, and on the father's side 堂哥 **táng gē**, 堂弟 **táng dì**, etc.

| 12.2 | **Brief duration** |

Brief duration can be conveyed by repeating the verb, sometimes after 一 **yī** 'one', or by using phrases like 一下 **yī xià** 'a moment' or 一会儿 **yī huìr** 'a short while' after the verb:

(1) Repetition of verbs:

(a) Monosyllabic verbs:

看看	**kànkàn**	have a look
看一看	**kàn yī kàn**	have a look
看了看	**kànle kàn**	had a look

(b) Disyllabic verbs (cannot be used with 一 **yī** or 了 **le**):

| 介绍介绍 | **jièshào jièshào** | give a brief introduction |

NOT:
| *介绍一介绍 | **jièshào yī jièshào** | give a brief introduction |
| *介绍了介绍 | **jièshàole jièshào** | gave a brief introduction |

(c) Verb object constructions (only the verb is repeated):

洗手	**xǐ shǒu**	wash hands
洗一洗手	**xǐ (yī) xǐ shǒu**	wash one's hands
扫地	**sǎo dì**	sweep the floor
扫了扫地	**sǎole sǎo dì**	swept the floor (briefly)

NOT: *洗手洗手   **xǐ shǒu xǐ shǒu**
or *扫地扫地   **sǎo dì sǎo dì**

(2) With 一下 **yī xià** or 一会儿 **yī huìr**:

| 让我看一下。 | **Ràng wǒ *kàn yī xià*.** | Let me have a look. |
| 咱们休息一会儿。 | **Zànmen *xiūxi yī huìr*.** | We'll rest for a while. |

Where the verb has an object, brief duration phrases, like other duration phrases, come before the object:

| 我们跳了一下舞。 | **Wǒmen tiàole *yī xià* wǔ.** | We danced for a while. |
| 我看了一会儿书。 | **Wǒ kànle *yī huìr* shū.** | I read for a while. |

 Brief duration and instrumental objects

Brief duration may also be expressed by employing an *instrumental object*, often part of the body, which follows the indirect object in a dative construction:

他打了我	**Tā dǎle wǒ**	(*lit.* He hit asp me one fist)
一拳。	**yī quán.**	He dealt me a blow.
我踢了他	**Wǒ tīle tā**	(*lit.* I kick asp him one foot)
一脚。	**yī jiǎo.**	I gave him a kick.
教练看了	**Jiàoliàn kànle**	(*lit.* coach look asp everybody one eye)
大家一眼。	**dàjiā yī yǎn.**	The coach cast a glance at everybody.
我们见过	**Wǒmen**	(*lit.* we see asp one face)
一面。	**jiànguo yī miàn.**	We met once.

Note: The last example may be reformulated as a dative construction: 我见过他一面。Wǒ jiànguo tā yī miàn. 'I met him once.'

 Frequency expressions

Frequency phrases, like duration phrases, come after the verb. They consist of a numeral combined with one of a number of common frequency measure words such as 次 cì, 遍 biàn, 回 huí and 趟 tàng. While 次 cì simply indicates an occurrence, 遍 biàn implies 'from beginning to end', 回 huí 'to and fro', and 趟 tàng 'back and forth from a place':

他们来	**Tāmen**	They've come/been here
过三次。	**láiguo sān cì.**	three times.
我念了一遍。	**Wǒ niànle yī biàn.**	I read [it] through once (from beginning to end).
我们见过	**Wǒmen jiànguo**	We have met him/her twice.
她两回。	**tā liǎng huí.**	
我去过几趟。	**Wǒ qùguo jǐ tàng.**	I have been [there] several times.

If the verb has a noun object, the frequency phrase is generally placed between the verb and the object.

我看过	**Wǒ kànguo**	(*lit.* I see asp two times opera)
两次歌剧。	**liǎng cì gējù.**	I have been twice to see an opera.
他坐过	**Tā zuòguo**	(*lit.* He sit asp three trip (air)plane)
三趟飞机。	**sān tàng fēijī.**	He has been on a plane three times.

If the object is a location phrase, however, the frequency phrase may be placed either between the verb and the location object or after the location object:

我去了两趟北京。	**Wǒ qùle *liǎng tàng* Běijīng.**	I went to
or, 我去了北京两趟。	**Wǒ qùle Běijīng *liǎng tàng.***	Beijing twice.
她来过一次我家。	**Tā láiguo *yī cì* wǒ jiā.**	She has been
or, 她来过我家一次。	**Tā láiguo wǒ jiā *yī cì.***	to my place once.

As with duration phrases, if the object is a pronoun, the frequency phrase is placed after the pronoun:

| 我找过他一次。 | **Wǒ zhǎoguo tā *yī cì.*** | I looked for/visited |
| NOT: *我找过一次他。 | **Wǒ zhǎoguo *yī cì* tā.** | him once. |

The above-mentioned rules regarding the position of the frequency phrase in relation to noun or pronoun objects always apply whatever the construction:

她帮过我 一次忙。	**Tā bāngguo wǒ yī cì máng.** (dative)	(*lit.* she help asp me one-time busy) She helped me once.
爸爸带我去 了一趟欧洲/ 爸爸带我去 了欧洲一趟。	**Bàba dài wǒ qùle yī tàng Ōuzhōu.** (causative)	(*lit.* Father take me go asp one-trip Europe/father take me go asp Europe one-trip) On one occasion, my father took me on a trip to Europe.
嫂嫂劝我 找他一次。	**Sǎosao quàn wǒ zhǎo tā yī cì.** (causative)	(*lit.* sister-in-law persuade me look for him one-time) My sister-in-law persuaded me to at least go and see him once.

13 Verbs and complements

13.1 Complements

As we have seen, Chinese verbs are seldom used without some form of marker or attachment. They are regularly modified (e.g. by time and location expressions) or complemented in some way. *Complements* in Chinese are those elements of a sentence which come after the verb (apart from the object) and which either describe the action of the verb or express its result.

A number of complements which occur with action verbs have already been encountered, for example, aspect markers, direction indicators and duration/frequency markers. Here we introduce a further range of complements, those indicating result, potential, manner, location/destination and degree.

| 13.2 | *Complements of result*

Complements of result are adjectives or verbs which follow immediately after the main verb. They indicate the direct result of an action, either what it achieves or what happens unintentionally. For example, the verb complement 见 **jiàn** 'to see' implies successful seeing or apprehension, as in 看见 **kàn jiàn** 'to see' (*lit.* look-see) and 听见 **tīng jiàn** 'to hear' (*lit.* listen-apprehend), while the adjective complement 错 **cuò** 'wrong' indicates a mistaken result, as in 听错 **tīng cuò** 'to mishear' (*lit.* listen-wrong) and 看错 **kàn cuò** 'to misread' (*lit.* look-wrong). Although most complements of result are monosyllabic, some of the adjectival ones are disyllabic (e.g. 清楚 **qīngchu** 'clear', 干净 **gānjìng** 'clean', etc.).

(1) Adjectives:

你猜错了。	**Nǐ cāi cuò le.**	(*lit.* you guess wrong p) You have guessed wrong.
他修好了那辆摩托车。	**Tā xiū hǎo le nèi liàng mótuōchē.**	(*lit.* He repair good asp that mw motorbike) He has repaired that motorbike.
他弄脏了她的裙子。	**Tā nòng zāng le tāde qúnzi.**	(*lit.* He make dirty asp her skirt) He has dirtied her skirt.
他没听清楚我的话。	**Tā méi tīng qīngchǔ wǒde huà.**	(*lit.* He not listen clear my words) He didn't hear clearly what I said.

(2) Verbs:

| 我已经做完了我的作业。 | **Wǒ yǐjing zuò wán le wǒde zuòyè.** | (*lit.* I already do finish asp my homework/coursework) I have already done my homework. |
| 你听懂了吗？ | **Nǐ tīng dǒng le ma?** | (*lit.* you listen understand asp p) Did you understand (what was said)? |

你六点钟 叫醒我。	**Nǐ liù diǎn zhōng** *jiào xǐng* **wǒ.**	(*lit.* you six o'clock call wake me) Wake me up at six.
他们拉开了 两个正在 打架的人。	**Tāmen** *lā kāi* **le liǎng gè zhèngzài dǎjià de rén.**	(*lit.* they pull separate asp two mw asp fight p person) They pulled apart two people who were fighting.

Many verb-and-complement expressions in fact are established
terms in the language:

人民的 生活水平 提高了。	**Rénmín de shēnghuó shuǐpíng** *tígāo* **le.**	(*lit.* people p life level raise-high p) The people's living standards have improved.
他打断了 我的发言。	**Tā** *dǎduàn* **le wǒde fāyán.**	(*lit.* He hit-broken-in-two asp my speech) He interrupted my speech.

Note: The most common complements of result, apart from the above, are:

(a)   *Adjectives*

坏 **huài**	bad	这个孩子弄坏了我的电脑。**Zhèi gè háizi** *nòng huài* **le wǒde diànnǎo.**
对 **duì**	right	你猜对了。**Nǐ** *cāi duì* **le.** You guessed right.
饱 **bǎo**	full (with eating)	我吃饱了。**Wǒ** *chī bǎo* **le.** I have eaten my fill/I'm full.
醉 **zuì**	drunk	我的朋友喝醉了。**Wǒde péngyou** *hē zuì* **le.** My friend is/was drunk.

(b)   *Verbs*

破 **pò**	break	我打破了眼镜。**Wǒ** *dǎ pò* **le yǎnjìng.** I broke my glasses.
到 **dào**	attain, achieve (purpose)	她找到了她的钱包。 **Tā** *zhǎo dào* **le tāde qiánbāo.** She's found her purse/wallet.

掉 **diào**	drop	他改掉了那个坏习惯。 **Tā gǎi diào le nèi gè huài xíguàn.** He's dropped that bad habit.
倒 **dǎo**	fall over	运动员摔倒了。**Yùndòngyuán shuāi dǎo le.** The athlete fell over.
住 **zhù**	stop, make firm	警察抓住了小偷。**Jǐngchá zhuā zhù le xiǎotōu.** The policeman (has) caught the thief. 记住这件事。**Jì zhù zhèi jiàn shì.** Try and remember this.

13.3 *Potential complements*

Ability or inability to do something is regularly expressed by a *poten-tial complement*. This is formed by placing 得 **de** (positive) or 不 **bù** (negative) between a verb and a complement of result. The potential complement, which is a distinctive feature of Chinese, implies that the result of the action can (or cannot) be achieved or happen, that is that the outcome is to some extent dependent on external circumstances beyond the speaker's control. (This contrasts with the use of the modal verb 能(够) **néng(gòu)** 'can', see 15.2 (5).)

(1) Adjectival potential complements:

他吃 不饱。	**Tā chī bù bǎo.**	(*lit.* He eat not full) He couldn't eat his fill. (i.e. there wasn't enough food to go round, he is such a big eater, etc.)
你站得 稳吗？	**Nǐ zhàn de wěn ma?**	(*lit.* you stand can stable p) Can you stand up (without falling)? (i.e. somebody has had too much to drink, has been ill, etc.)
这条牛仔 裤洗得 干净吗？	**Zhèi tiáo niúzǎikù xǐ de gānjìng ma?**	(*lit.* this mw jeans wash can clean p) Can these jeans be washed (clean)?

(2) Verbal potential complements:

她听得懂 我的话。	**Tā tīng de dǒng wǒde huà.**	(*lit.* She listen can understand my words) She could understand my words. (because they were not too profound, not strongly accented, etc.)

99

我走 不了了。	**Wǒ zǒu** **bù liǎo le.**	(*lit.* leave not achievable) I can't (possibly) leave. (i.e. there are no more trains, the work isn't finished yet, the weather is too bad, etc.)
大家都看 不见黑板 上的字。	**Dàjiā dōu** **kàn bù jiàn** **hēibǎn shang** **de zì.**	(*lit.* everybody all look not see blackboard-on p words/characters) Nobody can see the words/characters on the blackboard. (i.e. the blackboard is too far away, the words/characters are too small, etc.)
我走 不动了。	**Wǒ zǒu** **bù dòng le.**	(*lit.* I walk not move p) I can't walk any further (i.e. too tired, etc.)
这个人靠 得住吗?	**Zhèi gè rén** **kào de zhù** **ma?**	(*lit.* this mw person rely de fast p) Is this person reliable?

13.3.1 | Potential complements using direction indicators

Directional complements (see direction indicators discussed in 9.2) can also be used in the potential form:

我吃不 下了。	**Wǒ chī bù** **xià le.**	(*lit.* I eat not down) I can't eat any more. (i.e. too full, having already eaten too much, etc.)
我们 今天搬 不进去。	**Wǒmen** **jīntiān bān** **bù jìnqù.**	(*lit.* we today move not into-go) We can't move in today (e.g. into a flat, etc.). (i.e. the flat, etc. has not been vacated yet, etc.)
书要得 回来吗?	**Shū yào** **de huílái** **ma?**	(*lit.* book get can come-back p) Can I/you get the books back? (i.e. someone will or won't return them, etc.)

13.3.2 | Metaphorical meanings of potential complements

We have seen in 9.3 that direction indicators/complements may carry meanings beyond simply physical movement. Similar metaphorical usages are found with potential complement of direction:

这个礼堂 坐得下 一千人。	**Zhèi gè lǐtáng** **zuò de xià yī** **qiān rén.**	(*lit.* this mw auditorium sit can contain one thousand person) This hall can seat one thousand people.
我买不起 照相机。	**Wǒ mǎi bù qǐ** **zhàoxiàngjī.**	(*lit.* I buy not up camera) I can't afford a camera.

| 妈妈想
不起这
件事。 | **Māma** *xiǎng*
bù qǐ zhèi
jiàn shì. | (*lit.* mother think not up this mw matter) Mum can't recall this matter. (i.e. it happened a long time ago, her memory lets her down, etc.) |
| 她说不
下去了。 | **Tā** *shuō bù*
xiàqù le. | (*lit.* she speak not continue p) She can't carry on talking any more. (i.e. choked by emotion, having a sore throat, being shouted down, etc.) |

13.4 | *Complements of manner and of consequential state*

The *complements of manner and of consequential state* involve placing 得 de after a verbal or adjectival predicate followed by *either* an adjectival phrase (*normally indicating manner*) or a verbal phrase or clause (*usually indicating consequential state*). The adjectival phrase in a complement of manner describes the way in which an action is seen to be carried out. (This contrasts with adverbial modifiers which emphasise more the intention or demeanour of the initiator of the action – see 14.1 for further comment on this point.) The complement of consequential state can follow either an adjectival or a verbal predicate. It depicts an observed situation which arises from an action or an ongoing state but which is not necessarily an intended outcome.

13.4.1 | Modification of complement of manner

In the complement of manner, the adjective in the adjectival phrase must be either adverbially modified or followed by a degree complement (see 13.6 below):

她说得不 太清楚。	**Tā** *shuō de bù* *tài qīngchu.*	(*lit.* she speak p not too clear) She did not put it too clearly.
那匹马跑 得比较/ 最快。	**Nèi pǐ mǎ pǎo** *de bǐjiào/* *zuì kuài.*	(*lit.* that mw horse run p comparatively/most fast) That horse ran faster [than the others]/the fastest [of all].
歌咏队唱 得好极了。	**Gēyǒngduì** **chàng de** *hǎo jí le.*	(*lit.* chorus/choir sing p good extreme p) The chorus/choir sang extremely well.
我今天起 得早得多。	**Wǒ jīntiān qǐ** *de zǎo de duō.*	(*lit.* I today get-up p early much-more) I got up much earlier today.
战士们 站得很直。	**Zhànshìmen** **zhàn de** *hěn zhí.*	(*lit.* soldiers stand p very straight) The soldiers stood very straight.

那个姑娘	**Nèi gè gūniang**	(*lit.* that mw girl dress-up p very
打扮得<u>很</u>	**dǎbàn de *hěn***	beautiful) That young girl is dressed
漂亮。	**piàoliang.**	up very beautifully.

Note: The last two examples illustrate that with some verbs the manner complement borders on expressing consequential state.

| 13.4.2 | Complement of consequential state

The complement of consequential state is either a verbal phrase or a clause:

(1) Verbal phrase:

| 她跑得 | **Tā pǎo de** | (*lit.* she run p non-stop pant) |
| 直喘气。 | ***zhí chuǎnqì.*** | She ran till she was out of breath. |

| 她冷得 | **Tā lěng** | (*lit.* she cold p shiver p) She was so |
| 发抖了。 | **de *fādǒu le.*** | cold that she began to shiver. |

(2) Clause:

他走得	**Tā zǒu de**	(*lit.* He walk p leg all/also weak p)
脚都/也	***jiǎo dōu/yě***	He walked till his legs were
软了。	***ruǎn le.***	very weak.

他笑得	**Tā xiào de**	(*lit.* He smile/laugh p mouth all/also
嘴都/也合	***zuǐ dōu/yě hé***	close not together p)
不拢了。	***bù lǒng le.***	He grinned broadly.

我困得	**Wǒ kùn de**	(*lit.* I tired-and-sleepy p eye both also
眼睛都/也	***yǎnjing dōu/yě***	open not separate p) I was so sleepy
睁不开了。	***zhēng bù kāi le.***	that my eyes refused to open.

Note: For emphasis these complemental clauses often make use of the adverbs 都/也 *dōu/yě* 'all'/'also'. In addition, the preposition or coverb 连 *lián* 'even' may precede the subject in the clause. For instance, the second example above may be rewritten as: 他笑<u>得</u>连嘴都合不拢了。*Tā xiào de lián zuǐ dōu hé bù lǒng le.*

| 13.4.3 | Complements of manner or consequential state with a 'verb + object' verb

When a complement of manner or consequential state occurs with a 'verb + object' verb, the verb is repeated after the object and then followed by the complement:

她跳舞跳得很好。	**Tā tiàowǔ tiào de hěn hǎo.**	(*lit.* she dance-dances dance p very well) She danced very well.
他打字打得很快。	**Tā dǎzì dǎ de hěn kuài.**	(*lit.* he type-words type p very quick) He types very fast.
我跑步跑得浑身都热了。	**Wǒ pǎobù pǎo de húnshēn dōu rè le.**	(*lit.* I run-step run p whole-body all hot p) I ran (so much) that I was hot all over.

13.4.4 | Adjectival complements of manner in comparisons

Adjectival complements of manner may express comparison (note the general discussion of comparison, equivalence, etc., in 7.2 and 7.2.3). In such complements the '比 **bǐ** + (pro)noun', '跟 **gēn** + (pro)noun' and '没(有) **méi(yǒu)** + (pro)noun' expressions are placed either before the main verb, or before the adjective in the complement:

我跳得比他高。	**Wǒ tiào de bǐ tā gāo.**	(*lit.* I jump p compare he high) I jump higher than he does.
or, 我比他跳得高。	**Wǒ bǐ tā tiào de gāo.**	(*lit.* I compare he jump p high)
这匹马跑得跟那匹马一样快。	**Zhèi pǐ mǎ pǎo de gēn nèi pǐ mǎ yīyàng kuài.**	(*lit.* this mw horse run p and that mw horse same fast) This horse runs as fast as that one.
or, 这匹马跟那匹马跑得一样快。	**Zhèi pǐ mǎ gēn nèi pǐ mǎ pǎo de yīyàng kuài.**	(*lit.* this mw horse and that mw horse run p same fast)
我考得没(有)他那么好。	**Wǒ kǎo de méi(yǒu) tā nàme hǎo.**	(*lit.* I examine p not-have he so good) I did not do as well as he did in the examination.
or, 我没(有)他考得那么好。	**Wǒ méi(yǒu) tā kǎo de nàme hǎo.**	(*lit.* I not-have he examine p so good)

13.4.5 | Complement-of-manner comparison with a 'verb + object' verb

Where the complement-of-manner comparison occurs with a 'verb + object' verb, the same rule applies, with the '比 **bǐ** + (pro)noun', '跟 **gēn** + (pro)noun' or '没(有) **méi(yǒu)** + (pro)noun' phrase located either before the repeated verb or before the adjective in the complement:

他唱歌唱得 比我好听。	**Tā chànggē chàng** **de bǐ wǒ hǎotīng.**	(*lit.* s/he sing-songs sing p compare me good-to-hear) She sings better than I do.
or, 他唱歌比 我唱得好听。	**Tā chànggē bǐ wǒ** **chàng de hǎotīng.**	(*lit.* s/he sing-songs compare me sing p good-to-hear)
我说中文说 得没(有)他 那么流利。	**Wǒ shuō** **Zhōngwén shuō** **de méi(yǒu) tā** **nàme liúlì.**	(*lit.* I speak Chinese speak p not-have he (so) fluent) I don't speak Chinese as fluently as he does.
or, 我说中文 没(有)他说得 那么流利。	**Wǒ shuō Zhōngwén** **méi(yǒu) tā shuō de** **nàme liúlì.**	(*lit.* I speak Chinese not-have s/he speak p (so) fluent)

Note: The '比 **bǐ** + (pro)noun' and other comparative phrases cannot precede the first verb: e.g. *他比我唱歌唱得好听。*Tā bǐ wǒ chànggē chàng de hǎotīng.*

13.5	*Complement of location or destination*

Complements of location/destination occur with motion verbs and indicate the location where the subject ends up through the action of the verb.

汽车停 在车房。	**Qìchē tíng** **zài chēfáng.**	(*lit.* car stop at garage) The car was parked at the garage.
妈妈回 到家里。	**Māma huí** **dào jiā li.**	(*lit.* mother return to home in) Mother came home.

It would not be normal to say:

*他学习在 图书馆。	**Tā xuéxí zài** **túshūguǎn.**	(*lit.* he study at library)

because 学习 **xuéxí** 'study' does not express any spatial motion. It would be more natural to use an adverbial modifier before the verb:

他在图书馆 学习。	**Tā zài túshūguǎn** **xuéxí.**	(*lit.* he at library study) He studied at the library.

The location phrase as an adverbial placed before the verb indicates where the subject was before the action of the verb took place, i.e. one must get to the library before one can settle down to study there. In contrast, the location/destination phrase as complement indicates where the subject finishes up after the action has taken place.

Compare the following two sentences:

| 她走到公园去。 | **Tā zǒu dào gōngyuán qù.** | (*lit*. she walk to park go) She went to the park [on foot]. (i.e. she set out with the park as her destination.) |
| 她到公园去走走。 | **Tā dào gōngyuán qù zǒuzǒu.** | (*lit*. she get-to park go walk-walk) She went for a walk in the park. (i.e. she got to the park first and then took a walk there.) |

| 13.6 | *Degree complements* |

Degree complements follow and intensify adjectives. They are generally stronger in meaning than the degree adverbs and expressions introduced in 6.2.1 (e.g. 很 **hěn** 'very', 太 **tài** 'too', 相当 **xiāngdāng** 'rather', 够 **gòu** 'enough', 有点儿 **yǒu diǎnr** 'a bit', etc.). The most common degree complements are:

(1)	得很	de hěn	very
	冷得很	lěng de hěn	very cold
(2)	得多	de duō	much more
	好得多	hǎo de duō	much better
	多了	duō le	much more
	贵多了	guì duō le	much more expensive
(3)	极了	jí le	extremely
	高兴极了	gāoxìng jí le	extremely happy
(4)	透了	tòu le	thoroughly
	湿透了	shī tòu le	wet through
(5)	死了	sǐ le	extremely, terribly
	饿死了	è sǐ le	terribly hungry
(6)	得要命	de yàomìng	terribly
	热得要命	rè de yàomìng	terribly hot
(7)	得不得了	de bùdeliǎo	exceedingly
	坏得不得了	huài de bùdeliǎo	exceedingly bad
(8)	other 得 **de** + adjective/verb expressions:		
	得刺眼	de cìyǎn	eye-dazzling
	亮得刺眼	liàng de cìyǎn	dazzlingly bright
	得刺耳	de cì'ěr	ear-piercing
	响得刺耳	xiǎng de cì'ěr	ear-piercingly loud

Note: 得 de as used throughout this chapter in potential, manner, consequential state and degree complements is different from the attributive 的 de we have met earlier. The character for the 地 de which appears in Chapter 14 in adverbial modifiers is different again.

14 Verbs and adverbials

Adverbial modifiers are words or expressions, usually placed immediately before the verb or sometimes at the beginning of a sentence, which give additional information concerning the action or state expressed in the verb. They fall into three main categories: background, manner and attitude indicators. We have already discussed background indicators such as time and location expressions (see Chapters 10 and 11); here the focus is on adverbial modifiers of manner and attitude.

14.1 Adverbials of manner

Adverbials of manner consist of adjectives, normally two-syllable, followed by the particle 地 de:

| 她迅速地
跑过来。 | **Tā *xùnsù de*
pǎo guòlái.** | (*lit.* she speedy p run across)
She came over swiftly. |
| 她愉快地
笑了笑。 | **Tā *yúkuài de*
xiàole xiào.** | (*lit.* she happy p smile asp smile)
She smiled happily. |

The difference between an adverbial of manner and a complement of manner (see 13.4) is that the adverbial is concerned mainly with the 'demeanour', 'intention', etc., of the subject, while the complement is more concerned with the manner and result of the verb as observed by a third party. Compare:

Adverbial	Complement
他很快地跑着。	他跑得很快。
Tā *hěn kuài de* pǎozhe.	**Tā *pǎo de hěn kuài*.**
(*lit.* he very quick p run asp)	(*lit.* he run p very fast)
He ran *very fast*.	He ran *very fast*.
(i.e. He was intent on running fast)	(i.e. as apparent to an onlooker)
他十分出神地听着。	他听得十分出神。
Tā *shífēn chūshén de* tīngzhe.	**Tā *tīng de shífēn chūshén*.**
(*lit.* he extremely enchanted p listen asp)	(*lit.* he listen p extremely enchanted)
He listened *with great fascination*.	He listened *with great fascination*. (i.e. as could be observed)

| 14.1.1 | Monosyllabic adjectives as adverbials of manner |

A monosyllabic adjective must either be repeated or made disyllabic by the addition of a degree adverb to become an adverbial of manner:

| 她静静地
坐着。 | **Tā *jìngjìng de* zuòzhe.** | (*lit.* she quiet-quiet p sit p)
She sat (there) quietly. |
| 他很快地
转过身来。 | **Tā *hěn kuài de* zhuǎn guò shēn lái.** | (*lit.* he very quick p turn around body come) He quickly turned round. |

Note: Some disyllabic repetitions are established adverbial expressions and do not derive from monosyllabic adjectives:

悄悄地 **qiāoqiāo de**	quietly	他悄悄地告诉我。 **Tā *qiāoqiāo de* gàosù wò . . .** He told me quietly that . . .
偷偷地 **tōutōu de**	furtively	她偷偷地看了我一眼。 **Tā *tōutōu de* kànle wǒ yī yǎn.** She stole a glance at me.
默默地 **mòmò de**	silently	她默默地瞧着我。 **Tā *mòmò de* qiáozhe wǒ.** She looked at me silently.
渐渐地 **jiànjiàn de**	gradually	天气渐渐地暖和起来。 **Tiānqì *jiànjiàn de* nuǎnhuo qǐlái.** The weather gradually got warmer.

| 14.1.2 | Adverbials of manner with marked verbs |

As in the above sentences illustrating adverbials of manner, the verb preceded by an adverbial modifier usually has to be marked in some way, e.g. by a direction indicator or an aspect marker. In the following examples 站 **zhàn** is marked by 起来 **qǐlái** and 下 **xià** by 着 **zhe**.

| 我朋友慢慢地
站起来。 | **Wǒ péngyou *mànmàn de* zhàn qǐlái.** | (*lit.* my friend slow-slow p stand up) My friend stood up slowly. |
| 雪纷纷扬扬地
下着。 | **Xuě *fēnfēnyángyáng de* xiàzhe.** | (*lit.* snow hard-and-fast p fall asp) The snow came down thick and fast. |

14.1.3 Adverbials of manner with unmarked verbs

Adverbial modifiers may occur with unmarked verbs in expressions such as imperatives. 地 **De** is generally omitted, and the monosyllabic adverbial usually either reduplicated or extended by words such as 点儿 **diǎnr** or 些 **xiē** 'a bit'/'a little'.

快点儿来!	*Kuài diǎnr lái!*	(*lit.* quick a-bit come) Come here quickly!
早些回来。	*Zǎo xiē huílái.*	(*lit.* early a-little return-come) Come back a little earlier.
好好睡!	*Hǎohǎo shuì!*	(*lit.* good-good sleep) Go to sleep nicely! (parent to a child)
慢慢来!	*Mànmàn lái!*	(*lit.* slow-slow come) Take it easy!

14.1.4 Monosyllabic adverbial modifiers without **de**

Monosyllabic adverbial modifiers without 的 **de** occur in certain established expressions and imperatives:

慢走	*màn zǒu*	take care	*lit.* slow go (a polite expression when seeing guests off)
快起来	*kuài qǐlái*	up you get	*lit.* quick get-up (waking somebody in the morning)
多谢	*duō xiè*	many thanks	*lit.* much thank (an expression of gratitude)
多保重	*duō bǎozhòng*	look after yourself	*lit.* much take-care (a good wish at parting)

14.1.5 Particular types of adverbials of manner

Adverbials of manner are also formed from some particular types of phrase:

(1)　Onomatopoeic coinages:

风呼呼地吹着。	*Fēng hūhū de chuīzhe.*	(*lit.* wind onom p blow asp) The wind was howling.
蜜蜂在花丛中嗡嗡地飞着。	*Mìfēng zài huācóng zhōng wēng wēng de fēizhe.*	(*lit.* bee in flower-cluster middle onom p fly asp) The bees were humming amongst the flowers.

(2) Phonaesthetic expressions, in which a repeated syllable comes after an adjective, verb or noun to extend its descriptive quality through an association of sound and meaning:

他懒洋洋地躺着。	**Tā lǎnyāngyāng de tǎngzhe.**	(*lit.* he lazy-phon p lie asp) He *idly* lay there.
他兴冲冲地走进来。	**Tā xìngchōngchōng de zǒu jìnlái.**	(*lit.* he spirit-phon p walk in) He entered *in high spirits*.
她笑眯眯地点了点头。	**Tā xiàomīmī de diǎnle diǎn tóu.**	(*lit.* she smile-phon p nod asp nod head) She nodded *with a smile*.

(3) Quadrisyllabic idioms:

她无可奈何地耸了耸肩。	**Tā wúkě nàihé de sǒngle sǒng jiān.**	(*lit.* she without-able-do-what p shrug asp shrug shoulder) She shrugged her shoulders *helplessly*.
我情不自禁地叹了(一)口气。	**Wǒ qíng bù zì jìn de tànle (yī) kǒu qì.**	(*lit.* I feeling-not-self-forbid p sigh asp one mw:mouthful breath) I sighed *despite myself*.
我不知不觉地睡着了。	**Wǒ bù zhī bù jué de shuì zháo le.**	(*lit.* I not-know-not-feel p sleep achieve p) I fell asleep *without realising it*.

(4) Parallel constructions:

她一步一步地向前走去。	**Tā yī bù yī bù de xiàng qián zǒu qù.**	(*lit.* she one step one step p towards front walk go) She went forward *step by step*.
她一个字一个字地写着。	**Tā yī gè zì yī gè zì de xiězhe.**	(*lit.* she one mw character one mw character p write asp) She is writing [it] down *character by character*.

14.2   *Attitudinal adverbial expressions*

Attitudinal adverbial expressions are words or idioms used by the speaker to bring a tone of judgement or evaluation to the sentence. They occur either immediately after the subject or, if they are phrases, at the beginning of the sentence:

她当然不同意。	**Tā dāngrán bù tóngyì.**	(*lit.* she of-course not agree) She naturally disagreed.

| 我不一定去。 | **Wǒ bùyídìng qù.** | (*lit.* I not-certain go)
I can't say for sure that I will go. |
| 依我看，
她是对的。 | **Yī wǒ kàn,
tā shì duì de.** | (*lit.* according-I-see, she is right p)
As far as I can see, she is right. |

Note: Other common expressions of this type include: 甚至 **shènzhì** 'even', 总算 **zǒngsuàn** 'after all', 也许 **yěxǔ** 'perhaps', 可能 **kěnéng** 'probably', 肯定 **kěndìng** 'definitely', 对我来说 **duì wǒ lái shuō** 'as far as I am concerned', 在我看来 **zài wǒ kàn lái** 'as I see it', 毫无疑问 **háowú yíwèn** 'no doubt', 很不幸 **hěn bù xìng** 'unfortunately'.

| 我们总算
写完了。 | **Wǒmen zǒngsuàn
xiě wán le.** | We've finished writing [it] at last. |
| 他们也许听
得懂广州话。 | **Tāmen yěxǔ tīng de
dǒng Guǎngzhōuhuà.** | They can probably understand Cantonese. |

14.3 *Referential adverbs*

There are a number of monosyllabic adverbs which are placed directly before the main verb and have an important linking function in the meaning of the sentence. Since they refer forwards and/or backwards, we will call them *referential adverbs*. These referential adverbs also function as conjunctives linking clauses or predicates/comments in composite sentences (see Chapter 24), but here we deal with their place in simple sentences. Some are best discussed in pairs:

(1) 就 **Jiù** 'then' and 才 **cái** 'only then': 就 **jiù** emphasises a direct consequence, while 才 **cái** indicates that something ensued only at a particular time or under particular circumstances:

我们很早 就到了。	**Wǒmen hěn zǎo jiù dào le.**	(*lit.* we very early then arrive p) We arrived very early.
他们很晚 才来。	**Tāmen hěn wǎn cái lái.**	(*lit.* they very late only-then come) They didn't come till very late.
他们去年 就开始学 汉语了。	**Tāmen qùnián jiù kāishǐ xué Hànyǔ le.**	(*lit.* they last-year then begin learn Chinese p) They began to study Chinese (as early as) last year.
他们去年 才开始学 汉语。	**Tāmen qùnián cái kāishǐ xué Hànyǔ.**	(*lit.* they last-year only-then begin learn Chinese p) They did not begin to study Chinese until last year.

Note 1: Sentences with 就 jiù, as above, regularly end with 了 le, since
they almost certainly express a change in circumstances (see Chapter 16
for discussion of sentence 了 le). However, 了 le is not generally used
with 才 cái – see 16.3 (9).

Note 2: 便 Biàn 'then' may be used interchangeably with 就 jiù in this
sense, particularly in the written language.

就 Jiù can also emphasise immediacy:

我就来 (了)。	**Wǒ jiù lái (le).**	(*lit.* I immediately come (p)) I'm coming. (or I'll be right with you)
我去去就 回来(了)。	**Wǒ qùqù jiù huí lái (le).**	(*lit.* I go-go immediately back-come (p)) I'll be right back.

Note: 了 Le here is optional: without it, the sentence sounds somewhat
abrupt; with it, the tone is more reassuring.

(2) 都 Dōu 'all'/'both' always refers back to a preceding phrase, e.g.
the subject, a posed topic (i.e. object transposed to a pre-verbal
position – see 18.4), a frequency expression (e.g. with 每 měi
'every'). It never relates to what follows it or follows the verb:

大家都去 吃午饭了。	**Dàjiā dōu qù chī wǔfàn le.**	(*lit.* everybody all go eat lunch p) Everybody has gone for lunch.
他们两个 人都回 来了。	**Tāmen liǎng gè rén dōu huí lái le.**	(*lit.* they two mw people both back-come p) Both of them have come back.
这儿每年 冬天都 下雪。	**Zhèr měi nián dōngtiān dōu xià xuě.**	(*lit.* here every-year winter all come-down-snow) It snows here every winter.
我们北京、 西安、上海 都去过。	**Wǒmen Běijīng, Xī'ān, Shànghǎi dōu qùguo.**	(*lit.* we Beijing, Xi'an, Shanghai all go asp) We've been to Beijing, Xi'an and Shanghai.
那两个 电影我都 不喜欢。	**Nèi liǎng gè diànyǐng wǒ dōu bù xǐhuan.**	(*lit.* those two mw film I both not like) I don't like either of those two films.

(3) 只 Zhǐ 'only', in contrast with 都 dōu, generally refers to what
follows in the sentence:

我只去 香港。	**Wǒ zhǐ qù Xiānggǎng.**	(*lit.* I only go Hong Kong) I'm only going to Hong Kong.
我们只谈 过一次。	**Wǒmen zhǐ tánguo yī cì.**	(*lit.* we only talk asp one time) We talked [about it] only once.

(4) 也 Yě 'also' and 还 hái 'additionally' have similar meanings. 也 Yě generally refers back to the subject, though it may also point forward to the following verb and/or object:

她也 发烧了。	**Tā yě** **fāshāo le.**	(*lit.* she also start-burn p) She has a fever *too*.
我也 没(有)钱。	**Wǒ yě** **méi (yǒu) qián.**	(*lit.* I also not-have money) I haven't got any money *either*.

还 Hái, on the other hand, always refers to the following verb or object of that verb, implying an additional action or situation:

小偷 还偷了 电视机。	**Xiǎotōu** **hái tōule** **diànshìjī.**	(*lit.* thief in-addition steal asp television-set) The thief *also* stole the television. (i.e. in addition to other things)
大学还有 中文系。	**Dàxué** **hái yǒu** **Zhōngwénxì.**	(*lit.* university additionally have Chinese-department) The university has a Chinese Department *as well*.

Note 1: 还 Hái also has the meaning 'still':

她还在 这儿。	**Tā hái zài** **zhèr.**	(*lit.* she still at here) She is still here.
他们还 没回家。	**Tāmen hái** **méi huí jiā.**	(*lit.* they still not return home) They haven't gone home yet.

Note 2: In sentences with 谁 shéi/shuí 'everybody'/什么 shénme 'everything' as the subject, 也 yě can be used interchangeably with 都 dōu, and is generally preferred when the sentence is negative:

这件事 谁都/也 知道。	**Zhèi jiàn shì** **shéi dōu/yě** **zhīdao.**	(*lit.* this mw matter everybody all/also know) Everybody knows this.
这件事谁 也不知道。	**Zhèi jiàn shì shéi** **yě bù zhīdao.**	(*lit.* this mw matter everybody also not know) Nobody knows this.

Note 3: In another construction, 连 lián 'even' is used with 都 dōu or 也 yě in the pattern: subject + 连 lián + noun or verb phrase + 都 dōu or 也 yě + verb (or with '连 lián + noun or verb phrase' preceding the subject):

他连首相 都/也认识。	**Tā lián shǒuxiàng** **dōu/yě rènshi.**	(*lit.* he even prime-minister all/also know) He even knows the prime minister.
他连动 也不动。	**Tā lián dòng yě** **bù dòng.**	(*lit.* he even move also not move) He did not so much as move.
连一分钱 她也没有。	**Lián yī fēn qián** **tā yě méi yǒu.**	(*lit.* even one cent money she also not have) She doesn't (even) have a cent.

(5) 再 **Zài** and 又 **yòu** both mean 'again', but there is a subtle distinction between them. 又 **Yòu** expresses actual repetition, while 再 **zài** indicates projected repetition. This means that often 又 **yòu** is used in a past or continuous present context, whereas 再 **zài** is used in a future context:

我明天 再来。	**Wǒ míngtiān** **zài lái.**	(*lit.* I tomorrow again come) I'll come again tomorrow.
他们昨天 又来了。	**Tāmen zuótiān** **yòu lái le.**	(*lit.* they yesterday again come p) They came again yesterday.
那个孩子 又在看 电视了。	**Nèi gè háizi** **yòu zài kàn** **diànshì le.**	(*lit.* that mw child again asp watch television p) That child is watching television again.

As an indicator of projected repetition, 再 **zài** may also imply the postponement of an action:

我们明天 再谈。	**Wǒmen** **míngtiān** **zài tán.**	(*lit.* we tomorrow again talk) We'll discuss [it] tomorrow. (i.e. not today)
这个问题 以后再 考虑吧。	**Zhèi gè wèntí** **yǐhòu zài** **kǎolǜ ba.**	(*lit.* this mw question again consider p) We'll consider this question in future. (i.e. not now)

It is possible for 再 **zài** to be used in the past when repetition is anticipated rather than realised. That is why 再 **zài** occurs naturally in negative sentences where the anticipated repetition does not take place:

后来我们 不再去找 他们了。	**Hòulái wǒmen** **bù zài qù zhǎo** **tāmen le.**	(*lit.* afterwards we not again go look-up them p) Afterwards we did not go and look them up again.
他走了， 没(有)再 回来。	**Tā zǒu le,** **méi(yǒu)** **zài huí lái.**	(*lit.* he go p, not-have again back- come) He left and did not come back again.

Similarly, 又 **yòu** may occur in future contexts where repetition can be seen as part of a predetermined plan or course of action:

下个月我 们又要放 假了。	**Xià gè yuè** **wǒmen yòu** **yào fàngjià le.**	(*lit.* next mw month we again have-to start-holiday p) Our holiday comes round again next month.

我后天 又得去见 导师了。	**Wǒ hòutiān** **yòu děi qù** **jiàn dǎoshī le.**	(*lit.* I day-after-tomorrow again must go see tutor p) I'll have to go and see my tutor again the day after tomorrow.

(6) 倒 **Dào** and 却 **què** both mean 'but', 'however', 'on the other hand', or 'on the contrary'. They are almost interchangeable, though 却 **què** occurs more often in negative sentences:

小李倒 感冒了。	**Xiǎo Lǐ dào** **gǎnmào le.**	(*lit.* little Li however catch-cold p) However, Little Li caught a cold.
小李却 不喜欢 吃蔬菜。	**Xiǎo Lǐ què** **bù xǐhuan** **chī shūcài.**	(*lit.* Little Li however not like eat vegetables) Little Li, however, doesn't like (to eat) vegetables.

14.4 *Referential adverbs with negatives*

Referential adverbs generally precede the negative adverbs 不 **bù** and 没(有) **méi(yǒu)**:

明天我 就不来了。	**Míngtiān wǒ** **jiù bù lái le.**	(*lit.* tomorrow I then not come p) I won't come tomorrow then.
那次以后 他们才没(有) 去钓鱼。	**Nèi cì yǐhòu** **tāmen cái** **méi(yǒu) qù** **diào yú.**	(*lit.* that time after they only-then not-have go fishing) It was only after that that they did not go fishing again.

14.5 *Order of sequence of referential adverbs*

When two or more referential adverbs occur together or with negative adverbs, the sequence is as follows:

倒/却 **dào/què** 再 **zài** 也 **yě** 不/没(有) **bù/méi(yǒu)** 只 **zhǐ**

or

倒/却 **dào/què** 也 **yě** 都/就 **dōu/jiù** 不/没(有) **bù/méi(yǒu)** 再 **zài** 只 **zhǐ**

他们倒再也 不/没埋怨 我们了。	**Tāmen dào zài yě** **bù/méi mányuàn** **wǒmen le.**	(*lit.* they in-contrast again also not complain us p) After that they didn't complain about us any more.

Note: In the above sentence, 不 **bù** implies an intention (in this case a past rather than future intention) whereas 没 **méi** is simply factual.

哥哥也 就不 抽烟了。	**Gēge yě jiù bù chōuyān le.**	(*lit.* elder brother also then not inhale smoke p) My elder brother didn't smoke again after that either.
孩子们也 都不再 撒谎了。	**Háizimen yědōu bù zài sāhuǎng le.**	(*lit.* children also all not again tell lies p) The children also didn't tell lies any more.
大家就不 再只考虑 自己了。	**Dàjiā jiù bù zài zhǐ kǎolǜ zìjǐ le.**	(*lit.* everybody then not again only consider oneself p) Nobody thought only about themselves after that.

14.6 Order of adverbials in sequence

In this chapter and Chapters 10 and 11, we have discussed a whole range of adverbials. Where a number of adverbials occur in sequence before a verb, the general order is: 'attitude', 'time', 'referential', 'manner', 'location'. However, 'time' may change places with 'attitude', and 'location' with 'manner':

她很可能 这(个)时候 也认认真 真地在博 物馆看展 品呢。	**Tā hěn kěnéng zhèi (gè) shíhou yě rènrènzhēnzhēn de zài bówùguǎn kàn zhǎnpǐn ne.**	(*lit.* she very possible this (mw) time also conscientiously at museum see exhibit p) It is most likely that at this moment she is also looking conscientiously at the exhibits in the museum.

or, 她这(个)时候很可能也在 **Tā zhèi (gè) shíhou hěn kěnéng**
博物馆认认真真地看展品呢。 **yě zài bówùguǎn rènrènzhēnzhēn de kàn zhǎnpǐn ne.**

15 Modal and similar verbs

15.1 Modal, attitudinal, and intentional verbs

In this chapter we focus on verbs which precede the main verb in a sentence. Chief among these are *modal verbs* (e.g. 能 **néng** 'can', 要 **yào** 'want', 得 **děi** 'must', etc.). Other verbs of this type are those that express attitude in some way (e.g. 喜欢 **xǐhuan** 'like', 同意 **tóngyì** 'agree', etc.), which we refer to loosely as *attitudinal verbs*; there are also *intentional verbs* (e.g. 打算 **dǎsuàn** 'plan', 准备 **zhǔnbèi** 'prepare', etc.). Modal verbs, attitudinal verbs and most intentional verbs regularly appear with the negator 不 **bù** but never with 没(有) **méi(yǒu)**. The negator 不 **bù** usually comes before the modal, attitudinal or intentional verb, or occasionally after it, as required by meaning or emphasis:

我今天 不能来。	**Wǒ jīntiān** **bù néng lái.**	(*lit.* I today not can come) I can't come today.
我今天能 不来吗?	**Wǒ jīntiān** **néng bù lái ma?**	(*lit.* I today can not come p) Can I not come today?
你不能 不来。	**Nǐ bù néng** **bù lái.**	(*lit.* you not can not come) You must come (you cannot but come).

15.2 Modal verbs

Modal verbs express obligation, necessity, permission, possibility, ability, desire, admonition or daring. Note that: (1) they can precede any type of verb including attitudinal and intentional verbs, though they occur less commonly with 是 **shì** 'to be' or 有 **yǒu** 'to have'; (2) they are almost never preceded by another verb (see note below); (3) they are never immediately followed by a noun or pronoun object (though 要 **yào** 'want' can be used as a full verb when it may take an object). As we will see later (18.3.1), sentences with modal verbs are topic-comment rather than subject-predicate sentences.

Note: Modal verbs may be preceded by verbs expressing hope or aspiration, such as 希望 **xīwàng**, 盼望 **pànwàng**, 渴望 **kěwàng**, etc.

| 我希望能
再见到您。 | **Wǒ xīwàng néng**
zài jiàn dào nín. | (*lit.* I hope can again see polite:you)
I hope to see you again. |

See also note on 高兴 **gāoxìng** 'happy' at 15.3.2 below.

(1)   应该 **Yīnggāi** or, more colloquially, 该 **gāi** or 得 **děi** indicate *obligation* ('ought to', 'should', 'have to'):

你应该去 睡觉了。	**Nǐ yīnggāi qù** **shuìjiào le!**	(*lit.* you should go sleep p) You ought to go to bed./It's time you went to bed.
你不应该 在这儿 抽烟/吸烟。	**Nǐ bù yīnggāi** **zài zhèr** **chōuyān/xīyān.**	(*lit.* you not should at here inhale-smoke) You shouldn't smoke here.
我该/ 得走了。	**Wǒ gāi/** **děi zǒu le.**	(*lit.* I should leave p) I must be off.

你的新手表得报税。	**Nǐde xīn shǒubiǎo děi bàoshuì.**	(*lit.* your new watch should report-tax) You will have to declare your new watch [at customs].
旅客都得填写这张表格。	**Lǚkè dōu děi tiánxiě zhèi zhāng biǎogé.**	(*lit.* passengers all should fill-write this mw form) All passengers should fill in this form.

(2)　必须 **Bìxū** conveys *necessity* or *compulsion* ('must'):

你必须去打针。	**Nǐ bìxū qù dǎzhēn.**	(*lit.* you must go hit-needle) You must go and have an injection.
你必须回答我的问题。	**Nǐ bìxū huídá wǒde wèntí.**	(*lit.* you must answer my question) You must answer my question.

Note: 必须 **Bìxū** may be considered an adverb. Like modal verbs it is placed before the verb, but it cannot be used in an affirmative-negative form: *必须 不必须 bìxū bù bìxū.

The negation of 必须 **bìxū** is 不用 **bùyòng** or more formally 不必 **bùbì** ('there's no need'):

你不用/不必去接她。	**Nǐ bùyòng/bùbì qù jiē tā.**	(*lit.* you not need go meet her) There's no need for you to go and meet her.
我们不用告诉他们。	**Wǒmen bùyòng gàosù tāmen.**	(*lit.* we not need tell them) There's no need for us to tell them.

(3)　可以 **Kěyǐ** and 能 **néng** express *permission* ('may', 'can'):

我现在可以/能走了吗?	**Wǒ xiànzài kěyǐ/néng zǒu le ma?**	(*lit.* I now may/can leave p p) May I leave now?
你不可以/能在这儿停车。	**Nǐ bù kěyǐ/néng zài zhèr tíng chē.**	(*lit.* you not may/can at here stop car p) You may not park your car here.
我可以/能看看你的驾驶执照吗?	**Wǒ kěyǐ/néng kànkàn nǐde jiàshǐ zhízhào ma?**	(*lit.* I may/can look-look your driving licence p) May I have a look at your driving licence?
我可以/能提一个问题吗?	**Wǒ kěyǐ/néng tí yī gè wèntí ma?**	(*lit.* I may/can raise one mw question) May I ask a question?

(4) 会 **Huì** indicates either *possibility*/*probability* ('may', 'is likely to'):

今天会 刮风吗?	**Jīntiān *huì* guā fēng ma?**	(*lit.* today likely blow wind p) Is it likely to be windy today?
他们明天 不<u>会</u>来。	**Tāmen míngtiān bù *huì* lái.**	(*lit.* they tomorrow not likely come) They won't come tomorrow.

or, *ability* in the sense of an acquired skill ('can'):

导游会 说英语。	**Dǎoyóu *huì* shuō Yīngyǔ.**	(*lit.* tourist-guide can speak English) The tourist guide can speak English.
我不会 弹钢琴。	**Wǒ bù *huì* tán gāngqín.**	(*lit.* I not can play piano) I cannot play the piano.
你会打太 极拳吗?	**Nǐ *huì* dǎ tàijíquán ma?**	(*lit.* you can hit shadow-boxing p) Can you do shadow-boxing?

(5) 能 **Néng** and 能(够) **néng(gòu)** also convey *ability* but in the sense of physical strength or capability ('can'):

我一天 能(够)跑 十英里路。	**Wo yī tiān *néng(gòu)* pǎo shí yīnglǐ lù.**	(*lit.* I one day able run ten miles road/way) I can walk/run ten miles a day.
今天我不 能(够)去 上班。	**Jīntiān wǒ bù *néng(gòu)* qù shàngbān.**	(*lit.* today I not can go on-shift) I can't go to work today.

Note: In contrast to the potential complement, 能(够) **néng(gòu)** tends to imply that personal attitude, capacity or judgement, rather than external circumstances, determine ability (or inability).

(6) 想 **Xiǎng** and 要 **yào** expresses *wish* or *desire* ('want', 'would like to'):

我想买 (一)些食品 和饮料。	**Wǒ *xiǎng* mǎi (yī) xiē shípǐn hé yǐnliào.**	(*lit.* I want buy some food and drink) I'd like to buy some food and drink.
你想 去参观 工厂吗?	**Nǐ *xiǎng* qù cānguān gōngchǎng ma?**	(*lit.* you want go visit factory p) Do you want to go and visit a factory?
他要 学开车。	**Tā *yào* xué kāi chē.**	(*lit.* s/he want learn drive-car) S/he wants to take driving lessons.

| 她要在 广州呆(待) 两个礼拜。 | **Tā yào zài Guǎngzhōu dāi liǎng gè lǐbài.** | (*lit.* she want at Guangzhou stay two mw week) She wants to stay in Guangzhou for two weeks. |
| 我想换 五百元。 | **Wǒ *xiǎng* huàn wǔbǎi yuán.** | (*lit.* I want change five-hundred yuan) I would like to change five hundred yuan. |

Note 1: The 元 **yuán** (or more colloquially 块 **kuài**) is the basic unit of Chinese currency. It is divided into 10 角 **jiǎo** (more colloquially 毛 **máo**) and 100 分 **fēn**.

Note 2: 呆 **dāi** and 待 **dāi** can be used interchangeably to mean 'stay'.

However, in imperative sentences 要 **yào** and its negative form 不要 **bù yào** mean respectively *admonition* ('must') and *prohibition* ('don't'):

| 你要小心! | **Nǐ yào xiǎoxīn!** | (*lit.* you must small-concern) You must be careful! |
| 不要动! | ***Bù yào dòng!*** | (*lit.* not must move) Don't move! |

Note 1: With 要 **yào** in this sense the pronoun subject is normally present, but with 不要 **bù yào** it is optional.

Note 2: 要 **Yào** may also be used by itself as a transitive verb to mean 'want' or 'need', when it takes a noun or pronoun object:

| 我要茶, 不要咖啡。 | **Wǒ *yào* chá, bù *yào* kāfēi.** | I want tea, not coffee. |
| 坐车去只要 一个小时。 | **Zuò chē qù zhǐ *yào* yī gè xiǎoshí.** | It takes only an hour to go by car. |

别 **Bié** can be used as an alternative to 不要 **bù yào** for 'don't':

别动!	***Bié* dòng!**	Don't move!
别笑我!	***Bié* xiào wǒ!**	Don't laugh at me!
别进来!	***Bié* jìn lái!**	Don't come in!

(7) 愿意 **Yuànyi** and 肯 **kěn** indicate *willingness* ('be willing'):

| 校长愿意 退休。 | **Xiàozhǎng *yuànyi* tuìxiū.** | (*lit.* headmaster willing retire) The headmaster is willing to retire. |
| 他不愿意 谈宗教或 政治。 | **Tā bù *yuànyi* tán zōngjiào huò zhèngzhì.** | (*lit.* he not willing talk religion or politics) He is not willing to talk about religion or politics. |

119

| 经理不肯 见我。 | **Jīnglǐ bù kěn jiàn wǒ.** | (*lit.* manager not willing see me) The manager is not willing to see me. |
| 她肯教 你吗? | **Tā kěn jiāo nǐ ma?** | (*lit.* she willing teach you p) Is she willing to teach you? |

(8) 敢 Gǎn indicates either *bravery* or *audacity* ('dare'):

他不敢跳 进水里去。	**Tā bù gǎn tiào jìn shuǐ li qù.**	(*lit.* he not dare jump enter water in go) He did not dare to jump into the water.
你敢骂人!	**Nǐ gǎn mà rén!**	(*lit.* you dare scold people) How dare you use abusive language (to people)!
谁敢打他!	**Shéi gǎn dǎ tā!**	(*lit.* who dare hit him) Who dares to hit him! (i.e. nobody dares to hit him)

| 15.2.1 | Modal verbs and adverbs of degree

Modal verbs do not generally take adverbial modifiers. However, adverbs of degree (e.g. 很 **hěn**, 非常 **fēicháng**, etc.) naturally occur with 想 **xiǎng** 'want' and 愿意 **yuànyi** 'be willing':

| 我很想 去度假。 | **Wǒ hěn xiǎng qù dùjià.** | (*lit.* I very want go spend-holiday) I want very much to go away for a holiday. |
| 他们非 常愿意 帮助你。 | **Tāmen fēicháng yuànyi bāngzhù nǐ.** | (*lit.* they extremely willing help you) They are extremely willing to help you. |

Also, negative expressions are regularly softened by the addition of 太/大 **tài/dà** 'too':

明天不大 会下雨。	**Míngtiān bù dà huì xià yǔ.**	(*lit.* tomorrow not too likely fall-rain) It is not too likely to rain tomorrow.
他不太愿 意支持我。	**Tā bù tài yuàn yi zhīchí wǒ.**	(*lit.* he not too willing support me) He is not too willing to support me.
我不大敢 吃生蚝。	**Wǒ bù dà gǎn chī shēng háo.**	(*lit.* I not too dare eat raw-oyster) I'm a bit of a coward when it comes to eating raw oysters.

| 15.2.2 | Modal verbs and comparison

Comparisons can be expressed using modal verbs, with the '比 **bǐ** + (pro)noun' phrase preceding the modal verb (see 7.2 for comparison structures):

你比我 能吃。	**Nǐ *bǐ* wǒ *néng* chī.**	(*lit.* you compare me can eat) You can eat more than I can.
她比我会 说话。	**Tā *bǐ* wǒ *huì* shuōhuà.**	(*lit.* she compare me able speak) She can speak better than me.
她比谁 都愿意 帮助我。	**Tā *bǐ* shéi dōu *yuànyi* bāngzhù wǒ.**	(*lit.* she compare anybody all willing help me) She is willing to help me more than anybody else.

| 15.3 | *Attitudinal verbs* |

Attitudinal verbs may, like modal verbs, precede verbs, but they can
also be followed by nouns or pronouns. Unlike modal verbs, they regularly take adverbial modifiers of degree:

西方人 喜欢养狗。	**Xīfāngrén *xǐhuan* yǎng gǒu.**	(*lit.* Westerners like raise dog) Westerners like keeping dogs.
西方人很 喜欢狗。	**Xīfāngrén hěn *xǐhuan* gǒu.**	(*lit.* Westerners very like dog) Westerners like dogs very much.
他们非常 讨厌买 东西。	**Tāmen fēicháng *tǎoyàn* mǎi dōngxi.**	(*lit.* they extremely hate buy thing) They really hate shopping.
他们非常 讨厌那 个人。	**Tāmen fēicháng *tǎoyàn* nèi gè rén.**	(*lit.* they extremely hate that mw person) They really loathe that person.
我怕坐 缆车。	**Wǒ *pà* zuò lǎnchē.**	(*lit.* I fear sit cable-car) I am afraid to ride in a cable-car.
我怕鬼。	**Wǒ *pà* guǐ.**	(*lit.* I fear ghost) I am afraid of ghosts.
我很同意 选他。	**Wǒ hěn *tóngyì* xuǎn tā.**	(*lit.* I very agree elect him) I agree to vote for him.
我很同意 你的意见。	**Wǒ hěn *tóngyì* nǐde yìjiàn.**	(*lit.* I agree your opinion) I agree to your idea.
他们很 反对吃肉。	**Tāmen hěn *fǎnduì* chī ròu.**	(*lit.* they very oppose eat meat) They are opposed to eating meat.
他们反对 这个提议。	**Tāmen *fǎnduì* zhèi gè tíyì.**	(*lit.* they oppose this mw proposal) They are opposed to this proposal.

Wàngle and Jìde

Two commonly used verbs which may be categorised as attitudinal verbs are 忘了 wàngle 'to forget' and 记得 jìde 'to remember':

| 别忘了带钥匙。 | **Bié wàngle dài yàoshi.** | (*lit.* don't forget asp bring key) Don't forget to bring [your] keys [with you]. |
| 请记得锁门。 | **Qǐng jìde suǒ mén.** | (*lit.* please remember lock door) Please remember to lock the door. |

Note: 忘了 Wàngle 'to forget' invariably incorporates the aspect marker le.

Gāoxìng

The adjective 高兴 gāoxìng 'happy' can take on the function of an attitudinal verb and precede another verb:

| 我很高兴认识您。 | **Wǒ hěn gāoxìng rènshi nín.** | (*lit.* I very happy know polite: you) I am pleased to meet you. |
| 我们非常高兴有机会来这儿访问。 | **Wǒmen fēicháng gāoxìng yǒu jīhuì lái zhèr fǎngwèn.** | (*lit.* we extremely happy have opportunity come here visit) We are extremely happy to have the opportunity of coming here for a visit. |

Note: 高兴 Gāoxìng like 希望 xīwàng 'to hope' may precede a modal verb:

| 我很高兴能来中国留学。 | **Wǒ hěn gāoxìng néng lái Zhōngguó liúxué.** | (*lit.* I very happy can come China study-abroad) I am very happy to be able to come to study in China. |

Intentional verbs

Intentional verbs are always followed by verbs and do not take adverbial modifiers of degree:

| 我打算去旅行。 | **Wǒ dǎsuàn qù lǚxíng.** | (*lit.* I calculate go travel) I am planning to go travelling. |
| 我们的工厂打算装空调。 | **Wǒmen de gōngchǎng dǎsuàn zhuāng kōngtiáo.** | (*lit.* our factory calculate install air-conditioning) Our factory is planning to install air-conditioning. |

她准备 申请一份 工作。	**Tā zhǔnbèi shēnqǐng yī fèn gōngzuò.**	(*lit.* she prepare apply one mw job) She is planning to apply for a job.
你决定 吃什么?	**Nǐ juédìng chī shénme?**	(*lit.* you decide eat what) What have you decided to eat?

Note: Some of these verbs can be followed by nouns (e.g. 她在准备功课。**Tā zài zhǔnbèi gōngkè** 'She is preparing (for) the lesson') but they are then full verbs and carry no meaning of intention.

15.4.1	Negation of intentional verbs

Negating intentional verbs is slightly more complicated than negating modal or attitudinal verbs. The negator 不 **bù** can come either before or after the intentional verb, without there being any significant difference in meaning. For instance,

我不打算 参加比赛。	**Wǒ bù dǎsuàn cānjiā bǐsài.**	(*lit.* I not plan take-part-in contest) I am not planning to take part in the competition.
我打算不 参加比赛。	**Wǒ dǎsuàn bù cānjiā bǐsài.**	(*lit.* I plan not take-part-in contest) I am planning not to take part in the competition.

准备, 计划 **Zhǔnbèi, jìhuà** 'plan', etc., follow this pattern.
 Exceptionally, 决定 **juédìng** 'decide' can only be followed (not preceded) by the negator 不 **bù**:

我决定不 参加比赛。	**Wǒ juédìng bù cānjiā bǐsài.**	(*lit.* I decide not take-part-in contest) I have decided not to take part in the competition.
NOT: *我不决定参加比赛。	**Wǒ bù juédìng cānjiā bǐsài.**	

The negator 没(有)**méi(yǒu)**, usually preceded by 还 **hái** 'still', can be used before 决定 **juédìng**, however. The action verb which follows 决定 **juédìng** may then take an affirmative-negative format:

我还没(有) 决定参(加) 不参加 比赛。	**Wǒ hái méi(yǒu) juédìng cān(jiā) bù cānjiā bǐsài.**	(*lit.* I still not-have decide take-part- in not take-part-in contest) I haven't yet decided whether to take part in the competition or not.

Part III

Sentences

 Introduction

A distinctive characteristic of many Chinese sentences is the influential role of the particle **le** in their formulation. The addition of **le** at the end of a statement introduces an assertiveness of tone implying change, updating, etc. The presence of **le** may therefore convert a subject-predicate sentence into a topic-comment sentence (see Chapter 18). Other sentence particles, 吗 **ma**, 呢 **ne**, 吧 **ba**, etc., transform statements into various forms of question; imperatives may be signalled by 吧 **ba**; and exclamations are indicated by 啊 **a** and its variants.

Prepositional or coverbal phrases are a regular feature of Chinese sentences. The location phrases introduced in Part II are coverbal, and other coverbal phrases provide background information on method, direction, destination, etc. The coverb 把 **bǎ**, which expresses intentional manipulation or unintentional intervention, has the important function of moving an object to a pre-verbal position, leaving the post-verbal space clear for the complement. The coverb 被 **bèi**, rarely used except in narration, introduces the agent in a passive construction. (Passives are more readily formed, however, through topic-comment structures where sentence 了 **le** is generally indispensable.)

Serial constructions occur frequently in Chinese sentences. They bring together verbal elements through meaning relationships such as time-sequence, purpose, etc., rather than through syntax. Composite sentences, on the other hand, consist of more than one clause or predicate/comment, usually linked by conjunctions and/or conjunctives.

As a non-morphological language, Chinese relies heavily on its speakers'/listeners' knowledge of the real world. This makes for not only standard constructions like notional passives in the form of topic-comments but also frequent abbreviations and omissions in sentences so that sense depends on reference to non-linguistic contexts and verbal cotexts.

Emphasis is regularly generated by the use of the intensifier 是 **shì** which can focus stress on almost any element in the sentence. In addition, topicalisation may emphasise an object by transferring it to a topic position in a topic-comment sentence.

The subject-predicate and topic-comment dichotomy we have proposed offers insights into the organisation of Chinese sentences. The shift from subject-predicate to topic-comment through the introduction of sentence particle 了 **le**, modal verbs, the intensifier 是 **shì**, etc., represents a move by the speaker from a narrative to a descriptive, explanatory, or argumentative stance.

16 Statements and the sentence particle **le**

16.1 Le as a sentence particle

We have earlier discussed the function of **le** as an aspect marker suffixed to a verb of action to indicate the completion of the action (see 8.3.1). A second, important use of **le** is as a *sentence particle* placed at the end of a sentence and influencing its meaning as a whole. By adding **le** to a sentence, the speaker introduces some form of comment on the action or the situation, implying a commitment or involvement on his/her part. The speaker may be suggesting that circumstances have changed or are about to change, that things are not as the listener expects, or that circumstances have reached a particular point. When using **le** in this way, the speaker readily lets his/her enthusiasm, interest and involvement be known. Sentence **le** does occur in written Chinese, especially in letters, but its function makes it particularly common in speech. In effect, adding sentence **le** updates the situation; thus, underlying all such statements with **le** is the fundamental notion of change. For example,

| 我不抽烟。 | **Wǒ bù chōuyān.** | (*lit.* I not inhale-cigarette) I don't smoke. |
| 我不抽烟了。 | **Wǒ bù chōuyān le.** | (*lit.* I not inhale-cigarette p) I don't smoke any more. (i.e. I have given up smoking) |

The first statement is simply a statement of fact, whereas the second implies a change in habit from 'smoking' to 'non-smoking'.

16.2 Functions of sentence **le**

In the examples below, sentence 了 **le** conveys to the listener (or reader) a sense of updating, change, reversal, etc. of the previous situation.

(1) Sentences containing result or direction complements which in one way or another signal new situations or conditions:

她睡着了。	**Tā shuì zháo le.**	(*lit.* she sleep achieved p) She has fallen asleep.
爸爸喝醉了。	**Bàba hē zuì le.**	(*lit.* father drink intoxicated p) Father has got drunk.
她出去了。	**Tā chū qù le.**	(*lit.* she out go p) She has gone out.
太阳升起来了。	**Tàiyáng shēng qǐlái le.**	(*lit.* sun rise up-come p) The sun has risen.

(2) Sentences with verbs or indicators which mean 'begin', 'end', 'start', 'finish', 'emerge', 'disappear', 'change', etc., which by definition introduce new circumstances:

谈判开始了。	**Tánpàn *kāishǐ* le.**	(*lit.* negotiation begin p) The negotiations have begun.
会议结束了。	**Huìyì *jiéshù* le.**	(*lit.* meeting end p) The meeting has ended.
天气变了。	**Tiānqì *biàn* le.**	(*lit.* weather change p) The weather (has) changed.
她哭起来了。	**Tā *kū qǐlái* le.**	(*lit.* she cry/weep start p) She (has) started to cry.

Similarly, an adverbial in the sentence may indicate that something is about to take place:

飞机快要起飞了。	**Fēijī *kuài yào* qǐfēi le.**	(*lit.* plane quick about take-off p) The plane is about to take off.
天就要下雨了。	**Tiān *jiù yào* xià yǔ le.**	(*lit.* sky soon about fall-rain p) It is about to rain.

(3) Sentences with a monosyllabic action or state verb which naturally poses a contradiction to a previous action or state:

火车到了。	**Huǒchē dào le.**	(*lit.* train arrive p) The train has arrived.
她病了。	**Tā bìng le.**	(*lit.* she ill p) She has fallen ill.
天亮了。	**Tiān liàng le.**	(*lit.* sky bright p) It is light (now).

| 花儿开了。 | **Huār kāi le.** | (*lit.* flower open p) The flowers have come out. |
| 东西贵了。 | **Dōngxi guì le.** | (*lit.* things expensive p) Things are getting more expensive. |

(4) Sentences which have nominal predicates indicating age, height, weight, etc., and register change or updating:

我今年 六十岁了。	**Wǒ jīnnián liùshí suì le.**	(*lit.* I this-year sixty years-old p) I am sixty (years old) this year.
小伙子 一米八了。	**Xiǎohuǒzi yī mǐ bā le.**	(*lit.* young-man one metre eight p) The young man is one metre eight tall (now).
孩子 六个月了。	**Háizi liù gè yuè le.**	(*lit.* child six mw month p) The child is six months old (now).
我快七十 公斤了。	**Wǒ kuài qīshí gōngjīn le.**	(*lit.* I almost seventy kilogram p) I am almost seventy kilograms (in weight) (now).

16.2.1 | Summing-up function of **le**

Since the primary function of sentence 了 le is to emphasise updating or change of situation, a speaker narrating and commenting on a series of events will tend to delay 了 le to the end of the statement, thereby summing up the situation:

她把衣服 洗干净了。	**Tā bǎ yīfu xǐ gānjìng le.**	(*lit.* she grasp clothes wash clean p) She washed the clothes (clean).
她把衣服 洗干净, 晾出去了。	**Tā bǎ yīfu xǐ gānjìng, liàng chūqù le.**	(*lit.* she grasp clothes wash clean, hang out p) She washed the clothes and hung them out to dry.
她把衣服 洗干净, 晾 出去, 然后 寄信去了。	**Tā bǎ yīfu xǐ gānjìng, liàng chūqù, ránhòu jì xìn qù le.**	(*lit.* she grasp clothes wash clean, hang out, then post letter go p) She washed the clothes, hung them out to dry and then went to post a letter.

16.2.2 | **Le** as both sentence particle and aspect marker

When 了 le follows a verb phrase at the end of a sentence, it often functions both as aspect marker indicating completed action and as sentence particle:

他们来了。	**Tāmen lái le.**	(*lit.* they come asp+p) They've come. (i.e. they have arrived [completed action] and they are here now [updating, change of situation, etc.])
冬天 过去了。	**Dōngtiān guò qù le.**	(*lit.* winter pass go asp+p) The winter is over.
他们 结婚了。	**Tāmen jiéhūn le.**	(*lit.* they knot-marriage asp+p) They have got married.

Note: 结婚了 **Jiéhūn le** could also be expressed as 结了婚了 **jiéle hūn le** with the first **le** indicating completed action and the second **le** as a sentence particle.

| **16.3** | *Cases where sentence **le** is not used* |

Sentence 了 **le** is usually not used where the indication of 'change' is not the speaker's primary concern. For example, in:

(1) Sentences which indicate habitual actions, where the emphasis is more on persistence than change:

| 她常常 打网球。 | **Tā chángcháng dǎ wǎngqiú.** | (*lit.* she often-often hit net-ball) She plays tennis very often. |
| 我天天 钓鱼。 | **Wǒ tiāntiān diào yú.** | (*lit.* I day-day hook-fish) I go fishing every day. |

(2) Sentences with verbs marked by a continuous aspect marker or brief duration indicator, where the focus is on the continuity or brevity of the action:

| 她(正)在 听广播。 | **Tā (zhèng)zài tīng guǎngbō.** | (*lit.* she (just) asp: in-the-process-of listen broadcast) She is listening to the broadcast. |
| 他点了 点头。 | **Tā diǎnle diǎn tóu.** | (*lit.* he nod asp nod head) He nodded. |

(3) Sentences with verbs complemented by duration or frequency indicators or used with objects qualified by numeral and measure word phrases, where the interest is in what took place:

| 他学了 四年中文。 | **Tā xuéle sì nián Zhōngwén.** | (*lit.* he study asp four year Chinese) He studied Chinese for four years. |

她去过 中国两次。	**Tā qùguo Zhōngguó liǎng cì.**	(*lit.* she go asp China two times) She has been to China twice.
她吃了 三片面包。	**Tā chīle sān piàn miànbāo.**	(*lit.* she eat asp three mw bread) She ate three slices of bread.

Note: 了 **Le** can naturally be added to sentences like these where the speaker is providing updated or significantly changed information:

我学了四年 中文了。	**Wǒ xuéle sì nián Zhōngwén le.**	I have been studying Chinese for four years.
他喝了八杯 啤酒了。	**Tā hē le bā bēi píjiǔ le.**	He has drunk eight glasses of beer (and he does not look well, should not have done so, etc.).

(4) Sentences with location or manner complements, where attention is usually focused on the resulting location, situation, etc.:

她坐 在地上。	**Tā zuò zài dì shang.**	(*lit.* she sit at land on) She sat on the floor/ground.
雨下 得很大。	**Yǔ xià de hěn dà.**	(*lit.* rain fall p very big) The rain came down heavily.

(5) Sentences using adjectival predicates, where the interest is in the present state or situation of the subject:

我真笨!	**Wǒ zhēn bèn!**	(*lit.* I really foolish) I was really stupid./How stupid I was!
那个中年 人很胖。	**Nèi gè zhōngniánrén hěn pàng.**	(*lit.* that mw middle-aged-person very fat) That middle-aged man is very fat.

(6) Sentences using the verbs 是 **shì** or 有 **yǒu**, which by definition present a state of affairs:

她是画家。	**Tā shì huàjiā.**	(*lit.* she be painter) She is an artist.
这只猫是 雄的。	**Zhèi zhī māo shì xióng de.**	(*lit.* this mw cat be male p) This cat is a tom(cat).
她有很多 珠宝。	**Tā yǒu hěn duō zhūbǎo.**	(*lit.* she have very many pearl-jewel) She has got a lot of jewellery.

(7) Sentences expressing existence, emergence or disappearance, where the interest is in the object or entity that exists, emerges or disappears:

地毯上都 是灰尘。	**Dìtǎn shang dōu** **shì huīchén.**	(*lit.* carpet-on all be dust) There is dust all over the carpet.
花瓶里插 着玫瑰花。	**Huāpíng li chāzhe** **méiguìhuā.**	(*lit.* vase-in insert asp rose) There are roses in the vase.
去年下过 一场大雪。	**Qùnián xiàguo** **yī cháng dà xuě.**	(*lit.* last-year fall asp one mw big snow) There was a heavy snowfall last year.
礼堂里 坐满了人。	**Lǐtáng li zuò** **mǎn le rén.**	(*lit.* auditorium-in sit full asp people) The auditorium is full (of people).

(8) Sentences in which a manner adverb is the centre of interest:

气球慢慢地 飘上天空去。	**Qìqiú *mànmàn*** ***de* piāo shàng** **tiānkōng qù.**	(*lit.* balloon slow-slow p float up sky go) The balloon rose slowly into the sky.
母亲紧紧地 抱住孩子。	**Mǔqīn *jǐnjǐn*** ***de* bào zhù** **háizi.**	(*lit.* mother tight-tight p embrace firm child) The mother held the child firmly in her arms.

(9) Sentences with the referential adverb 才 **cái** which emphasise the
time or condition referred to:

她很晚才 回家。	**Tā hěn wǎn** ***cái* huí jiā.**	(*lit.* she very late until-then return home) She returned home very late.
他喝醉了 才写得出 好诗。	**Tā hē zuì le** ***cái* xiě de** **chū hǎo shī.**	(*lit.* s/he drink intoxicated p only-then write p out good poem) Only when s/he is drunk can s/he produce good poems.

16.4	*Ultimate versatility of sentence* **le**

Nevertheless, 了 **le** may be used with almost any sentence if the speaker
wishes to impart his/her awareness of development or difference in a
situation (see note under 16.3 (3) above). Naturally sentence **le** occurs
in some circumstances more than others, but it is possible to find it
added to unlikely sentences if the situation demands. For example:

我天天	**Wǒ tiāntiān**	(*lit.* I day-day wash-bath p) I take a bath
洗澡了。	**xǐzǎo le.**	every day nowadays. (i.e. I didn't use to,
		but I have changed my habits, etc.)

花园里	**Huāyuán li**	(*lit.* garden in grow full asp vegetable p)
种满了	**zhòng mǎn**	The garden is now full of vegetables. (i.e.
菜了。	**le cài le.**	it used to be overgrown with weeds, etc.)

那个人是	**Nèi gè rén**	(*lit.* that mw person be male p p) That
男的了。	**shì nán**	person is now a man. (i.e. he has
	de le.	undergone a sex change, etc.)

17   **Questions**

Questions in Chinese take a number of different forms: question-word
questions; general questions (with **ma**); surmise questions (with **ba**);
affirmative-negative questions; alternative questions; rhetorical questions, etc.

17.1   *Question-word questions*

Question-word questions make use of question words or expressions,
of which the following are the most obvious examples:

谁	**shéi** (or **shuí**)	Who or whom
谁的	**shéide** (or **shuíde**)	Whose
什么	**shénme**	What
什么时候/几时	**shénme shíhou** (or **jǐ shí**)	When
几点钟	**jǐ diǎn** (**zhōng**)	What time (of day)
哪儿	**nǎr** (or **shénme dìfang**)	Where
怎么/怎么样	**zěnme, zěn(me)yàng**	How
哪	**nǎ/něi** + (numeral) + measure word	Which
为什么	**wèi shénme**	Why

Note: See earlier reference to interrogative pronouns in 4.4.

Question words or expressions occur in the sentence at the point where
the answer is expected. There is no change in word order as in English.

Q: 她是谁?   **Tā shì *shéi*?**   (*lit.* she be who) Who is she?

A: 她是   **Tā shì**   (*lit.* she be my fellow student)
我同学。   ***wǒ tóngxué.***   She is my fellow student.

Q: 谁来过?   ***Shéi* láiguo?**   (*lit.* who come asp) Who has been?

A: 张先生   ***Zhāng xiānsheng***   (*lit.* Zhang Mr come asp)
来过。   **láiguo.**   Mr Zhang has been.

Q: 你见到   **Nǐ jiàn dào**   (*lit.* you bump into asp whom)
了谁?   **le *shéi*?**   Who did you bump into?

A: 我见到了   **Wǒ jiàn dào**   (*lit.* I see achieve asp Li Miss)
李小姐。   **le *Lǐ xiǎojie*.**   I bumped into Miss Li.

Q: 这是   **Zhè shì**   (*lit.* this be whose dog)
谁的狗?   ***shéide* gǒu?**   Whose dog is this?

A: 这是我   **Zhè shì *wǒ***   (*lit.* this be my neighbour p dog)
邻居的狗。   ***línjū* de gǒu.**   This is my neighbour's dog.

Q: 你想喝(一)   **Nǐ xiǎng hē (yī)**   (*lit.* you want drink a little what)
点儿什么?   **diǎnr *shénme*?**   What would you like to drink?

A: 我想喝(一)   **Wǒ xiǎng hē**   (*lit.* I want drink a little coke)
点儿可乐。   **(yì) diǎnr *kělè*.**   I would like to have some coke.

Q: 你今天上   **Nǐ jīntiān shàng**   (*lit.* you today attend what class)
什么课?   ***shénme* kè?**   What classes do you have today?

A: 我今天上   **Wǒ jīntiān**   (*lit.* I today attend literature class)
文学课。   **shàng *wénxué***   I have literature classes today.
   kè.

Q: 你什么   **Nǐ *shénme***   (*lit.* you when go China)
时候去   ***shíhou* qù**   When are you going to China?
中国?   **Zhōngguó?**

A: 我下个月   **Wǒ *xià gè yuè***   (*lit.* I next month go China)
去中国。   **qù Zhōngguó.**   I'm going to China next month.

Q: 你几点钟   **Nǐ *jǐ diǎn***   (*lit.* you what time back-come)
回来?   **(zhōng) huí lái?**   What time are you coming back?

A: 我八点(钟)   **Wǒ *bā diǎn***   (*lit.* I eight o'clock about
左右回来。   **(zhōng) zuǒyòu**   back-come) I'm coming back
   huí lái.   around eight.

Q:	你在哪儿 等我?	**Nǐ zài nǎr děng wǒ?**	(*lit.* you at where wait me) Where will you wait for me?
A:	我在火车 站等你。	**Wǒ zài huǒchēzhàn děng nǐ.**	(*lit.* I at train-station wait you) I'll wait for you at the (railway) station.
Q:	四十一路 车站在 哪儿?	**Sìshí yī lù chēzhàn zài nǎr?**	(*lit.* forty one route stop at where) Where is the 41 bus stop?
A:	四十一路 车站在 前面。	**Sìshí yī lù chēzhàn zài qiánmian.**	(*lit.* forty one route stop at front) The 41 bus stop is just ahead.
Q:	你准备 怎么样 去伦敦?	**Nǐ zhǔnbèi zěnmeyang qù Lúndūn?**	(*lit.* you plan how go London) How are you going to London?
A:	我准备 坐长途 汽车去。	**Wǒ zhǔnbèi zuò chángtú qìchē qù.**	(*lit.* I plan sit coach go) I am taking a coach.

Note: For discussion of coverbs like 坐 zuò 'travel by', see Chapter 19.

Q:	他为什么 没来?	**Tā wèi shénme méi lái?**	(*lit.* he why not come) Why didn't he turn up?
A:	他有事 没来。	**Tā yǒu shì méi lái.**	(*lit.* he have business not come) He didn't turn up because he had something to do.

Note: 为什么 Wèi shénme 'why' is asking for an explanation rather than an identification, and the most common responses to it are therefore clauses beginning with 因为 yīnwèi 'because'. (See Chapter 4.)

Q:	你觉得 这件外套 怎(么)样?	**Nǐ juéde zhèi jiàn wàitào zěn(me)yàng?**	(*lit.* you feel this mw jacket how) What do you think of this jacket?
A:	我觉得很好。	**Wǒ juéde hěn hǎo.**	(*lit.* I feel very good) I think [it is] very nice.
Q:	哪本小说最 有趣?	**Nǎ/něi běn xiǎoshuō zuì yǒuqù?**	(*lit.* which mw novel most interesting) Which novel is the most interesting?

| A: 那本小说最
有趣。 | **Nà/nèi běn
xiǎoshuō zuì
yǒuqù.** | (*lit.* that mw novel most
interesting) That novel is
the most interesting. |

17.1.1 | **Zěnmeyàng**

怎么样 Zěnmeyàng 'how' can be used as a predicate by itself without a verb (see also 17.6 below).

Q: 电影怎么样?	**Diànyǐng zěnmeyàng?**	(*lit.* film how/what like) How was the film?/What was the film like?
A: 电影很动人。	**Diànyǐng hěn dòngrén.**	(*lit.* film very moving) The film was very moving.
Q: 价钱怎么样?	**Jiàqián zěnmeyàng?**	(*lit.* price how/what like) What about the price?
A: 价钱很公道。	**Jiàqián hěn gōngdào.**	(*lit.* price very reasonable) The price was very reasonable.
Q: 咖啡馆的 服务员 怎么样?	**Kāfēiguǎn de fúwùyuán zěnmeyàng?**	(*lit.* café p assistant how/what like) What are the waiters at the café like?
A: 他们很友好。	**Tāmen hěn yǒuhǎo.**	(*lit.* they very friendly) They are very friendly.

17.1.2 | **Duō** in questions

A number of question expressions are formed with 多 **duō** 'how', 'to what extent':

多久 (多长时间)	**duō jiǔ** (or **duō cháng shíjiān**)	how long
多远	**duō yuǎn**	how far
多大	**duō dà**	how old
多	**duō** + gradable adjective	how + gradable adjective

There is also the common question word 多少 **duōshǎo** (*lit.* many-few) 'how many'/'how much'. 'How many' (but not 'how much') in pragmatically smaller numbers or quantities can also be represented by 几 **jǐ**.

As above, these question expressions are placed in the sentence where the answer is expected:

Q: 你想要 多少？	**Nǐ xiǎng yào duōshǎo?**	(*lit*. you want have how-many) How many do you want?
A: 我想要 两个。	**Wǒ xiǎng yào liǎng gè.**	(*lit*. I want have two mw) I would like (to have) two.
Q: 你用了 多少钱？	**Nǐ yòngle duōshǎo qián?**	(*lit*. you use asp how-much money) How much (money) did you spend?
A: 我用了 三十镑(钱)。	**Wǒ yòngle sānshí bàng (qián).**	(*lit*. I use asp thirty pound money) I spent thirty pounds.
Q: 你等了 多久了？	**Nǐ děngle duō jiǔ le?**	(*lit*. you wait asp how-long p) How long have you been waiting?
A: 我等了一个 小时了。	**Wǒ děngle yī gè xiǎoshí le.**	(*lit*. I wait asp one mw hour p) I have been waiting (for) an hour.
Q: 你家离 这儿多远？	**Nǐ jiā lí zhèr duō yuǎn?**	(*lit*. you home from here how-far) How far is your home from here?
A: 我家离这儿 二十英里。	**Wǒ jiā lí zhèr èrshí yīnglǐ.**	(*lit*. my home from here twenty mile) My home is twenty miles from here.
Q: 你妹妹 今年 多大了？	**Nǐ mèimei jīnnián duō dà le?**	(*lit*. your younger sister this-year how big p) How old is your younger sister this year?
A: 她今年 十八岁了。	**Tā jīnnián shí bā suì le.**	(*lit*. she this-year eighteen years- of-age p) She is eighteen years old this year.
Q: 你弟弟 多高？	**Nǐ dìdi duō gāo?**	(*lit*. your younger-brother how tall) How tall is your younger brother?
A: 他一米 七五。	**Tā yī mǐ qī wǔ.**	(*lit*. he one metre seven five) He is one metre seventy-five.
Q: 你在上海 呆了几天？	**Nǐ zài shànghǎi dāile jǐ tiān?**	(*lit*. you in Shanghai stay asp how many days) How many days did you stay in Shanghai?

A:	我在上海 呆了<u>三天</u>。	**Wǒ zài shànghǎi dāile *sān tiān*.**	(*lit.* I in Shanghai stay asp three days) I stayed there three days.
Q:	你买了 <u>几磅</u>苹果?	**Nǐ mǎile *jǐ bàng* píngguǒ?**	(*lit.* you buy asp how many pounds apple) How many pounds of apples did you buy?
A:	我买了 <u>五磅</u>(苹果)。	**Wǒ mǎile *wǔ bàng* (píngguǒ).**	(*lit.* I buy asp five pounds (apple)) I bought five pounds (of apples).
Q:	你弟弟 今年读 (小学) <u>几年级</u>?	**Nǐ dìdi jīnnián dú (xiǎoxué) *jǐ niánjí*?**	(*lit.* your younger brother this year read (primary school) how many year-grade) What year is your younger brother in at primary school (this year)?
A:	我弟弟/ 他今年读 (小学) <u>四年级</u>。	**Wǒ dìdi/ Tā jīnnián dú (xiǎoxué) *sì niánjí*.**	(*lit.* my younger brother/he this year read (primary school) four year-grade) He's in the fourth year.
Q:	你妹妹 今年<u>几岁</u> (了)?	**Nǐ mèimei jīnnián *jǐ suì* (le)?**	(*lit.* your younger sister this year how many years-of-age (p)) How old is your younger sister (this year)?
A:	我妹妹/ 她今年 <u>八岁</u>(了)。	**Wǒ mèimei/ Tā jīnnián *bā suì* (le).**	(*lit.* my younger sister/she this year eight years-of-age (p)) She's eight.

| 17.1.3 | **Ne** in questions |

The particle 呢 **ne** can be added to the end of a question-word question usually to convey a slightly quizzical tone:

书在哪儿?	**Shū zài nǎr?**	Where is the book?
书在哪儿<u>呢</u>?	**Shū zài nǎr *ne*?**	Where can the book be?
他为什么没来?	**Tā wèi shénme méi lái?**	Why didn't he come?
他为什么没来<u>呢</u>?	**Tā wèi shénme méi lái *ne*?**	Why didn't he come then?

17.2 *General questions with* **ma**

General questions in Chinese can be formed by adding the particle
吗 **ma** to the end of the sentence. There is no change in word order.
The answer to such questions is likely to be 'yes' or 'no'; this is usually
expressed by repeating the verb or adjective used in the question, in the
case of 'no' with the negative (不 **bù** or 没 **méi**). If the question has a
modal verb, the response uses the modal verb:

Q: 您是张云吗?	**Nín shì Zhāng Yún ma?**	Are you Zhang Yun?
A: 是。(我是张云。)	**Shì. (Wǒ shì Zhāng Yún.)**	Yes. (I'm Zhang Yun.)
Q: 这是终点站吗?	**Zhè shì zhōngdiǎn zhàn ma?**	Is this the terminus?
A: 不是。	**Bù shì.**	No.
Q: 你同意吗?	**Nǐ tóngyì ma?**	Do you agree?
A: 同意。	**Tóngyì.**	Yes. (*lit.* agree)
Q: 他有一个弟弟吗?	**Tā yǒu yī gè dìdi ma?**	Has he got a younger brother?
A: 没有。(他没有弟弟。)	**Méi yǒu. (Tā méi yǒu dìdi.)**	No. (He doesn't have a younger brother.)
Q: 你姐姐抽烟吗?	**Nǐ jiějie chōuyān ma?**	Does your elder sister smoke?
A: 抽。	**Chōu.**	Yes. (*lit.* smoke)
Q: 汽车加了油吗?	**Qìchē jiāle yóu ma?**	Have you filled the car with petrol?
A: 加了。	**Jiāle.**	Yes. (*lit.* filled)
Q: 你当过兵吗?	**Nǐ dāngguo bīng ma?**	Have you ever been a soldier?
A: 没有。(没当过。)	**Méiyǒu. (Méi dāngguo.)**	No. (I have never been (one).)

Q: 你会说 中文吗?	**Nǐ huì shuō Zhōngwén ma?**	Can you speak Chinese?
A: 不会。	**Bù huì.**	No. (*lit.* cannot)
Q: 你要喝 杯茶吗?	**Nǐ yào hē bēi chá ma?**	Would you like a cup of tea?
A: 要。	**Yào.**	Yes. (*lit.* like)
Q: 那个节目 有趣吗?	**Nèi gè jiémù yǒuqù ma?**	Was that programme interesting?
A: <u>很</u>有趣。	*Hěn yǒuqù.*	Yes, very interesting.
Q: 你最近 忙吗?	**Nǐ zuìjìn máng ma?**	Have you been busy recently?
A: 不<u>太</u>忙。	**Bù *tài* máng.**	Not very. (*lit.* not too busy)
Q: 那儿冷吗?	**Nàr lěng ma?**	Was it cold there?
A: 冷<u>极了</u>。	**Lěng *jí le*.**	Extremely cold.

Note: As in the last three examples, a degree adverb or complement of some kind normally precedes or follows the adjectival predicate in the response. We have seen earlier (6.2.1 and 13.6) that adjectival predicates do not usually occur without some form of marker.

When the question is enquiring about a state of affairs rather than an action, the initial response is usually 是(的) **shì(de)** 'yes' or 不(是) **bù (shì)** 'no':

Q: 你感冒了吗?	**Nǐ gǎnmào le ma?**	(*lit.* you get-cold asp p) Have you got a cold?
A: 是(的)。 我感冒了。	**Shì (de). Wǒ gǎnmào le.**	(*lit.* be [p]. I get-cold p) Yes. I've got a cold.
Q: 你回来得 很早吗?	**Nǐ huí lái de hěn zǎo ma?**	(*lit.* you back-come p very very late) Did you come back early?
A: 不(是)。 我回来 得很晚。	**Bù (shì). Wǒ huí lái de hěn wǎn.**	(*lit.* not [be] I back-come p early p) No, I came back quite late.

| Q: 她结了婚 了吗？ | **Tā jiéle hūn le ma?** | (*lit.* she get asp married p p) Is she married? |
| A: 不, 她还 没(有)结婚。 | **Bù, tā hái méi(yǒu) jiéhūn.** | (*lit.* no, she still not have marry) No, she is not married yet. |

It should be noted that in Chinese the response to a question posed in the negative is to affirm or deny the negative, whereas in English the convention is to link the 'yes' or 'no' with the response:

Q: 你不 高兴吗？	**Nǐ bù gāoxìng ma?**	(*lit.* you not happy p) Aren't you pleased?
A: 不, 我很 高兴。	**Bù, wǒ hěn gāoxìng.**	(*lit.* no, I very happy) Yes, I am.
or, 是(的), 我不高兴。	**Shì (de), wǒ bù gāoxìng.**	(*lit.* yes, I not happy) No, I'm not.
Q: 你明天 不来吗？	**Nǐ míngtiān bù lái ma?**	(*lit.* you tomorrow not come p) Aren't you coming tomorrow?
A: 不, 我来。	**Bù, wǒ lái.**	(*lit.* no, I come) Yes, I am.
or, 是(的), 我不来。	**Shì (de), wǒ bù lái.**	(*lit.* yes, I not come) No, I'm not.
Q: 你没见过 他们吗？	**Nǐ méi jiànguo tāmen ma?**	(*lit.* you not see asp them p) Haven't you met them before?
A: 不, 见过。	**Bù, jiànguo.**	(*lit.* no, see asp) Yes, I have.
or, 是(的), 没见过。	**Shì (de), méi jiànguo.**	(*lit.* yes, not see asp) No, I haven't.

Note: These questions can be made more *rhetorical* by introducing 难道 *nándào* 'do you mean to say', 'is it really the case' before or after the subject:

| 你难道不 想家吗？ | **Nǐ nándào bù xiǎng jiā ma?** | Don't you really miss your family? |
| 难道你不知道 这回事吗？ | **Nándào nǐ bù zhīdao zhèi huí shì ma?** | Didn't you really know this? |

| 17.3 | *Surmise questions with* **ba** |

To ask a general question, where the answer is expected or assumed, 吧 **ba** is used in place of 吗 **ma**. Such questions are similar to English tag questions with phrases like 'is(n't) it', 'are(n't) they', etc., at the end. We will call these questions *surmise questions*:

你会骑 摩托车吧?	**Nǐ huì qí mótuōchē ba?**	(*lit.* you can ride motorcycle p) You can ride a motorbike, can't you?
你不吃 蛇吧?	**Nǐ bù chī shé ba?**	(*lit.* you not eat snake p) You don't eat snake, do you?

The answers to surmise questions (吧 **ba** questions) follow the same lines as those to 吗 **ma** questions. If the enquiry is about a state of affairs, 是 (的) **shì (de)** 'yes' or 不 (是) **bù (shì)** 'no' can be used:

Q: 你会 溜冰吧?	**Nǐ huì liūbīng ba?**	(*lit.* you can slide-ice p) You can skate, can't you?
A: 不。我不会。	**Bù. Wǒ bù huì.**	(*lit.* no I not can) No, I can't.
Q: 他懂广州 话吧?	**Tā dǒng Guǎngzhōuhuà ba?**	(*lit.* he understand Cantonese p) He knows Cantonese, doesn't he?
A: 是(的)。 他懂。	**Shì (de). Tā dǒng.**	(*lit.* be [p]. he understand) Yes, he does.

Where the question is posed in the negative, the response affirms or denies that negative, as with negative 吗 **ma** questions (see 17.2):

Q: 你不是 张先生吧?	**Nǐ bù shì Zhāng xiānsheng ba?**	(*lit.* you not be Zhang mister p) You aren't Mr Zhang, are you?
A: 是(的)。 我不是。 or, 不。我是 张先生。	**Shì (de). Wǒ bù shì.** or **Bù. Wǒ shì Zhāng xiānsheng.**	(*lit.* yes, I not be) No, I am not. (*lit.* no, I be Zhang mister) Yes, I am Mr Zhang.

17.4 | *Affirmative-negative questions*

Another common way to make a general enquiry is to use *affirmative-negative questions*. These take the form of an affirmative verb or adjective immediately followed by its negative, i.e. 'verb/adjective + 不 **bù** verb/adjective'. In the case of 有 **yǒu**, the negative is, of course, 没 **méi**.

Q: 你是不是 张小姐?	**Nǐ *shì bù shì* Zhāng xiǎojie?**	Are you Miss Zhang (or not)?
A: 是。/不是。	**Shì./Bù shì.**	Yes./No.
Q: 你身上 有没有钱?	**Nǐ shēn shang *yǒu méi yǒu* qián?**	Have you got any money on you?
A: 有。/没有。	**Yǒu./Méi yǒu.**	Yes./No.
Q: 他明天 来不来?	**Tā míngtiān *lái bù lái?***	Is he coming tomorrow?
A: 来。/不来。	**Lái./Bù lái.**	Yes./No.
Q: 你想不想 喝啤酒?	**Nǐ *xiǎng bù xiǎng* hē píjiǔ?**	Would you like some beer?
A: 想。/不想。	**Xiǎng./Bù xiǎng.**	Yes./No.
Q: 杯子够不够?	**Bēizi *gòu bù gòu?***	Are there enough cups/ glasses?
A: 够。/不够。	**Gòu./Bù gòu.**	Yes./No.
Q: 银行远不远?	**Yínháng *yuǎn bù yuǎn?***	Is the bank far [from here]?
A: 很远。/ 不很远。	**Hěnyuǎn./ Bù hěn yuǎn.**	Yes./No.

If the verb or adjective is disyllabic, the second syllable may be dropped
from the first verb or adjective:

Q: 那儿安(静)不安静?	**Nàr *ān(jìng) bù ānjìng?***	Is it quiet there?
A: 安静。/不安静。	**Ānjìng./Bù ānjìng.**	Yes./No.
Q: 她愿(意)不愿意?	**Tā *yuàn(yi) bù yuànyi?***	Is she willing?
A: 愿意。/不愿意。	**Yuànyi./Bù yuànyi.**	Yes./No.

This also happens with 'verb + object' expressions:

Q: 你起不起床?	**Nǐ *qǐ bù qǐchuáng?***	Are you getting up?
A: 起床。/不起床。	**Qǐchuáng./ Bù qǐchuáng.**	Yes./No.

Q: 你洗不洗澡? **Nǐ xǐ bù xǐzǎo?** Are you going to take a bath?

A: 洗。/不洗。 **Xǐ./Bù xǐ.** Yes./No.

If the verb is preceded by a modal verb or 来/去 lái/qù, then only the modal verb or 来/去 lái/qù is made affirmative-negative:

Q: 你会不会
拉小提琴? **Nǐ huì bù huì
lā xiǎotíqín?** Can you play the violin?

A: 会。/不会。 **Huì./Bù huì.** Yes./No.

Q: 明天会不
会下雨? **Míngtiān huì
bù huì xià yǔ?** Will it rain tomorrow?

A: 会。/不会。 **Huì./Bù huì.** Yes./No.

Q: 你下午去
不去游泳? **Nǐ xiàwǔ qù bù
qù yóuyǒng?** Are you going swimming
this afternoon?

A: 去。/不去。 **Qù./Bù qù.** Yes./No.

Where the verb indicates a completed action or past experience, the affirmative-negative pattern can be created either by putting 没有 **méiyǒu** at the end of the question or by placing 有没有 **yǒu méiyǒu** before the verb:

Q: 你学过中文没有?/

or, 你有没有学过
中文? **Nǐ xué guo
Zhōngwén méiyǒu?
Nǐ yǒu méiyǒu
xuéguo Zhōngwén?** Have you ever
learned
Chinese?

A: 学过。/没有。/
没学过。 **Xuéguo./Méiyǒu./
Méi xuéguo.** Yes./No.

Q: 你吃了药没有?
or, 你有没有吃药? **Nǐ chīle yào méiyǒu?
Nǐ yǒu méiyǒu
chī yào?** Did you take
your medicine?

A: 吃了。/没有。
or 没(有)吃。 **Chīle./Méiyǒu.
Méi(yǒu) chī.** Yes./No.

Q: 你收到了回信没有?

or 你有没有收到回信? **Nǐ shōu dào le
huíxìn méiyǒu?
Nǐ yǒu méiyǒu
shōu dào huíxìn?** Have you got a
reply to your
letter?

A: 收到了。/没有。
or 没(有)收到。 **Shōu dào le./Méiyǒu
Méi(yǒu) shōu dào.** Yes./No.

143

Note: As seen in 8.3.1, the aspect marker **le** is not used in a negative statement with 没(有) **méi(yǒu)**. It would therefore be incorrect to say: *你有没有吃了药？ **Nǐ yǒu méiyǒu chīle yào?**

17.5 Alternative questions with **háishì**

Alternative questions are posed by using 还是 **háishì** 'or' as a pivot between two balanced verbal clauses to suggest alternative possibilities:

你今天走还是 明天走？	**Nǐ jīntiān zǒu *háishì* míngtiān zǒu?**	Are you leaving today or tomorrow?
你坐汽车去还是 坐火车去？	**Nǐ zuò qìchē qù *háishì* zuò huǒchē qù?**	Are you going by coach or by train?
他们想跳舞 还是想看戏？	**Tāmen xiǎng tiàowǔ *háishì* xiǎng kànxì?**	Do they want to go to a dance or to see a play?
你来还是她来？	**Nǐ lái *háishì* tā lái?**	Are you coming or is she coming?

Note 1: 还是 **Háishì** is used to mean 'or' only in questions. In other sentences the word for 'or' is 或者 **huòzhě** (see 24.2.1 (2)).

Note 2: The adverbs 究竟 **jiūjìng** and 到底 **dàodǐ**, meaning 'after all', are often used for emphasis with alternative questions, affirmative-negative questions and with some question-word questions. They are always placed before the first verb:

他究竟想学汉语 还是想学日语？	**Tā *jiūjìng* xiǎng xué Hànyǔ háishì xiǎng xué Rìyǔ?**	What does he really want to learn – Chinese or Japanese?
你到底有 没有空？	**Nǐ *dàodǐ* yǒu méi yǒu kòng?**	Are you free after all?
他们究竟 什么时候到？	**Tāmen *jiūjìng* shénme shíhou dào?**	When exactly do they arrive?
你究竟要去 哪儿呢？	**Nǐ *jiūjìng* yào qù nǎr ne?**	Where do you really want to go?

17.6 Tags indicating suggestion

Suggestions in the form of questions can be made by adding a tag expression such as 好不好 **hǎo bù hǎo**, 好吗 **hǎo ma** or 怎么样 **zěnmeyàng** at the end of the sentence:

咱们去爬山，好不好？	Zánmen qù pá shān, *hǎo bù hǎo?*	Shall we go climbing?
请关上窗户，好吗？	Qǐng guān shàng chuānghu, *hǎo ma?*	Could you please close the window?
请说得慢点儿，好吗？	Qǐng shuō de màn diǎnr, *hǎo ma?*	Would you please speak a little slower?
咱们喝一杯，怎么样？	Zánmen hē yī bēi, *zěnmeyàng?*	How about (having) a drink?
请你帮我修一修, 好吗？	Qǐng nǐ bāng wǒ xiū yī xiū, *hǎo ma?*	Can you please (help) fix [it] for me?

A positive answer to all these questions will usually be 好 hǎo 'fine'/ 'OK'/'good'. A negative response will obviously involve explanation but will often begin with 对不起 duìbuqǐ 'sorry'.

17.7 Tags seeking confirmation

Confirmation can often be sought by adding the tag expression 是吗 shì ma or 是不是 shì bù shì at the end of a statement:

Q: 她病了, 是吗？	Tā bìng le, *shì ma?*	She is ill, isn't she?
A: 是的。她病了。	Shì de. Tā bìng le.	Yes. She's ill.
Q: 你下个星期考试, 是不是？	Nǐ xià gè xīngqī kǎoshì, *shì bù shì?*	You'll have exams next week, won't you?
A: 不是。是这个星期。	Bù shì. Shì zhèi gè xīngqī.	No. It's this week.

Note: For discussion of 是 shì as an intensifier, see Chapter 22.

17.8 Rhetorical questions

Rhetorical questions, for which no answers are expected, can be formulated by inserting expressions such as 难道 nándào (*lit.* 'difficult to say'), using pronouns such as 谁 shéi 'who/nobody', 什么 shénme 'what/ anything', or referential adverbs such as 才 cái 'only then', etc.:

| 你难道不知道这件事吗？ | Nǐ nándào bù zhīdào zhèi jiàn shì ma? | (*lit.* you difficult-to-say not know this mw matter p) Don't you know about this?! |

谁知道？	**Shéi zhīdào?**	(*lit.* who know) Who knows?!
怎样才行？	**Zěnyàng cái xíng?**	(*lit.* how only-then OK) What then?!/ Where do we go from here?!/What do we do now?!
你懂什么？	**Nǐ dǒng shénme?**	(*lit.* you understand what) What do you know?!

18 Subject and predicate; topic and comment

18.1 Dual patterning of sentence structures

Chinese sentences may be divided into two broad categories: *subject-predicate* and *topic-comment*. These two categories are markedly distinct both in terms of definite and indefinite reference and in their use of different types of verb with or without aspect markers. The transformation of a subject-predicate structure into a topic-comment one, with modal verbs or the sentence particle **le**, is a key feature of Chinese sentence construction.

This dual patterning of syntax enables flexible and succinct expression, with less dependence on formal grammatical features and sharper focus on meaning in relation to the real world. For instance:

| 东西都放在 柜子里了。 | **Dōngxi dōu fàng zài guìzi li le.** | (*lit.* things all put at cupboard-in p) Everything has been put in the cupboard. |

This sentence does not need to be couched in the passive voice, though its English equivalent does. By relying on real-world knowledge, the Chinese speaker can be confident that no misunderstanding will arise, since the listener cannot possibly assume that the 'things' in the sentence are the subject and responsible for the action of putting. (Compare 18.4.1.)

18.2 Subject-predicate sentences

A *subject-predicate* sentence usually relates an event and is therefore used for narrative purposes. It has the following features:

(1)   The subject is often a noun or pronoun representing the initiator or recipient of the action (or non-action) expressed by the verb:

大家都带 了雨伞。	*Dàjiā dōu* *dàile yǔsǎn.*	Everybody carried an umbrella with them.
他们收到了 不少礼物。	*Tāmen shōu dàole* *bù shǎo lǐwù.*	They received quite a lot of presents.
弟弟不吃鱼。	*Dìdi bù chī yú.*	My younger brother doesn't eat fish.
他没(有)去 过印度。	*Tā méi(yǒu)* *qùguo Yìndù.*	He has never been to India.

(2) The subject must be of *definite reference*:

她在洗碗。	*Tā zài xǐ wǎn.*	She is washing the dishes.
老师走进 了教室。	*Lǎoshī zǒu jìn* *le jiàoshì.*	The teacher came into the classroom.
孩子们在 马路上踢球。	*Háizimen zài* *mǎlù shang tī qiú.*	The children are playing football on the road.
妈妈丢掉了 她的钱包。	*Māma diū diào* *le tāde qiánbāo.*	Mother has lost her purse.

A noun at the beginning of such a sentence, even if unqualified
by a demonstrative (this, that), will have definite reference (e.g.
老师 **lǎoshī** 'the teacher' in the above). A personal pronoun is
naturally of definite reference, and a pronoun like 大家 **dàjiā**
refers to 'everybody of a definite group'. A noun of indefinite
reference cannot normally be the subject of a subject-predicate
construction, and it would therefore be unusual to say:

| *一个学生
站了起来。 | **Yī gè xuésheng*
zhànle qǐlái. | (*lit.* A student stood up.) |

However, it is possible to begin the sentence with the verb 有 **yǒu**
so that the noun of indefinite reference comes after a verb:

| 有一个学生
站了起来。 | *Yǒu yī gè xuésheng*
zhànle qǐlái. | A student stood up. |

This accounts for the fact that many narrative sentences begin
with a time or location expression followed by 有 **yǒu**:

| 这时候有
(一)辆车
开了过来。 | *Zhèi shíhou*
yǒu (yī) liàng
chē kāile guòlái. | (*lit.* this time there-was (one)
mw car drive asp across-
come) At this moment a car
approached. |

| 今天晚上
有(一)个
朋友来
我家坐。 | **Jīntiān wǎnshang
yǒu (yī) gè
péngyou lái
wǒ jiā zuò.** | (*lit.* today evening there-will-be
(one) mw friend come my
home sit) A friend is coming
round to my place this evening. |
| 外面有人
找你。 | **Wàimiàn yǒu
rén zhǎo nǐ.** | (*lit.* outside there-is person
look-for you) There is someone
outside looking for you. |

(3) The predicate verb is an action verb. Aspect markers are therefore almost always present in subject-predicate sentences (see
Chapter 8).

我喝了 一杯牛奶。	**Wǒ hēle yī bēi niúnǎi.**	I drank/had a glass of milk.
他看过杂技。	**Tā kànguo zájì.**	He has seen acrobatics.
他们正在 谈判。	**Tāmen zhèngzài tánpàn.**	They are negotiating right now.
她戴着一顶 白帽子。	**Tā dàizhe yī dǐng bái màozi.**	She is wearing a white hat.

Note: Some action verbs can be followed by **zhe** to indicate a persistent
state that results from the action of the verb. See the last example above
and 8.3.4.

(4) It may be a sentence with a passive marker (e.g. 被 **bèi**, 让 **ràng**,
叫 **jiào**, etc.) or with 把 **bǎ** (implying intentional manipulation or
unintentional intervention; see also Chapter 20):

| 信封被弄
得很脏。 | **Xìnfēng bèi
nòng de
hěn zāng.** | (*lit.* envelope by handle p very
dirty) The envelope has been
made very dirty. |
| 他们把汽车
停在路边。 | **Tāmen bǎ
qìchē tíng
zài lù biān.** | (*lit.* they grasp car stop at
road-side) They parked their
car by the side of the road. |

(5) The predicate verb may be causative or dative (see 8.5 and
21.5).

| 她请我吃饭。 | **Tā qǐng wǒ
chī fàn.** | She invited me to a meal.
(*causative*) |
| 我送他一个
礼物。 | **Wǒ sòng tā
yī gè lǐwù.** | I gave him a present. (*dative*) |

18.3 | Topic-comment sentences

A *topic-comment* sentence, while usually following a structure with a noun phrase followed by a verb phrase similar to that of a subject and predicate, provides a description or offers an opinion, rather than narrating an action or event. It is therefore a construction designed for descriptive, explanatory or argumentative purposes. The following features differentiate it from the subject-predicate sentence:

(1) The topic may be of any word class or any structure (e.g. a phrase or even a clause):

字典很有用。	*Zìdiǎn* hěn yǒuyòng. (*noun*: 'dictionaries')	(*lit.* dictionary very useful) Dictionaries are useful.
懒惰是不对的。	*Lǎnduò* shì bù duì de. (*adjective*: 'lazy')	(*lit.* lazy is not right p) Being lazy is wrong.
做事应该认真。	*Zuò shì* yīnggāi rènzhēn. (*verbal phrase*: 'doing anything')	(*lit.* do things should conscientious) One should be conscientious when doing anything.
他不来不要紧。	*Tā bù lái* bù yàojǐn. (*clause*: 'he does not come')	(*lit.* he not come not urgent) It does not matter if he does not turn up.

(2) The topic may be of definite or indefinite reference:

工具应该放在这儿。	*Gōngjù* yīnggāi fàng zài zhèr.	(*lit.* tool should put at here) The tools should be placed here.
一个人不能不讲理。	*Yī gè rén* bù néng bù jiǎng lǐ.	(*lit.* one mw person not able not talk reason) A person must be reasonable.

(3) The comment can be an adjectival predicate, or it can contain the verbs 是 shì or 有 yǒu:

这个孩子很聪明。	*Zhèi gè háizi* hěn cōngmíng.	This child is (very) intelligent.
今天是我的生日。	*Jīntiān shì* wǒde shēngrì.	Today is my birthday.
每个人都有一个名字。	*Měi gè rén dōu yǒu yī gè míngzi.*	Every person has a name.

Further ways to form topic-comment sentences

In addition, topic-comments can be created in the following circumstances:

(1) When a *modal verb* is present, since a modal verb naturally signals a comment:

她<u>会</u>说 中文。	**Tā *huì* shuō Zhōngwén.**	She can speak Chinese.
谁都<u>应该</u> 遵守纪律。	**Shéi dōu *yīnggāi* zūnshǒu jìlǜ.**	Everybody should observe discipline.
学生也 <u>可以</u>参加。	**Xuésheng yě *kěyǐ* cānjiā.**	Students may also take part.

(2) By the addition of the *sentence particle* 了 le. This can convert most subject-predicates into topic-comments since by definition it expresses a comment on the action, updating, indicating change, etc. (see 16.1):

弟弟 吃鱼<u>了</u>。	**Dìdi chī yú *le*.**	(*lit.* younger-brother eat fish p) My younger brother eats fish now.
病人醒 过来<u>了</u>。	**Bìngrén xǐng guòlái *le*.**	(*lit.* patient wake across-come p) The patient has regained consciousness.
别人都 离开<u>了</u>。	**Biérén dōu líkāi *le*.**	(*lit.* others all depart p) The others have all left.

18.4 Topic | subject-predicate sentences

A posed topic may be followed by a subject-predicate structure. There are therefore a large number of sentences where both a topic and a subject are present. These '*topic | subject-predicate*' structures are often used for explanatory purposes:

那本侦探 小说我们 卖完了。	**Nèi běn zhēntàn xiǎoshuō	wǒmen mài wán le.**	(*lit.* that mw detective novel | we sell finish p) We have sold out of that detective/crime novel.
信她寄 出去了。	**Xìn	tā jì chūqù le.**	(*lit.* letter | she post out-go p) She has posted the letter.
<u>你的裤子</u> <u>我</u>烫好了。	**Nǐde kùzi	wǒ tàng hǎo le.**	(*lit.* your trousers | I iron good p) I've ironed your trousers.

18.4.1   Notional passive sentences

The subject in these 'topic + subject-predicate' structures may be omitted if its sense is understood from the context. Sentences of this type superficially become 'topic + predicate' structures and can be seen as *notional passive* sentences in which the topic is notionally the object of the verb. The three examples in 18.4 may be re-formulated without the subject as:

那本侦探 小说卖 完了。	*Nèi běn zhēntàn* *xiǎoshuō	mài* *wán le.*	(*lit.* that mw detective novel | sell finish p) That detective novel is sold out.
信寄 出去了。	*Xìn	jì chūqù le.*	(*lit.* letter | post out-go p) The letter has been sent/posted.
你的裤子 烫/熨好了。	*Nǐde kùzi	tàng/* *yùn hǎo le.*	(*lit.* your trousers | iron good p) Your trousers have been ironed.

Other examples are:

这个戏演了 两个月了。	*Zhèi gè xì |* *yǎnle liǎng* *gè yuè le.*	(*lit.* this mw play | perform asp two mw month p) This play has been on for two months.
包裹 收到了。	*Bāoguǒ |* *shōu dào le.*	(*lit.* parcel | receive arrive p) The parcel has been received.
代表团的 访问日程 安排好了。	*Dàibiǎotuán* *de fǎngwèn* *rìchéng	ānpái* *hǎo le.*	(*lit.* delegation p visit itinerary | arrange good p) The itinerary for the delegation's visit has been arranged.
你要的东西 买回来了。	*Nǐ yào de* *dōngxi	mǎi* *huílái le.*	(*lit.* you want p things | buy back-come p) The things you want have been bought.

18.5   *Subject | topic-comment sentences*

Conversely, a subject may be followed by a topic-comment structure to create a '*subject | topic-comment*' sentence. At first sight these sentences seem to have two subjects, but in fact what looks like a second subject is a topic (relating to the subject) on which a comment is expressed:

他身体 不好。	*Tā	shēntǐ* bù hǎo.	(*lit.* he | body not good) His health is not good.
我工作 很忙。	*Wǒ	gōngzuò* hěn máng.	(*lit.* I | work very busy) I am busy with my work.
董事长 薪水 十分高。	*Dǒngshìzhǎng	* *xīnshuǐ* *shífēn gāo.*	(*lit.* board-director | salary extremely high) The director of the board has an extremely high salary.
广东省 经济发展 非常快。	*Guǎngdōngshěng	* *jīngjì fāzhǎn* *fēicháng kuài.*	(*lit.* Guangdong province | economic development extremely fast) The economy of Guangdong developed/is developing very fast.

It is also possible for the possessive 的 de to be used after the subject, thereby changing the subject–topic sequence into a simple topic and leaving the sentence in the topic-comment form:

| 我的工作
很忙。 | **Wǒde gōngzuò |**
hěn máng. | (*lit.* my work \| very busy)
I am busy with my work. |
| 广东省的
经济发展
非常快。 | **Guǎngdōngshěng**
de jīngjì fāzhǎn |
fēicháng kuài. | (*lit.* Guangdong province p economic
development \| extremely fast) The
economy of Guangdong developed/is
developing very fast. |

19 Prezpositions and coverbs

19.1 Coverbs

We have seen in 11.4 how the preposition 在 zài 'in', 'at' followed by a location noun, pronoun or postpositional phrase can be placed before the verb as a location phrase:

| 妈妈在
厨房里
做饭。 | **Māma zài**
chúfáng li
zuò fàn. | (*lit.* mother at kitchen in make rice-
meal) Mother is preparing the meal/
doing the cooking in the kitchen. |

There are a number of prepositions that grammatically function like 在 zài. As they can also be used as full verbs, they may be called *coverbs*, i.e. verbs that occur in sequence with other verbs in a sentence. The coverb with its object can be referred to as a *coverbal phrase*. In the above example, 在 zài is the coverb, and the location phrase 在厨房里 zài chúfáng li, in syntactic terms, is a coverbal phrase.

Note: We have observed in 11.3 that zài can be a full verb as in 他们现在在
美国。Tāmen xiànzài *zài* Měiguó 'They are in America now'.

The coverbal phrase normally comes after the subject and before the
main verb; it provides background information about the place, time,
methods, service, reference, reason, etc., associated with the main verb.
Generally modal verbs (e.g. 能 néng, 要 yào) and the negators 不 bù
and 没有 méi(yǒu) come before the coverbal phrase, though occasionally,
when they relate only to the main verb, they come after it (e.g. in the
case of 离 lí 'away from'). The main types of coverb are listed below.

| 19.1.1 | Coverbs of place and time |

(1)   在 **Zài** 'in, at'

她在	**Tā** *zài*	(*lit.* she at airport act interpreter)
(飞)机场	*(fēi)jīchǎng*	She serves as an interpreter at
当翻译。	**dāng fānyì.**	the airport.

我在大使馆	**Wǒ** *zài*	(*lit.* I at embassy deal visa) I was
办签证。	***dàshǐguǎn* bàn**	applying for a visa at the embassy.
	qiānzhèng.	

我可以在	**Wǒ kěyǐ** *zài*	(*lit.* I can at here inhale-smoke p)
这儿抽烟/	*zhèr* **chōuyān/**	May I smoke here?
吸烟吗?	**xīyān ma?**	

(2)   到 **Dào** 'to'

下学期到	**Xià xuéqī**	(*lit.* next term cv:to April only-
四月份才	*dào* **sìyuèfèn**	then begin) Next term doesn't
开始。	**cái kāishǐ.**	begin till April.

课程到明年	**Kèchéng** *dào*	(*lit.* course cv:to next year June
六月份就	**míngnián**	then end p) The course will end
结束了。	**liùyuèfèn jiù**	next June/June next year.
	jiéshù le.	

Note: 月份 yuèfèn is used as an alternative to 月 yuè when referring to
months of the year.

他们明天	**Tāmen**	(*lit.* they tomorrow to Russia
到俄国去。	**míngtiān** *dào*	go) They are going to Russia
	***Éguó* qù.**	tomorrow.

他没到医院	**Tā méi** *dào*	(*lit.* he not to hospital come see
来看我。	**yīyuàn lái**	me) He did not come to the
	kàn wǒ.	hospital to see me.

153

| 我们不
到饭馆去
吃饭。 | **Wǒmen bù
dào fànguǎn
qù chīfàn.** | (*lit.* we not to restaurant go
eat-rice) We are not dining out
at a restaurant. |

As can be seen from the last example, a 到 **dào** coverbal phrase with 来 **lái** 'come' or 去 **qù** 'go' may often be followed by another verb to indicate purpose.

(3) 往 **Wǎng,** 向 **xiàng,** 朝 **cháo** 'towards'

汽车往南 开去。	**Qìchē wǎng nán kāi qù.**	(*lit.* car towards south drive go) The car is heading south.
她朝我 点了点头。	**Tā cháo wǒ diǎn le diǎn tóu.**	(*lit.* she towards me nod asp nod head) She nodded to me.
他向俱乐部 走来。	**Tā xiàng jùlèbù zǒu lái.**	(*lit.* s/he towards club walk come) S/he came towards the club.

(4) 从 **Cóng** 'from'

这个音乐剧 从去年就开 始上演了。	**Zhèi gè yīnyuèjù cóng qùnián jiù kāishǐ shàngyǎn le.**	(*lit.* this mw music opera cv:from last year then begin stage p) This musical has been on since last year.
风从西边 吹来。	**Fēng cóng xībian chuī lái.**	(*lit.* wind from west-side blow come) The wind blew from the west.
你从这儿 向北走。	**Nǐ cóng zhèr xiàng běi zǒu.**	(*lit.* you from here towards north walk) You go north from here.

Note: In this last example, there are two coverbal phrases: 从这儿 **cóng zhèr** and 向北 **xiàng běi**.

(5) 离 **Lí** '(distance) from (in terms of place or time)'

| 我家离大学
很远。 | **Wǒ jiā lí dàxué
hěn yuǎn.** | (*lit.* my home from university
very far) My home is very far
from the university. |
| 我的办公室
离市中心
很近。 | **Wǒde
bàngōngshì lí shì
zhōngxīn hěn jìn.** | (*lit.* my office from city centre
very near) My office is very
close to the city centre. |

Note 1: 离 **Lí** 'from' simply indicates *distance* between two fixed objects, while 从 **cóng** 'from' is always associated with *movement* from one place to another.

Note 2: The negator 不 **bù** comes before the main predicate verb or
adjective and not before 离 **lí**: 我家离大学<u>不远</u>。Wǒ jiā lí dàxué *bù yuǎn*
'My home is not far from the university.' NOT: *我家不离大学远。Wǒ
jiā bù lí dàxué yuǎn.

我家离 上海有 二十公里。	**Wǒ jiā lí** **Shànghǎi yǒu** **èrshí gōnglǐ.**	(*lit.* my home from Shanghai have twenty kilometres) My home is twenty kilometres from Shanghai.
现在离 圣诞节 还有 两个月。	**Xiànzài lí** **Shèngdànjié** **hái yǒu liǎng** **gè yuè.**	(*lit.* now from Christmas still have two mw month) There are still two months from now to Christmas.

Note: When the actual distance or time is specified, the verb 有 **yǒu** is
normally required.

(6) 沿着 **Yánzhe** 'along'

我们沿着那 条街走去。	**Wǒmen** **yánzhe nèi** **tiáo jiē zǒu qù.**	(*lit.* we along that mw street walk go) We went along that street.
船沿着运河 开来。	**Chuán yánzhe** **yùnhé kāi lái.**	(*lit.* boat along canal sail come) The boat came along the canal.

Note: 沿 **Yán** on its own is only found in such expressions as 沿路 **yán lù**
'all along the road', 沿海 **yán hǎi** 'all along the coast', etc., which are
generally used to indicate existence rather than movement:

沿路都 是麦田。	**Yán lù dōu** **shì màitián.**	There are wheatfields all along the road.

19.1.2 Coverbs of methods and means

(1) 用 **Yòng** 'with, using'

她用毛笔 画画儿。	**Tā yòng máobǐ** **huà huàr.**	(*lit.* she use Chinese-brush paint picture) She paints with a Chinese brush.

(2) 坐 **Zuò** '(travelling) on/by' (*lit.* sit)

我常常坐 地铁上班。	**Wǒ chángcháng** **zuò dìtiě** **shàngbān.**	(*lit.* I often sit underground-rail go-to-work) I often go to work by underground.

| 我们很想
坐火车/
公共汽车/
飞机/船去。 | **Wǒmen hěn
xiǎng zuò
huǒchē/gōnggòng
qìchē/fēijī/
chuán qù.** | (*lit.* we very want sit train/bus/
plane/boat go) We'd very much
like to go by train/bus/plane/boat. |

Note: An alternative coverb for travel is 乘 **chéng**:

| 我常常乘
出租汽车上班。 | **Wǒ chángcháng chéng
chūzū qìchē shàngbān.** | (*lit.* I often take hire-car
go-to-work) I often go to
work by taxi. |

| **19.1.3** | Coverbs of human exchange and service |

(1) 对 **Duì** '(speaking) to', '(behaving) towards'

| 他对我
说... | **Tā duì wǒ
shuō...** | (*lit.* he to me said...)
He said to me... |
| 他们对我
很好。 | **Tāmen duì
wǒ hěn hǎo.** | (*lit.* they towards me very good)
They are very kind to me. |

Note: 对 **Duì** is also commonly used to mean 'with regard to':

| 我对美术/
音乐没(有)
兴趣。 | **Wǒ duì
měishù/yīnyuè
méi(yǒu) xìngqù.** | (*lit.* I regarding fine-art/music not-
have interest) I have no interest in
fine art/music. |

(2) 给 **Gěi** 'to', 'for'

我今天晚上 给你打 电话。	**Wǒ jīntiān wǎnshang gěi nǐ dǎ diànhuà.**	(*lit.* I today evening to you make telephone-call) I will call/ring you tonight.
我每周都 给爸爸 写信。	**Wǒ měi zhōu dōu gěi bàba xiě xìn.**	(*lit.* I every week all to father write letter) I write to my father every week.
请你给我 开(一)张 收据。	**Qǐng nǐ gěi wǒ kāi (yī) zhāng shōujù.**	(*lit.* please you to me write (one) mw receipt) Please write a receipt for me.

(3) 为/替 **Wèi/tì** 'for', 'on behalf of'

| 姐姐替我
理发。 | **Jiějie tì wǒ
lǐ fà.** | (*lit.* elder-sister for me cut hair)
My elder sister cut my hair
for me. |

| 门房为我
叫了一辆
的士/
出租汽车。 | **Ménfáng wèi**
wǒ jiào le yī
liàng díshì/
chūzū qìchē. | (*lit.* porter for me call asp
one mw taxi) The porter
called a taxi for me. |

(4) 跟/和/同 **Gēn/hé/tóng** . . . 一起 **yīqǐ** '(together) with'

| 我跟父母
一起去
度假。 | **Wǒgēn fùmǔ**
yīqǐ qù dùjià. | (*lit.* I with father-mother together go
spend-holiday) I spent my holiday
with my parents. |

Note: 跟 **Gēn** may also be used colloquially like 对 **duì** above:

| 她跟我说 . . . | **Tā gēn wǒ shuō** . . . | She said to me . . . |

19.1.4 Coverbs of reference

(1) 按/照/按照 **Àn/zhào/ànzhào** 'according to'

| 请你按/
照/按照
规定去办
这件事。 | **Qǐng nǐ àn/**
zhào/ànzhào
guīdìng qù bàn
zhèi jiàn shì. | (*lit.* please you according-to
regulation go manage this
mw matter) Please do this
according to the regulations. |

(2) 就 **Jiù** 'with reference to'

| 我们就
这个问题
讨论一下。 | **Wǒmen jiù**
zhèi gè wèntí
tǎolùn yī xià. | (*lit.* we with-reference-to this mw
question discuss a-moment) Let's have
a discussion of/discuss this question. |

19.1.5 Coverbs and comparison

比 **Bǐ** and 跟 **gēn** in comparison expressions (as discussed in 7.2 and
7.2.3) are in fact coverbs.

| 她比我大。 | **Tā bǐ wǒ dà.** | She is older than me. |
| 这个跟那个
一样贵。 | **Zhèi gè gēn nèi**
gè yīyàng guì. | This one is as expensive as that
one. |

把 **Bǎ** in manipulation constructions and 被 **bèi** for passive voice
(analysed in Chapter 20) are also coverbs.

19.2 Disyllabic prepositions

There are a number of disyllabic *prepositions* which, though similar to
coverb prepositions, are not strictly in that category, since they may be

followed not only by nominal expressions but also in most cases by verbal phrases. These prepositional constructions usually come at the beginning of the sentence:

(1) 根据/据 **Gēnjù/jù** 'on the basis of'

根据路牌 我们找到 了她的家。	**Gēnjù lùpái** **wǒmen zhǎo** **dào le tāde jiā.**	(*lit.* basing-on road-sign we look-for-and-find asp her home) We found her home with the help of road signs.
据她所说， 他们已经 走了。	**Jù tā suǒ shuō,** **tāmen yǐjing** **zǒu le.**	(*lit.* basing-on she p say, they already leave p) According to her, they have already left.

(2) 关于 **Guānyú** 'as for', 'as regards'

关于这一点， 我已经提出 过我的意见。	**Guānyú zhèi** **yī diǎn, wǒ** **yǐjing tíchūguo** **wǒde yìjian.**	(*lit.* as-for this one point, I already raise-out asp my opinion) As regards this point, I have already put forward my opinion.

(3) 由于 **Yóuyú** 'because of'

由于大雪， 球赛暂停。	**Yóuyú dà xuě,** **qiúsài zàntíng.**	(*lit.* because-of heavy snow, ball-contest temporary-stop) The ball game was temporarily suspended because of the heavy snow.

Note: 由于 **Yóuyú** may also be regarded as a conjunction when it is followed by a clause. (See Chapter 24.)

(4) 为了 **Wèile** 'for the sake of'

为了这件事， 我去了三趟。	**Wèile zhèi** **jiàn shì, wǒ** **qù le sān tàng.**	(*lit.* for this mw matter, I go asp three trip) I made three trips there for this business.
为了看望 老祖母， 她每星期 都回家。	**Wèile kànwàng** **lǎo zǔmǔ, tā** **měi xīngqī dōu** **huí jiā.**	(*lit.* in-order-to visit old grandma, she every week all return home) She goes home every week in order to see her old grandma.

Note: We have consciously used the term 'preposition' for this group of words in order to illustrate the uniformity of their function.

| 20.1 | *The* **bǎ** *construction* |

The 把 **bǎ** *construction* is a grammatical feature unique to the Chinese language. In this construction, the coverb 把 **bǎ**, which as a verb has the meaning 'to grasp', has the function of shifting the object of the verb to a pre-verbal position in the pattern of 'subject + **bǎ** + object + verb'. Three interrelated features of the construction can be identified:

(1) As seen in 1.3.2, an unqualified object after the verb will gener- ally be of indefinite reference. Employment of the coverb 把 **bǎ**, which moves the object in front of the verb, automatically con- verts the noun to definite reference:

| 我去买书。 | **Wǒ qù** | (*lit.* I go buy book) I am going |
| | **mǎi shū.** | to buy a book/some books. |

我去把书	**Wǒ qù *bǎ* shū**	(*lit.* I go grasp book buy back-come)
买回来。	**mǎi huílái.**	I am going to buy *the* book/books
		(and come back with it/them).

(2) In the discussion of complements in 13.4.3, it was apparent that with complements adjustments have to be made when the verb is followed by an object:

这个人	**Zhèi gè rén**	(*lit.* this mw person say words say
说话说	*shuō* **huà** *shuō*	p very fast) This person speaks
得很快。	**de hěn kuài.**	very fast.

In this example, the repetition of the verb 说 **shuō** enables it to deal with the object and the complement one at a time. The coverb 把 **bǎ** is used to similar effect, moving the object before the verb and leaving the post-verbal position clear for the complement.

她把书	**Tā bǎ *shū***	(*lit.* she grasp book put good p)
放好了。	**fàng *hǎo* le.**	She placed the books in good
		order.

她把它搁	**Tā bǎ *tā* gē *zài***	(*lit.* she grasp it leave at book-
在书架上。	*shūjià* **shang.**	shelf on) She placed it on the
		bookshelf.

Note: 它 **Tā** 'it' cannot be omitted after 把 **bǎ**.

(3)　把 **Bǎ**, which as noted derives from a verb meaning 'to grasp', also implies *intentional* (or sometimes unintentional) *manipulation* of the object on the part of the subject. In the latter case, 给 **gěi** may sometimes be added before the main verb.

她把衣服 洗干净了。	**Tā bǎ yīfu** **xǐ gānjìng le.**	(*lit.* she grasp clothes wash clean p) She has washed the clothes./ She has done the washing.
他把衬衫 (给)弄脏了。	**Tā bǎ chènshān** **(gěi)nòngzāng le.**	(*lit.* he grasp shirt handle dirty p) He dirtied his shirt.

The subject of a 把 **bǎ** construction deliberately (or unwittingly) handles or deals with the object in such a way that some kind of consequence is registered in the complement that follows the verb.

The 把 **bǎ** construction, therefore, cannot be used if any of the above conditions are not met. In other words, a 把 **bǎ** construction must have an object of definite reference (shifted now to a pre-verbal position directly after 把 **bǎ**); a complement of some kind after the verb to indicate the result achieved by the action of the verb, either intentionally or unintentionally, on the part of the subject. The following sentences are therefore unacceptable:

(a)　*我把舞跳　**Wǒ *bǎ* wǔ tiào**　(*lit.* I danced once)
　　了一次。　　**le yī cì.**

(The noun 舞 **wǔ** 'dance' is not of definite reference in this context.)

(b)　*我把书放。　**Wǒ *bǎ* shū fàng.**　(*lit.* I put the books)

(There is no complement and therefore no indication of any result achieved by the action of the verb 放 **fàng** 'put'.)

(c)　*我把电影看　**Wǒ *bǎ* diànyǐng kàn**　(*lit.* I took two hours to
　　了两个钟头。　**le liǎng gè zhōngtóu.**　watch the film)

(It is clearly beyond the power of the subject to decide how long the film will be. There are of course occasions when the subject can control the duration of something – see 20.1.1 below.)

(d)　*我把这本书　**Wǒ *bǎ* zhèi běn shū**　(*lit.* I like this book very
　　喜欢得很。　　**xǐhuan de hěn.**　much)

(The verb 喜欢 **xǐhuan** 'like' expresses the inclination of the subject and the complement 的很 **de hěn** 'very much' indicates the degree or extent of the liking; these cannot be regarded as a manipulative action and an achieved result.)

| 20.1.1 | The **bă** construction and complements |

Complements in a 把 **bă** construction may take various forms:

我把垃圾倒掉了。	**Wǒ bǎ lā jī dào diào le.** (result – verb)	(lit. I grasp litter pour off p) I have dumped the rubbish.
她把信封好了。	**Tā bǎ xìn fēng hǎo le.** (result – adjective)	(lit. she grasp letter seal good p) She has sealed the letter.
他把画挂起来了。	**Tā bǎ huà guà qǐlái le.** (direction)	(lit. he grasp picture hang up-come p) He hung the picture.
弟弟把课文复习了两遍。	**Dìdi bǎ kèwén fùxí le liǎng biàn.** (frequency)	(lit. younger-brother grasp text revise asp two times) My younger brother revised the text twice.
警察把小偷关了两个月。	**Jǐngchá bǎ xiǎotōu guān le liǎng gè yuè.** (duration)	(lit. police grasp thief imprison asp two mw month) The police kept the thief in prison for two months.
姐姐把房间收拾了一下。	**Jiějie bǎ fángjiān shōushí le yī xià.** (brief duration)	(lit. elder-sister grasp room tidy asp one stroke) My elder sister tidied up the room.
她把椅子拉到桌子旁边。	**Tā bǎ yǐzi lā dào zhuōzi pángbiān.** (destination)	(lit. she grasp chair pull to table side) She pulled the chair to the side of the table.
我把大衣挂在衣架上。	**Wǒ bǎ dàyī guà zài yījià shang.** (location)	(lit. I grasp overcoat hang at clothes-hanger on) I hung my overcoat on the clothes-hanger.
我们把礼物送给她。	**Wǒmen bǎ lǐwù sòng gěi tā.** (dative)	(lit. we grasp gift present give her) We presented the gift to her.
他们把屋子打扫得干干净净的。	**Tāmen bǎ wūzi dǎsǎo de gāngānjìngjìng de.** (manner)	(lit. they grasp room sweep p clean-clean p) They swept the room clean.

Note: Reduplicated adjectival complements are usually followed by 得 **de**.

| 她把我气得话都说不出来了。 | **Tā bǎ wǒ qì de huà dōu shuō bù chūlái le.** (consequential state) | (lit. she grasp me anger p words all speak not out-come p) She made me so angry that I could not speak a word. |

20.1.2 **Le and zhe as complements in bǎ sentences**

The aspect markers 了 le and 着 zhe may also be used as complements in 把 bǎ sentences.

(1) 了 Le (indicating completed action with verbs which have an inherent meaning of result):

| 她把茶喝<u>了</u>。 | **Tā bǎ chá hē*le*.** | (*lit.* she grasp tea drink asp) She drank up/finished the tea. |
| 谁把门锁<u>了</u>。 | **Shéi bǎ mén suǒ*le*?** | (*lit.* who grasp door lock asp) Who has locked the door? |

(2) 着 Zhe (indicating persistence in an *imperative* sentence):

| 请把灯拿<u>着</u>。 | **Qǐng bǎ dēng ná*zhe*.** | (*lit.* please grasp lamp hold asp) Please hold the lamp. |
| 把菜留<u>着</u>。 | **Bǎ cài liú*zhe*.** | (*lit.* grasp dishes keep asp) Keep the food. (i.e. don't throw it away or eat it) |

20.1.3 **Bǎ and resultative complements**

One type of complement regularly used with 把 bǎ is the resultative complement beginning with 成 chéng, 作 zuò or 为 wéi all meaning 'become', 'act as':

| 作家把
自己写的
故事翻译
<u>成</u>法文。 | **Zuòjiā *bǎ* zìjǐ xiě de gùshì fānyì *chéng* Fǎwén.** | (*lit.* writer grasp self write p story translate become French) The writer translated his/her own story into French. |
| 她<u>把</u>我当
作最好的
朋友。 | **Tā *bǎ* wǒ dàng *zuò* zuì hǎo de péngyou.** | (*lit.* s/he grasp me regard become most good p friend) S/he regarded me as her best friend. |

20.1.4 **Nòng and Gǎo in bǎ sentences**

弄 Nòng and 搞 gǎo are two versatile colloquial verbs meaning loosely 'to handle' which feature regularly in 把 bǎ sentences:

| 我把盒子(给)
<u>弄</u>破了。 | **Wǒ bǎ hézi (gěi) *nòng* pò le.** | (*lit.* I grasp box handle break p) I broke the box. |
| 别把机器(给)
<u>搞</u>坏了。 | **Bié bǎ jīqì (gěi) *gǎo* huài le.** | (*lit.* don't grasp machine handle bad p) Don't damage the machine. |

20.1.5 Negative **bă** sentences

In negative 把 **bă** sentences, the negator must precede 把 **bă**:

音乐家还 没(有)把 他的歌曲 灌成唱片。	**Yīnyuèjiā hái** **méi(yǒu) bă tāde** **gēqǔ guàn chéng** **chàngpiàn.**	(*lit.* musician still not-have grasp his song record become record) The musician has not yet recorded his song.
别把花瓶 碰倒。	**Bié bă huāpíng** **pèng dǎo.**	(*lit.* don't grasp vase bump fall-over) Don't knock the vase over.
他从不把 被子叠好。	**Tā cóng bù bă** **bèizi dié hǎo.**	(*lit.* he always not grasp quilt fold- good) He never folds up [his] quilt properly.

Note: 不 **Bù** with 把 **bă** is comparatively rare, occurring normally with verbs indicating habitual action or sometimes intention. It also occurs in composite sentences (see 24.3).

20.1.6 **Bă** and modal verbs

Modal verbs may come before 把 **bă**:

我能把 窗户 打开吗？	**Wǒ néng bă** **chuānghu dǎ** **kāi ma?**	(*lit.* I can grasp window hit open p) May I open the window?
你可以把 工具收 起来了。	**Nǐ kěyǐ bă** **gōngjù shōu** **qǐlái le.**	(*lit.* you can grasp tool collect up- come p) You can put the tools away [now].

The negator 不 **bù** generally precedes the modal verb in a 把 **bă** construction, though it may occasionally come after it if required by meaning:

她不肯 把词典 借给他。	**Tā bù kěn** **bă cídiǎn jiè** **gěi tā.**	(*lit.* she not willing grasp dictionary lend give him) She was not willing to lend her dictionary to him.
你能不把 垃圾倒在 这儿吗？	**Nǐ néng bù** **bă lājī dào** **zài zhèr ma?**	(*lit.* you can not grasp litter dump at here p) Can you not tip [your] litter here?

20.1.7 **Bă** and indefinite reference

We have emphasised in this section that the object of the coverb 把 **bă** must be of definite reference. This is certainly true, particularly in narrative or descriptive sentences. Sometimes even when the object is indefinite in form, it is still of definite reference in meaning:

她把一条 好好的裙子 撕破了。	**Tā bǎ yī tiáo hǎohǎode qúnzi sī pò le.**	(*lit.* she grasp one mw good de skirt tear-break p) She tore a nice skirt into pieces.

This definite reference would of course have been made clearer if the speaker had said:

她把那么/ 这么一条 好好的裙子 撕破了。	**Tā bǎ nàme/ zhème yī tiáo hǎohǎode qúnzi sī pò le.**	(*lit.* she grasp like-that/like-this one mw good de skirt tear-break p) She tore a nice skirt like that/like this into pieces.

However, where 把 **bǎ** is followed by a noun in a generic sense, it is to be understood as of indefinite (i.e. generic) reference. A sentence like this tends to sound more argumentative:

她(老是) 把钱藏在 枕头下。	**Tā (lǎoshì) bǎ qián cáng zài zhěntou xià.**	(*lit.* she (always) grasp money hide cv:in/at pillow below) She always hides her money under the pillow.
他们(竟然) 把书本放 在冰箱里。	**Tāmen (jìngrán) bǎ shū běn fàng zài bīngxiāng li.**	(*lit.* they contrary-to-expectation grasp books place cv:in/at refrigerator inside) They even put books in the fridge.
别把朋友 当成敌人。	**Bié bǎ péngyou dàngchéng dírén.**	(*lit.* don't grasp friend regard become enemy) Don't regard your friends as enemies.

20.2 The **bèi** construction

The 被 **bèi** *construction* in Chinese is similar to the *passive voice* in English, though it is not as commonly used. The coverb 被 **bèi** 'by' marks the agent and with it forms a coverbal phrase, which like other coverbal phrases comes after the subject and before the verb. The agent may be either definite or indefinite reference.

The 被 **bèi** construction has features in common with the 把 **bǎ** construction: the verb is usually one of 'manipulation', involving action, handling, changing, etc., and is normally complex, that is, followed by some form of complement. Additionally, the 被 **bèi** construction often conveys the sense that something has gone wrong:

她被经理 批评了一顿。	**Tā** *bèi* **jīnglǐ** **pīpíngle yī dùn.**	(*lit.* she by manager criticise asp one mw) She was criticised by the manager.
他被人打了 一拳。	**Tā** *bèi* **rén dǎle** **yī quán.**	(*lit.* he by someone hit asp one fist) He was struck by someone.
他被老板 解雇了。	**Tā** *bèi* **lǎobǎn** **jiěgù le.**	(*lit.* he by boss dismiss p) He was dismissed by [his] boss.

20.2.1 | **Ràng** and **jiào**

In colloquial speech, 让 **ràng** or 叫 **jiào** may be used instead of 被 **bèi**:

香蕉让孩子 吃掉了。	**Xiāngjiāo** *ràng* **háizi chī diào le.**	(*lit.* banana by child eat off p) The banana was eaten by the child.
我的雨伞叫 人借走了。	**Wǒde yǔsǎn** *jiào* **rén jiè** **zǒu le.**	(*lit.* my umbrella by someone borrow away p) My umbrella was borrowed by someone.

In addition, 给 **gěi** may be added before the verb:

足球迷叫 流氓给 打伤了。	**Zúqiúmí** *jiào* **liúmáng** *gěi* **dǎ shāng le.**	(*lit.* football-fan by hooligan by hit hurt p) The football fan was beaten up by hooligans.

20.2.2 | The **bèi** construction with an agent

It is possible for the construction to be used without an agent. In these cases, 被 **bèi** (or 给 **gěi**, but not 让 **ràng** or 叫 **jiào**), is placed before the verb:

他们被关在 外头了。	**Tāmen** *bèi* **guān** **zài wàitou le.**	(*lit.* they by shut at outside p) They were shut outside.
他给踢了 一脚。	**Tā** *gěi* **tīle** **yī jiǎo.**	(*lit.* he by kick asp one mw) He was kicked.

20.2.3 | Negative **bèi** sentences

As with the 把 **bǎ** structure, the negator and modal verbs precede 被 **bèi**:

他们的主张 没(有)被 接受。	**Tāmende** **zhǔzhāng** *méi(yǒu)* **bèi** **jiēshòu.**	(*lit.* their proposal not-have by accept) Their proposal was not accepted.

| 别让他
给骗了。 | **Bié ràng tā**
gěi piàn le. | (*lit.* don't by him by cheat p)
Don't be fooled by him. |
| 计算机会
被人偷
走吗？ | **Jìsuànjī huì**
bèi rén tōu
zǒu ma? | (*lit.* computer likely by someone
steal away p) Is the computer
likely to be stolen by someone? |

Note: 不 **bù** is not normally used in 被 **bèi** sentences.

20.3 The **bèi** construction versus the notional passives

While the 被 **bèi** construction, usually describing an event, parallels the passive voice, sentence forms of the topic-comment variety (see 18.3) may be defined as *notional passives*. In these sentences, the topic is often inanimate (or non-human), and therefore no ambiguity arises as to the relationship between the topic and the verb. For example, in the first sentence below, the *letter* cannot possibly be taken as initiating the action of *writing* itself.

信写完了。	**Xìn xiě** **wán le.**	(*lit.* letter write finish p) The letter has been written.
杯子打破了。	**Bēizi dǎ** **pò le.**	(*lit.* cup/mug hit broken p) The cup/mug was broken.
窗户都漆成 绿色了。	**Chuānghu** **dōu qī chéng** **lǜsè le.**	(*lit.* window all paint become green p) All the windows have been painted green.
床单和被套 都洗干净， 折叠好了。	**Chuángdān hé** **bèitào dōu xǐ** **gānjìng, zhédié** **hǎo le.**	(*lit.* bedsheets and blanket-cover all wash clean, fold good p) All the bedsheets and quilt covers have been washed [and] neatly folded up.

---

21 Serial constructions

21.1 General features of serial constructions

Chinese, unlike English, does not have the grammatical means to construct participles or infinitives, nor sets of prepositions capable of diversified meanings. Instead, it makes use of sequences of verbal phrases in what we will call serial constructions.

A *serial construction* normally consists of two (or more) verbal predicates or comments which share the same subject or topic and follow one another without any conjunction(s). A serial construction may have adjectival as well as verbal predicates.

| 21.2 | *Semantic varieties in serial constructions* |

The semantic relations between serial predicates or comments may belong to any of the following categories:

(1) *Sequence*: The action of the first verb takes place before that of the second. The first verb often carries the aspect marker 了 le:

| 他下了课 | **Tā** *xià le kè* | (*lit.* he finish asp class return home |
| 回家去了。 | *huí jiā qù le.* | go p) He finished class and went home. |

| 她吃了药 | **Tā** *chī le yào* | (*lit.* she eat asp medicine go sleep p) |
| 去睡觉了。 | *qù shuìjiào le.* | She took her medicine and went to bed. |

Note: As discussed in 8.3.1, if an unqualified noun follows a verb carrying the aspect marker 了 le, the sentence needs to be completed with another clause or verbal phrase.

(2) *Purpose*: The action described by the second verb is the purpose of the first verb (often 来 lái 'to come' or 去 qù 'to go'):

| 他们来伦敦 | **Tāmen** *lái Lúndūn* | (*lit.* they come London visit us) |
| 探望我们。 | *tànwàng wǒmen.* | They came to London to visit us. |

| 我去商店 | **Wǒ** *qù shāngdiàn* | (*lit.* I go shop buy things) |
| 买东西。 | *mǎi dōngxi.* | I am going to the shops to do some shopping. |

咱们约	**Zánmen** *yuē*	(*lit.* we appoint (one) mw time
(一)个时间	*(yī) gè shíjiān*	talk (one) talk p) Let's make an
谈(一)谈吧。	*tán (yī) tán ba.*	appointment to have a talk.

| 我代表大家 | **Wǒ** *dàibiǎo dàjiā* | (*lit.* I represent everybody |
| 向您祝贺。 | *xiàng nín zhùhè.* | to polite:you congratulate) On behalf of everybody I congratulate you. |

Note: Coverbal phrases indicating 'service' may often be used after 来 lái 'come' or 去 qù 'go' in a purpose serial construction:

| 她来替我 | **Tā** *lái tì wǒ* | (*lit.* she come for me iron |
| 熨衣服。 | *yùn yīfu.* | clothes) She came to iron my clothes for me. |

| 我去给 | **Wǒ** *qù gěi* | (*lit.* I go for him arrange-hair) |
| 他理发。 | *tā lǐfà.* | I'll go and cut his hair. |

Sometimes 来 **lái** may lose its motion meaning and simply indic-ate an intention:

我来谈谈。	**Wǒ *lái* tántán.**	(*lit.* I come talk-talk) I'll say a few words.
我来给你们 介绍一下。	**Wǒ *lái* gěi nǐmen jièshào yī xià.**	(*lit.* I come for you introduce one time) Let me introduce you.

To enhance the meaning of purpose (or lack of purpose), words such as 以便 **yǐbiàn** 'so as to' and 以免 **yǐmiǎn** 'so as not to' are used before the second verbal expression.

她学习 中文, 以便 到中国去 旅游/旅行。	**Tā xuéxí Zhōngwén, *yǐbiàn* dào Zhōngguó qù lǚyóu/lǚxíng.**	(*lit.* she studies Chinese, so-that to China go travel) She is studying Chinese so that she can go and travel in China.
我没(有) 把这件事 告诉他, 以免使 他难过。	**Wǒ méi(yǒu) bǎ zhèi jiàn shì gàosu tā, *yǐmiǎn* shǐ tā nánguò.**	(*lit.* I not grasp this mw matter tell him, so-as-not-to make him sad) I did not tell him about this matter so as not to make him sad.

(3) In constructions we have met which are essentially serial con-structions, for example:

(a) Using coverbs 用 **yòng**, 坐 **zuò**, etc.:

我们坐电梯 上三楼。	**Wǒmen *zuò* diàntī shàng sān lóu.**	(*lit.* we sit lift go-up three floor) We went up to the second floor by lift.
你能用 中文说吗?	**Nǐ néng *yòng* Zhōngwén shuō ma?**	(*lit.* you can use Chinese say p) Can you say [it] in Chinese?

(b) Using the aspect marker 着 **zhe**:

她握着我的手 说: '谢谢你'。	**Tā *wòzhe* wǒde shǒu shuō: 'Xièxie nǐ'.**	(*lit.* she grasp asp my hand say: thank-thank you) Shaking my hand, she said: 'Thank you'.

(c) 把 **bǎ**, 被 **bèi**, 比 **bǐ** constructions (see Chapters 7 and 20).

(4) Where the main verbal phrase is followed by a second verbal phrase which conveys no new information but reiterates the

same idea from a different perspective by means of a *negative*, *antonymous expression*:

他抓住 我<u>不</u>放。	**Tā zhuā zhù wǒ *bù fàng*.**	(*lit.* he catch hold me not let-go) He held me firmly and didn't let me go.
我咬了一口 面包<u>没(有)</u> <u>吞</u>下去。	**Wǒ yǎole yī kǒu miànbāo *méi(yǒu)* *tūn xiàqù*.**	(*lit.* I bite asp one mw bread not-have swallow down-go) I took a bite from the bread but did not swallow it.

(5) Where the verb 有 **yǒu**, indicating possession or existence, is followed by its object and then by another verb (sometimes preceded by a modal verb) expressing *intentional action* directed back to the object:

我<u>没有</u>钱<u>用</u>。	**Wǒ *méiyǒu* qián *yòng*.**	(*lit.* I not-have money use) I haven't got any money to spend.
我<u>有</u>一封信 <u>要写</u>。	**Wǒ *yǒu* yī fēng xìn *yào xiě*.**	(*lit.* I have one mw letter want write) I have got a letter to write.
你<u>有</u>什么 衣服<u>要熨</u>吗?	**Nǐ *yǒu* shénme yīfu *yào yùn* ma?**	(*lit.* you have what clothes want ironing p) What clothes have you got [for me] to iron?
哪儿<u>有</u> (香)烟<u>卖</u>?	**Nǎr *yǒu* (xiāng)yān *mài*?**	(*lit.* where there-are cigarette sell) Where do they sell cigarettes?

If the object of 有 **yǒu** is an abstract noun, the following verb phrase may be of any length, expressing the need (or lack of need) for further action:

我没有责任 告诉她。	**Wǒ *méiyǒu* *zérèn* gàosu tā.**	(*lit.* I not-have responsibility tell her) I'm not responsible for letting her know.
你有理由 不同意。	**Nǐ *yǒu lǐyóu* bù tóngyì.**	(*lit.* you have reason not agree) You have reasons to disagree.
你没有权利 每天到这儿 来胡说八道。	**Nǐ *méiyǒu* *quánlì* měi tiān dào zhèr lái húshuō bādào.**	(*lit.* you not-have right every day to here come talk-nonsense) You don't have the right to come here and talk nonsense every day.

| 21.3 | *Adjectives or state verbs in serial constructions* |

Adjectives or state verbs may be placed at any position in a serial construction to introduce a descriptive element into the narrative:

| 小猫跳上跳下，
可爱极了。 | **Xiǎo māo tiào
shàng tiào xià,
kě'ài jí le.**
(*adjective*) | (*lit.* little kitten jump up jump
down, lovable to-the-extreme p)
The kitten was extremely lovable
as it jumped up and down. |
| 大家静了下来，
坐着不动。 | **Dàjiā jìngle
xiàlái, zuòzhe
bù dòng.**
(*state verb*) | (*lit.* everybody quieten asp down,
sit asp not move) Everybody
quietened down and remained
motionless in their seats. |

| 21.4 | *Dative constructions* |

Dative verbal expressions regularly feature in serial constructions. A verb taking a *direct object* is followed by the verb 给 gěi with an *indirect object*:

| 爸爸买了
一辆汽车
给我。 | **Bàba mǎile
yī liàng qìchē
gěi wǒ.** | (*lit.* father buy asp one mw car
give me) Father bought a car
for me. |
| 我寄了一张
明信片给同事。 | **Wǒ jì le yī zhāng
míngxìnpiàn
gěi tóngshì.** | (*lit.* I post asp one mw
postcard give colleague) I sent
a postcard to my colleague. |

This extended dative construction with 给 gěi generally does not apply in the case of verbs expressing speech activity:

| 我告诉你
一个秘密。 | **Wǒ gàosu nǐ
yī gè mìmì.** | (*lit.* I tell you one mw secret)
I'll tell you a secret. |
| NOT *我告诉
一个秘密给你。 | **Wǒ gàosu yī gè
mìmì gěi nǐ.** | (*lit.* I tell one mw secret
give you) |

Note: See 8.5 for a fuller discussion of direct and indirect objects.

| 21.5 | *Causative constructions* |

A common form of serial construction is the *causative construction*, in which the object of the first verb becomes the subject of the second verb/adjective:

我请他吃饭。	**Wǒ** *qǐng* **tā** *chī* **fàn.**	I invited him to dinner.	Serial constructions
我们选他 当主席。	**Wǒmen** *xuǎn* **tā** *dāng* **zhǔxí.**	We elected him president.	
这使我 很高兴。	**Zhè** *shǐ* **wǒ** **hěn gāoxìng.**	This made me very happy.	
他们要 我别去。	**Tāmen** *yào* **wǒ** *bié* **qù.**	They wanted me not to go.	

Note 1: Verbs which produce a causative construction include those in the following semantic categories:

(i)   Request or command: 请 qǐng 'ask', 叫 jiào 'make', 派 pài 'send', 命令 mìnglìng 'order'.

他叫我把 护照拿出来。	**Tā** *jiào* **wǒ bǎ** **hùzhào** *ná* **chūlái.**	He asked me to take out my passport.

(ii) Wish: 要 yào 'want'.

她要我到 (飞)机场 去接她。	**Tā** *yào* **wǒ dào** **(fēi)jīchǎng** *qù* **jiē tā.**	She wanted me to go and meet her at the airport.

(iii) Persuasion or requirement: 劝 quàn 'persuade, urge', 催 cuī 'press', 要求 yāoqiú 'require'.

我劝她 学打拳。	**Wǒ** *quàn* **tā** *xué* **dǎ quán.**	I urged her to learn shadow-boxing.
老师要求 学生注意 安全。	**Lǎoshī** *yāoqiú* **xuésheng** *zhùyì* **ānquán.**	The teacher required the students to pay attention to safety.

(iv) Permission: 让 ràng 'let', 允许 yǔnxǔ 'allow', 准 zhǔn 'permit'.

爸爸允许 我去跳舞。	**Bàba** *yǔnxǔ* **wǒ** *qù* **tiàowǔ.**	Father allowed me to go dancing.

(v)   Coercion: 逼 bī 'force', 强迫 qiángpò 'compel'.

强盗逼我 把钱拿 出来给他。	**Qiángdào** *bī* **wǒ bǎ qián** *ná* **chūlái gěi tā.**	The robber forced me to get out my money and hand it over to him.

(vi) Prevention: 禁止 jìnzhǐ 'forbid, ban', 阻止 zǔzhǐ 'prevent'.

这条路禁止 货车通过。	**Zhèi tiáo lù** *jìnzhǐ* **huòchē** *tōngguò.*	(*lit.* this mw road forbid lorry go through) Lorries are not allowed to use this road.

(vii)   Others: 等 **děng** 'wait', 听 **tīng** 'listen to'.

| 我等你来。 | **Wǒ děng nǐ lái.** | I'll wait till you come. |
| 听我说 | **Tīng wǒ shuō.** | Listen to me. |

Note 2: Causative verbs do not take aspect markers:

| *我逼了他
去看医生。 | **Wǒ bīle tā
qù kàn yīshēng.** | (*lit.* I force asp him go see
doctor) I forced him to go and
see the doctor. |

If necessary, the second verb may incorporate aspect markers:

| 她请我们看了
一场电影。 | **Tā qǐng wǒmen
kànle yī cháng
diànyǐng.** | (*lit.* she invite us look asp one
mw film) She invited us to go
and see a film. |
| 我请他们
吃了一顿饭。 | **Wǒ qǐng tāmen
chīle yī dùn fàn.** | (*lit.* I invite them eat asp one mw
food) I invited them for a meal. |

| 21.5.1 | **Qǐng** in a causative construction |

Polite requests are often a serial construction using the causative verb
请 **qǐng** 'ask politely' (cf. 8.6).

(1)   With an object:

| 请你把证件
拿出来。 | **Qǐng nǐ bǎ
zhèngjiàn
ná chūlái.** | (*lit.* ask you grasp document
take out-come) Please take out
your documents. |
| 请大家安静
一点儿。 | **Qǐng dàjiā
ānjìng yī diǎnr.** | (*lit.* ask everybody quiet a
little) Please be quiet,
everyone./ Would everyone
please be quiet. |

(2)   Without an object:

请再说 一遍。	**Qǐng zài shuō yī biàn.**	(*lit.* ask again say one time) Please say it again.
请说得 慢一点儿。	**Qǐng shuō de màn yī diǎnr.**	(*lit.* ask say p slow a little) Please speak more slowly.
请别用 手摸展品。	**Qǐng bié yòng shǒu mō zhǎnpǐn.**	(*lit.* ask don't use hand touch exhibits) Please don't touch the exhibits with your hands.

21.5.2   Extended causative constructions

In an extended causative construction, the second verb (i.e. next but
one) after the causative verb may refer to either the object or the subject of the causative verb:

(1)   Referring to the subject:

我约她在   **Wǒ yuē tā zài**   (*lit.* I make-appointment her at
图书馆等我,   **túshūguǎn**   library wait-for me, have one
有一封信   **děng wǒ, yǒu**   mw letter want hand-over
要交给她。   **yī fēng xìn yào**   give her) I asked her to wait
                jiāo gěi tā.   for me at the library, [as] I had
                                        a letter to pass on to her.

(2)   Referring to the object:

我请她   **Wǒ qǐng tā**   (*lit.* I asked her help me, teach
帮助我,   **bāngzhù wǒ,**   me how read those two mw
教我怎么   **jiāo wǒ zěnme**   Chinese-characters) I asked
读/念那   **dú/niàn nà/nèi**   her to help me and teach me
两个(汉)字。   **liǎng gè (hàn)zì.**   how to read those two
                                        Chinese characters.

21.6   *Extended serial constructions*

All the predicate (or comment) types mentioned above may, of course,
combine in longer serial constructions:

我洗了澡,   **Wǒ xǐle zǎo,**   (*lit.* I wash asp bath, change asp
换了衣服,   **huànle yīfu,**   clothes, bring asp younger-brother
带着弟弟   **dàizhe dìdi**   drive car to Xiao Li home, ask him
开车到   **kāi chē dào**   with us together go see film) Having
小李家,   **Xiǎo Lǐ jiā,**   taken a bath and changed my clothes,
请他跟   **qǐng tā gēn**   I drove with my younger brother to
我们一起   **wǒmen yīqǐ qù**   Xiao Li's place and asked him to go
去看电影。   **kàn diànyǐng.**   with us to see a film.

22   **Emphasis and the intensifier shì**

22.1   **Shì** *as an intensifier*

Emphasis in language can be conveyed in various ways. The most common is to focus on a particular word or phrase through sentence stress,

word order or other intensifying devices. Sentence stress is the concern of phonology, and we will not dwell on it here. In our discussion of subject-predicate and topic-comment constructions, we have seen how change in word order can bring about different emphases. What concerns us here is the use of the verb 是 shì as an *intensifier* to highlight specific elements in a sentence. We will distinguish between its use in sentences referring to the past (i.e. with 的 de) and in those referring to the continuous present or future (i.e. generally without 的 de). (In the literal translations of the examples in this chapter, 是 shì appears as int[ensifier].)

22.2 The shì . . . de construction

Where an event or action took place in the past, 是 shì may be used in conjunction with 的 de to highlight the adverbials or modifying elements in a sentence, e.g. time expressions; coverbal phrases indicating location, method or instrument; adverbial phrases of manner; or 'purpose' constructions beginning with 来 lái or 去 qù. It is as if a statement with the 是 . . . 的 shì . . . de *construction* represents an answer to a question about when, where, how, to what purpose, at the hands of whom, etc., an action took place. 是 Shì is placed immediately before the adverbial expression or verb followed by purpose expression/complement, and 的 de generally comes at the end of the sentence.

(1) Time expressions:

我是昨天 来的。	**Wǒ shì zuótiān lái de.**	(*lit.* I int yesterday come p) I came *yesterday.*/It was yesterday that I came.
你是去年 还是今年 到的？	**Nǐ shì qùnián háishi jīnnián dào de?**	(*lit.* you int last-year or this- year arrive p) Did you arrive here last year or this year?

(2) Coverbal phrases indicating location, method, instrument, etc.:

她是在 新加坡 生/出世的。	**Tā shì zài Xīnjiāpō shēng/ chūshì de.**	(*lit.* she int at Singapore be-born p) She was born in *Singapore.*
我们是从 朝鲜来的。	**Wǒmen shì cóng Cháoxiān lái de.**	(*lit.* we int from Korea come p) We come from Korea.
你是坐车 还是走路 来的？	**Nǐ shì zuò chē háishi zǒulù lái de?**	(*lit.* you int sit car or walk-road come p) Did you come by car or on foot?

| 我是用毛笔
写这封信的。 | Wǒ *shì* yòng
máobǐ xiě zhèi
fēng xìn *de*. | (*lit.* I int use pen-brush write
this mw letter p) I wrote this
letter with a writing brush. |

(3) 'Purpose' constructions beginning with 来 lái or 去 qù:

| 我是来
看病的。 | Wǒ *shì* lái
kàn bìng *de*. | (*lit.* I int come see illness p)
I've come to see the doctor. |
| 他是去
找你的。 | Tā *shì* qù
zhǎo nǐ *de*. | (*lit.* he int go find you p)
He went to look for you. |

(4) 被 Bèi or similar phrase introducing an agent:

| 洗衣机
是被她
弄坏的。 | Xǐyījī *shì*
bèi tā nòng
huài *de*. | (*lit.* washing-machine int by her
mess-with bad p) The washing-
machine was damaged by her. |
| 汽车是
让司机
给修好的。 | Qìchē *shì*
ràng sījī gěi
xiū hǎo *de*. | (*lit.* car int by driver by repair
good p) The car was repaired
by the driver. |

(5) Adverbial phrases of manner:

| 她是
老老实实地
告诉我的。 | Tā *shì*
lǎolǎoshíshí de
gàosu wǒ *de*. | (*lit.* she int honest p tell me p)
She told me honestly. |
| 船是慢慢地
沉到海底
去的。 | Chuán *shì*
mànmàn de chén
dào hǎi dǐ qù *de*. | (*lit.* boat int slow p sink to the
bottom go p) The boat slowly
sank to the bottom of the sea. |

(6) Complements of manner:

| 我们是谈
得很投机的。 | Wǒmen *shì* tán
de hěn tóujī *de*. | (*lit.* we int talk p very
congenial p) We had a very
congenial conversation. |
| 他们是玩儿
得非常
高兴的。 | Tāmen *shì* wánr
de fēicháng
gāoxìng *de*. | (*lit.* they int play p extremely
high-spirited p) They had an
extremely good time. |

Note: In colloquial speech, 是 shì may often be omitted from the 是 . . . 的 shì . . . de structure:

| 他昨天来的。 | Tā zuótiān lái *de*. | He came *yesterday*. |
| 他们坐飞机
去的吗? | Tāmen zuò fēijī
qù *de* ma? | Did they go by plane? |

| 22.2.1 | Subject and object emphasis in **shì . . . de** sentences |

The 是 . . . 的 **shì . . . de** construction may also be used to emphasise either the subject or the object of the verb.

(1) If the emphasis is on the subject, 是 **shì** is placed directly before the subject:

是我打破 这个杯子<u>的</u>。	**Shì wǒ dǎ pò zhèi gè bēizi de.**	(*lit.* int I hit break this mw cup/mug) I was the one who broke this cup/mug.
是警察抓 住小偷的。	**Shì jǐngchá zhuā zhù xiǎotōu de.**	(*lit.* int policeman/woman catch hold thief p) It was the policeman/ woman who caught the thief.
这本小说 <u>是</u>谁写<u>的</u>?	**Zhèi běn xiǎoshuō shì shéi/shuí xiě de?**	(*lit.* this mw novel int who write p) Who wrote this novel?/Who was this novel written by?
那杯咖啡 是我倒给 你<u>的</u>。	**Nèi bēi kāfēi shì wǒ dào gěi nǐ de.**	(*lit.* that mw coffee int I pour give you p) (It was) I (who) poured that cup of coffee for you.

Note: The last two sentences above are *topic | subject-predicate* constructions (see 18.4). The subject embedded in this structure can be emphasised, but the topic is emphatic by definition and cannot be intensified by a 是 . . . 的 **shì . . . de** construction. Therefore, the sequence '是 **shì** topic | subject-predicate 的 **de**' is impossible:

*是信我寄的。 **Shì xìn wǒ jì de.** (*lit.* int letter I post p)

(2) If the emphasis is on the object of a verb, 是 **shì** is placed before the verb, while 的 **de** comes before the object instead of at the end of the sentence:

| 我<u>是</u>买
<u>的</u>肥皂。 | **Wǒ shì mǎi
de féizào.** | (*lit.* I int buy p soap)
I bought some *soap*. |
| 她<u>是</u>喝
<u>的</u>桔子水。 | **Tā shì hē de
júzishuǐ.** | (*lit.* she int drink p orange-juice)
She drank *orange juice*. |

| 22.2.2 | **Shì . . . de** construction and **bù** |

The 是 . . . 的 **shì . . . de** construction, though it refers to past events, may only be negated by 不 **bù** (not by 没(有) **méi(yǒu)**). 不 **Bù** comes before 是 **shì**:

我不是来借钱的。	**Wǒ bù shì lái jiè qián de.**	(*lit.* I not int come borrow money p) I've not come to borrow money.
不是我告诉她这件事的。	**Bù shì wǒ gàosu tā zhèi jiàn shì de.**	(*lit.* not int I tell her this mw matter p) I wasn't the one who told her about this.
我们那天不是吃的鱼。	**Wǒmen nèi tiān bù shì chī de yú.**	(*lit.* we that day not int eat p fish) We didn't eat *fish* that day.

22.3 | **Shì** *without* **de** *for progression and projection*

When 是 **shì** is used for emphasis in relation to present continuous or projected events or actions, it generally occurs alone without 的 **de**.

22.3.1 | Contexts for **shì** (without **de**) sentences

是 **Shì** can be employed in the contexts listed under 22.2 (1), (2) and (3) for the 是 . . . 的 **shì** . . . **de** structure (i.e. with time expressions, coverbal phrases and 'purpose' constructions), and to emphasise either subject or object:

我是明天来。	**Wǒ shì míngtiān lái.**	(*lit.* I int tomorrow come) I'll be coming *tomorrow*.
他们是到海边去度假。	**Tāmen shì dào hǎibiān qù dùjià.**	(*lit.* they int go seaside spend-holiday) They are going to the *seaside* for [their] holidays.
我们不是坐电车去。	**Wǒmen bù shì zuò diànchē qù.**	(*lit.* we not int travel-by tram go) We won't be going by tram.

If the emphasis is on the subject, 是 **shì** is placed immediately before the subject:

| 是你去吗? | **Shì nǐ qù ma?** | (*lit.* int you go p) Will *you* be going? |
| 是她应该向大家道歉。 | **Shì tā yīnggāi xiàng dàjiā dàoqiàn.** | (*lit.* int she must towards everybody say-sorry) *She's* the one who should apologise to everybody. |

If the emphasis is on the object, 是 **shì** is placed immediately before the predicate verb, but the object will naturally be stressed in speech:

我是去看她。	**Wǒ** *shì* **qù kàn tā.**	(*lit.* I int go see her) I am going to see *her*.
他们是想吃冰激凌/冰淇凌。	**Tāmen** *shì* **xiǎng chī bīngjilíng/ bīngqílíng.**	(*lit.* they int want eat ice-cream) It is ice-cream that they want to eat.

22.3.2 | **Shì** and comparison

是 **Shì** is also used alone to emphasise a comparison construction. It is placed immediately before 比 **bǐ** in affirmative and 没(有) **méi(yǒu)** in negative comparisons:

你的房子是比我的大。	**Nǐde fángzi** *shì* **bǐ wǒde dà.**	(*lit.* your house int compare mine big) Your house really *is* bigger than mine.
我说中文是没(有)你说得好。	**Wǒ shuō Zhōngwén** *shì* **méi(yǒu) nǐ shuō de hǎo.**	(*lit.* I speak Chinese int not-have you speak p good) I really *don't* speak Chinese as well as you do.

22.3.3 | **Shì** and negation

The negative of 是 **shì** sentences, like that of 是 . . . 的 **shì . . . de** sentences, is formed by placing 不 **bù** before 是 **shì**:

我们不是走路去。	**Wǒmen** *bù shì* **zǒulù qù.**	(*lit.* we not int on foot go) We are not going on foot.
我不是去吵架。	**Wǒ** *bù shì* **qù chǎojià.**	(*lit.* I not int go quarrel) I am not going (in order) to have a row.

22.4 | **Shì** *and topic-comment sentences*

The above discussion has focused on 是 **shì** as an intensifier of elements in the predicate that modify the verb (adverbials, 'purpose' constructions, etc.) or subjects/objects of the verb. In addition, 是 **shì** as an intensifier may occur alone in topic-comment sentences with gradable adjectives or state verbs.

(1) Gradable adjectives:

| 她<u>是</u>很矮。 | **Tā** *shì* **hěn ǎi.** | (*lit.* she int very short) She *is* short. |
| 他们是 不高兴。 | **Tāmen** *shì* **bù gāoxìng.** | (*lit.* they int not happy) They *are* unhappy. |

(2) State verbs:

| 我<u>是</u>病了。 | **Wǒ** *shì* **bìng le.** | (*lit.* I ill p) I *am* ill. |
| 我们<u>是</u>错了。 | **Wǒmen** *shì* **cuò le.** | (*lit.* we int wrong p) We *are* wrong./It's *our* fault. |

It can also be introduced in a subject-predicate sentence where the emphasis is on the whole predicate. Its presence in effect makes the sentence topic-comment:

我们是 去了三次。	**Wǒmen** *shì* **qùle sān cì.**	(*lit.* we int go asp three-times) We (really) *did* go three times.
我是吃过 蜗牛。	**Wǒ** *shì* **chīguo wōniú.**	(*lit.* I int eat snail) I *have* eaten snails.
他们是 不知道。	**Tāmen** *shì* **bù zhīdao.**	(*lit.* they int not know) They *really* don't know.
这个问题是 可以提出来。	**Zhèi gè wèntí** *shì* **kěyǐ tí chūlái.**	(*lit.* this mw question int can raise out-come) This question *can* be raised.

22.4.1 **Shì** implying reservation

The sentences in 22.4, in fact, all have an undertone of reservation or contradiction. It is often the case that the implicit reservation in such sentences is immediately made explicit by a contradictory statement:

| 他是聪明, 不过太 骄傲了。 | **Tā** *shì* **cōngming,** *bùguò* **tài jiāo'ào le.** | (*lit.* he int clever, but too proud p) He *is* clever, *but* he's too conceited. |
| 这个工作 我是喜欢, 可是薪水 太少。 | **Zhèi gè gōngzuò wǒ** *shì* **xǐhuan,** *kěshì* **xīnshuǐ tài shǎo.** | (*lit.* this mw job I int like, but salary too little) I *do* like this job, *but* the salary is too little. |

22.4.2 'Verb/Adjective + **shì** + Verb/Adjective' implying reservation

The pattern of this last structure (in 22.4.1) in colloquial speech can take the form of 'verb-是 shì-verb' or 'adjective-是 shì-adjective':

这个工作我 喜欢是喜欢, 但是 ...	**Zhèi gè gōngzuò wǒ *xǐhuan* shì *xǐhuan*, dànshì ...**	(*lit.* this mw job/work I like int like, but ...) I *do* like this job, but ...
那本书好是好, 不过太贵了。	**Nèi běn shū *hǎo* shì *hǎo*, bùguò tài guì le.**	(*lit.* that mw book good int good, nevertheless too expensive p) (It is true) that book *is* good, but it is too expensive.

22.5 *Repetition and emphasis*

Apart from the use of the intensifier 是 **shì**, emphasis in Chinese may also be expressed through repetition. This occurs particularly when agreement, disagreement, thanks or welcome are expressed:

A: 这样行吗?	**Zhèi yàng xíng ma?**	(*lit.* this type OK p) Will this do?
B: 行, 行, 行。	**Xíng, xíng, xíng.**	(*lit.* OK, OK, OK) It is perfectly all right.
A: 我来帮你忙	**Wǒ lái bāng nǐ máng.**	(*lit.* I come help you busy) I'll come and help you.
B: 不, 不, 不, 我自己来。	**Bù, bù, bù. Wǒ zìjǐ lái.**	(*lit.* no, no, no. I self come) No, no, no. I'll manage myself.
A: 你英文 说得真好。	**Nǐ Yīngwén shuō de zhēn hǎo.**	(*lit.* you English speak p really good) You speak really good English.
B: 不, 不, 不。	**Bù, bù, bù.**	(*lit.* no, no, no) Not at all. (being modest)

Note: When praised, an English speaker is likely to say 'thank you', while a Chinese person will probably make a modest denial such as 不, 不, 不 **bù, bù, bù**.

欢迎, 欢迎。	**Huānyíng, huānyíng.**	Welcome.
请进, 请进。	**Qǐng jìn, qǐng jìn.**	Please come in.
哪里, 哪里。	**Nǎli, nǎli.**	It was nothing. (polite response to thanks)

23 Abbreviation and omission

23.1 Three types of abbreviation

Like most languages, Chinese has a considerable number of *conventional* phrases or constructions which habitual usage has made acceptable despite apparent grammatical incompleteness. Similarly, Chinese makes use of abbreviated expressions when allowed or demanded by the *context* (i.e. the actual situation in which the utterance takes place). There is also a tendency, already observed, for Chinese to omit words from a sentence that are not strictly necessary for the meaning. This is possible because the sentence is formulated within a *cotext* (i.e. the spoken or written text that precedes and/or follows). For example, the subject and/or object may be omitted in response to a question (see 17.2). There is, of course, likely to be some overlap between context and cotext.

23.2 Conventional abbreviations as subjectless sentences

Conventional abbreviations normally take the form of *subjectless sentences* and occur in the following types of expression:

(1)   Thanks, good wishes, apologies, etc.:

谢谢, *or* 谢谢你。	**Xièxie,** **Xièxie nǐ.**	(*lit.* thank-thank, *or* thank-thank you) Thanks, *or* Thank you.
不谢, *or* 不客气。	**Bù xiè,** **Bù kèqi.**	(*lit.* not thank, *or* not polite) You're welcome. (in response to 谢谢 **xièxie**)
别客气, *or* 不要客气。	**Bié kèqi,** **Bù yào kèqi.**	(*lit.* don't polite) Don't stand on ceremony, *or* Make yourself at home.
对不起。	**Duìbuqǐ.**	(*lit.* face not rise) Sorry.
很/真抱歉。	**Hěn/zhēn** **bàoqiàn.**	(*lit.* very/really be-apologetic) [I] must apologise.
恭喜, 恭喜。	**Gōngxǐ,** **gōngxǐ.**	(*lit.* respectfully-[wish]-happy, respectfully-[wish]-happy) Congratulations!

Others include: 慢走 **màn zǒu** 'take care' (*lit.* slow walk) (said when seeing off a guest), 辛苦了 **xīnkǔ le** 'you must be tired (after such a long journey)/ sorry to have put you to so much trouble' (*lit.* tiring p), 一路平安 **yī lù píng'ān** 'have a safe/pleasant journey' (*lit.* all way peace-safe), 祝你身体

健康 **zhù nǐ shēntǐ jiànkāng** 'wish you good health' (*lit.* wish you body healthy), 敬你一杯 **jìng nǐ yī bēi** 'your health'! (*lit.* respectfully-[offer] you one cup/glass), 再见 **zàijiàn** 'goodbye' (*lit.* again-see), 干杯 **gān bēi** 'bottoms up, cheers' (*lit.* dry glass).

(2)   Approval, commendation, etc.:

对!	**Duì!**	(*lit.* correct) (You're) right!
好。	**Hǎo.**	(*lit.* good) That's good/All right.
不要紧。	**Bù yàojǐn.**	(*lit.* not important) It doesn't matter.

Others include: 没关系 **méi guānxì** 'never mind/it doesn't matter' (*lit.* no concern), 没问题 **méi wèntí** 'no problem', 真巧啊 **zhēn qiǎo a** 'what a coincidence' (*lit.* really coincidental p), 好香啊 **hǎo xiāng a** 'how sweet (of smell)/how tasty' (*lit.* very fragrant/savoury p).

(3)   Requests, warnings, etc.:

请便。	**Qǐngbiàn.**	(*lit.* please convenient) Please yourself, *or* Do as you please.
请指正。	**Qǐng zhǐzhèng.**	(*lit.* please point-correct) Please make comments/corrections. (usually when presenting a piece of writing, etc. and politely seeking opinion)
小心。	**Xiǎoxīn.**	(*lit.* small concern) Be careful, *or* Take care.
记得关门。	**Jìde guān mén.**	(*lit.* remember close door) Remember to close the door.

Others include: 看好 **kàn hǎo** 'look out/watch out' (*lit.* look well), 开会了 **kāihuì le** 'let's start (the meeting)' (*lit.* start/hold meeting p), 救命啊 **jiùmìng a** 'help!' (*lit.* save life p).

(4)   Standard prohibitions, often found as public notices:

请勿吸烟!	**Qǐng wù xīyān!**	(*lit.* please no inhale-smoke) No smoking!
请勿随地丢垃圾!	**Qǐng wù suídì diū lājī!**	(*lit.* please no over-all-floor throw rubbish) No litter!
不准停车!	**Bù zhǔn tíng chē!**	(*lit.* not allow stop car) No parking (on these premises).
禁止入内!	**Jìnzhǐ rù nèi!**	(*lit.* forbid enter inside) No entry.

(5) Proverbial sayings:

活到老， 学到老。	**Huó dào lǎo,** **xué dào lǎo.**	(*lit.* live till old, learn till old) It's never too late to learn./You're never too old to learn
己所不欲， 勿施于人。	**Jǐ suǒ bù yù,** **wù shī yú rén.**	(*lit.* self that-which not want, do-not impose on people) Do unto others as you would be done by.

(6) Sentence starters, characteristic of oral or written narrative:

想不到会在 这儿见到你。	*Xiǎngbudào* *huì zài zhèr* *jiàn dào nǐ.*	(*lit.* think-not-reach can at here bump into you) [I] never thought/expected [I] would see you here.
不知道他 明天来不来。	*Bùzhīdao tā* *míngtiān* *lái bù lái.*	(*lit.* not know he tomorrow come not come) [I] don't know whether he is coming tomorrow or not.
恐怕我 感冒了。	*Kǒngpà wǒ* *gǎnmào le.*	(*lit.* afraid I catch-cold p) [I] am afraid I have caught a cold.

Others include: 记得 . . . jìde . . . '[I] remember . . .' (*lit.* remember), 不料 . . . bù liào . . . 'unexpectedly . . .' (*lit.* not expect), 听说 . . . tīng shuō . . . '[I] have heard that . . .' (*lit.* hear say).

(7) Statements about the weather (often including a change in the weather, or a realisation about the state of the weather on the part of the speaker – see discussion on sentence 了 le in Chapter 16):

下雨了。	*Xià yǔ le.*	(*lit.* fall rain p) It's raining.
出太阳了。	*Chū tàiyáng le.*	(*lit.* out sun p) The sun is out.

Others include: 刮风了 guā fēng le 'it's windy', 起雾了 qǐ wù le 'it's getting foggy', 打霜了 dǎ shuāng le 'it's frosty/there's a frost', 打雷了 dǎ léi le 'it's thundering', 闪电了 shǎn diàn le 'it's lightning'.

23.3 | *Contextual abbreviation*

Contextual abbreviation usually takes the form of a one-word (or two-word) expression.

(1) Calling out to somebody:

喂!	**Wèi!**	Hello! Hey! (or on the telephone, Hello)
老李!	**Lǎo Lǐ!**	Old Li!
服务员!	**Fúwùyuán!**	Waiter!

(2) Calling attention to something:

火!	**Huǒ!**	Fire!
信。	**Xìn.**	A letter (for you).
票。	**Piào.**	Tickets. (said perhaps by a bus conductor)

(3) Enquiring about the 'whereabouts' of something or the 'condition' of somebody:

鞋呢?	**Xié ne?**	Where are the shoes?
钱呢?	**Qián ne?**	Where is the money?
你呢?	**Nǐ ne?**	How about you?
他们呢?	**Tāmen ne?**	How about them?

(4) Written instructions:

男(厕)	**nán(cè)**	gentlemen (*lit.* man-lavatory)
女(厕)	**nǚ(cè)**	ladies (*lit.* female-lavatory)
无人	**wú rén**	vacant (of lavatory) (*lit.* no people)
有人	**yǒu rén**	engaged (of lavatory) (*lit.* have people)
推	**tuī**	push
拉	**lā**	pull

23.4 *Cotextual omissions*

Cotextual omissions take a number of forms. As observed earlier, numbers/demonstratives with measures and attributives with 的 **de** do not need to be followed by a noun once that noun has been identified:

这个	**zhèi gè**	this one
第三个	**dì sān gè**	the third one
我的	**wǒde**	mine

王先生的	**Wáng xiānsheng de**	Mr Wang's
黄色的	**huáng sè de**	yellow one(s)
昨天买的	**zuótiān mǎi de**	the one(s) bought yesterday

23.4.1 Cotextual omissions and headwords

Where a noun is made up of a defining element and a headword, once
the noun is identified, subsequent reference may be to the headword
alone. Thus when it is already clear that references are to respectively
公共汽车 gōnggòng qìchē 'bus', 直升飞机 zhíshēng fēijī 'helicopter', and
精神病院 jīngshénbìng yuàn 'mental hospital', the following sentences
can occur:

我们在	**Wǒmen zài**	Where do we wait for
哪儿等车?	**nǎr děng chē?**	the bus?
我们几点(钟)	**Wǒmen jǐdiǎn**	When do we board the
登机?	**(zhōng) dēng jī?**	helicopter?
他已经	**Tā yǐjing**	He has already been admitted
入院了。	**rù yuàn le.**	to the mental hospital.

23.4.2 Cotextual omissions in answers

As seen in 17.2, positive or negative answers to a question are regularly
expressed by repeating the verb in the question. With cotextual abbreviations, usually the verb is retained as the core element, and repetition of
other parts of the sentence, especially pronouns, becomes unnecessary:

Q: 你喜欢这件毛衣吗?   A: 喜欢。**Xǐhuan.**
    Nǐ xǐhuan zhèi jiàn máoyī ma?   (*lit.* like) Yes.
    (*lit.* you like this mw sweater p)   不喜欢。**Bù xǐhuan.**
    Do you like this sweater?   (*lit.* not like) No.

Q: 你认识她吗?   A: 认识。**Rènshi.**
    Nǐ rènshi tā ma?   (*lit.* know) Yes.
    (*lit.* you know her p)   不认识。**Bù rènshi.**
    Do you know her?   (*lit.* not know) No.

23.4.3 Contextual/cotextual omissions in extended passages

In written or spoken passages, omissions of previous references are
similarly possible, because the reader or listener is able to make sense
of the material on the basis of contextual/cotextual evidence:

我用中文	**Wǒ yòng**	(*lit.* I use Chinese write asp one mw
写了一篇	**Zhōngwén**	essay give my teacher look, say look
文章给	**xiěle yī piān**	after, please correct, afterwards can
我老师看,	**wénzhāng gěi**	re-write) I wrote an essay in Chinese
说看后,	**wǒ laǒshī kàn,**	and gave [it] to my teacher to look
请指正,	**shuō kàn hòu,**	at, saying that after [she] had read [it]
今后可以	**qǐng zhǐzhèng,**	could [she] please correct [it],
重写。	**jīnhòu kěyǐ**	(so that) afterwards [I] could
	chóngxiě.	re-write [it].

The seven bracketed pronouns in the translation are not present in the Chinese original. Such omissions are possible because the speaker/writer is confident that the passage is intelligible on the basis of contextual/cotextual evidence.

24 Composite sentences: conjunctions and conjunctives

24.1 Types of composite sentence

In Chapter 21, we looked at serial constructions, in which a subject (or topic) is followed by more than one verb (or adjective) without any linking device(s). Here we deal with *composite sentences*. We use this term to describe sentences which have either (1) more than one clause in a coordinated or subordinated relationship, or (2) more than one predicate or comment pertaining to the same subject or topic. The common feature of these two types of composite sentence is that their parts are usually linked by *conjunctions* and/or *conjunctives*.

It is possible, however, for the first type of construction to have no conjunctions or conjunctives; the clauses are then bound together in rhythmic or lexical balance or contrast (see 24.3 below). When the second type of construction has no conjunctions or conjunctives, it becomes a serial construction. We deal here first with sentences marked by conjunctions or conjunctives.

Note: We have discussed conjunctions that link words and expressions, e.g. 和 hé, 跟 gēn, etc. (see Chapter 1), but not those that link clauses.

24.2 Conjunctions and conjunctives

Conjunctions in Chinese occur independently (e.g. 但是 dànshì, 可是 kěshì, 不过 bùguò 'but'; 否则/不然 fǒuzé/bùrán 'otherwise'; 所以/因此 suǒyǐ/yīncǐ 'therefore', etc.) or in related pairs (e.g. 虽然 ... 但是

... suīrán ... dànshì ... 'although ... (however) ...'; 因为 ... 所以 ... yīnwèi ... suǒyǐ ... 'because ... (therefore) ...' etc.):

我们退让了，可是他们还不同意。	**Wǒmen tuìràngle, kěshì tāmen hái bù tóngyì.**	(*lit.* we give-way asp, but they still not agree) We gave way *but* they still would not agree.
因为妈妈病了，所以我呆/待在家里看护她。	**Yīnwèi māma bìng le, suǒyǐ wǒ dāi zài jiā li kānhù tā.**	(*lit.* because mother ill asp, therefore I stay at home in nurse her) *Because* mother was ill, (*therefore*) I stayed at home to nurse her.
虽然那个孩子很聪明，但是学习不够努力。	**Suīrán nèi gè háizi hěn cōngming, dànshì xuéxí bù gòu nǔlì.**	(*lit.* though that mw child very intelligent, but study not sufficient hard) *Though* that child is very clever, (*however*) he does not study hard enough.

From the second and third examples above, it can be seen that pairs of related conjunctions (e.g. 因为 yīnwèi and 所以 suǒyǐ, 虽然 suīrán and 但是 dànshì) are split such that one is placed at the beginning of the first clause and the other at the beginning of the second. The conjunction in the first clause may alternatively come after the subject, generally when the two clauses share the same subject:

那个孩子虽然很聪明，但是学习不够努力。	**Nèi gè háizi suīrán hěn cōngming, dànshì xuéxì bù gòu nǔlì.**	(*lit.* that mw child though very intelligent, but study not sufficient hard) *Though* that child is very clever, (*however*) he does not study hard enough.

Conjunctives, on the other hand, are adverbs such as 就 jiù 'then', 才 cái 'only then', etc., which function as *referential adverbs* in simple sentences (see 14.3), but in compound sentences occur at the beginning of the second (main) clause after the subject to link that clause to the previous (subordinate) clause. The previous clause may include a conjunction such as 如果 rúguǒ, 要是 yàoshi, 假如 jiǎrú 'if', 除非 chúfēi 'unless', etc.). Conjunctives also occur as related pairs (e.g. 一 ... 就 ... yī ... jiù ... 'as soon as ..., ...', 又 ... 又 ... yòu ... yòu ... 'both ... and ...', etc.).

你如果没空，我们就改天谈吧。	**Nǐ rúguǒ méi kòng, wǒmen jiù gǎitiān tán ba.**	(*lit.* you if not free, we then change-day talk p) *If* you are busy, we'll talk [about it] another day.

Sometimes a second conjunction may be included with the conjunctive in the second clause:

你如果没空, 那么我们就 改天谈吧。	**Nǐ** *rúguǒ* **méi kòng,** *nàme* **wǒmen** *jiù* **gǎitiān tán ba.**	(*lit.* you if not free, in-that-case we then change-day talk p) *If* you are busy, (then) we'll talk [about it] another day.

24.2.1 | Meanings and functions of composite sentences

Composite sentences have a wide range of meanings and functions. We will give examples in the following categories: contrast, choice, addition, cause and effect, inference, condition, 'non-condition', supposition, concession, preference, and time relations:

(1) *Contrast*:

他想睡 一会儿, 可是 睡不着。	**Tā xiǎng shuì yī huìr,** *kěshì* **shuì bù zháo.**	(*lit.* he want sleep one while, but sleep not attain) *He* wanted to have a sleep *but* could not go to sleep.

(*conjunction*: 可是 kěshì 'but')

快走吧, 否则你会 迟到的。	**Kuài zǒu ba,** *fǒuzé* **nǐ huì chídào de.**	(*lit.* quick go p, otherwise you probably late-arrive p) Be quick, *or* you'll be late.

(*conjunction*: 否则 fǒuzé 'otherwise')

我没有钱, 不然我就买 微波炉了。	**Wǒ méi yǒu qián,** *bùrán* **wǒ** *jiù* **mǎi wēibōlú le.**	(*lit.* I not-have money, otherwise I then buy microwave-stove p) I don't have any money, *otherwise* I would have bought a microwave.

(*conjunction*: 不然 bùrán 'otherwise', reinforced by *conjunctive*: 就 jiù 'then')

我们的 房子很小, 不过有(一)个 很漂亮 的花园。	**Wǒmen de fángzi hěn xiǎo,** *bùguò* **yǒu (yī) gè hěn piàoliàng de huāyuán.**	(*lit.* our house very small, but have (one) mw very beautiful garden) Our house is small, *but* we have a beautiful garden.

(*conjunction*: 不过 bùguò 'however')

她虽然很饿，但是不想吃饭。	Tā *suīrán* hěn è, *dànshì* bù xiǎng chī fàn.	(*lit.* she though very hungry, but not want eat rice) *Though* she was very hungry, (*however*) she did not want to touch any food.

(*paired conjunctions*: 虽然 suīrán 'though' and 但是 dànshì 'but')

他不但不责备自己，反而责怪别人。	Tā *bùdàn* bù zébèi zìjǐ, *fǎn'ér* zéguài biérén.	(*lit.* he not-only not blame oneself, on-the-contrary blame others) *Not only* did he not blame himself *but* he laid blame on others.

(*paired conjunctions*: 不但 bùdàn 'not only' and 反而 fán'ér 'on the contrary')

(2) *Choice*:

你可以付现金或者开支票。	Nǐ kěyǐ fù xiànjīn *huòzhě* kāi zhīpiào.	(*lit.* you may pay cash or write cheque) You may pay cash *or* by cheque.

(*conjunction*: 或者 huòzhě 'or')

他不是抽烟就是喝酒。	Tā *bùshì* chōuyān *jiùshì* hējiǔ.	(*lit.* he not-be inhale-cigarette then-be drink-wine) *If* he is not drinking, (*then*) he is smoking.

(*paired conjunctions*: 不是 bùshì 'if not' and 就是 jiùshì 'then')

不是他们来，就是我们去。	*Bùshì* tāmen lái, *jiùshì* wǒmen qù.	(*lit.* not-be they come, then-be we go) *If* they didn't come, (*then*) we would go./Either they would come or we would go.

(3) *Addition*:

她很聪明，而且很用功。	Tā hěn cōngming, *érqiě* hěn yònggōng.	(*lit.* she very intelligent, moreover very hardworking) She is very intelligent, *and also* extremely diligent.

(*conjunction*: 而且 érqiě 'moreover')

他不仅/不但	Tā bùjǐn/bùdàn	(lit. he not-only scold people
骂人而且	mà rén érqiě	but-also hit people) He not
打人。	dǎ rén.	only used abusive language
		but also resorted to blows.

(*paired conjunctions*: 不仅/不但 bùjǐn/bùdàn 'not only' and 而且 érqiě 'but also')

(4) *Cause and effect*:

他病了,因此	Tā bìng le, yīncǐ	(lit. he ill p, therefore not
没来参加	méi lái cānjiā	come attend banquet)
宴会。	yànhuì.	He was ill and so did not
		come to the banquet.

(*conjunction*: 因此 yīncǐ 'therefore')

因为他们	Yīnwèi tāmen	(lit. because they not bring
没带地图,	méi dài dìtú,	map, therefore lose-way p)
所以迷路了。	suǒyǐ mílù le.	Because they did not have
		a map with them, they lost
		their way.

(*paired conjunctions*: 因为 yīnwèi 'because' and 所以 suǒyǐ 'therefore')

由于天气	Yóuyú tiānqì	(lit. owing-to weather not
不好,比赛	bù hǎo, bǐsài	good, contest suspend)
暂停。	zàntíng.	Owing to bad weather, the
		contest was postponed.

(*conjunction*: 由于 yóuyú 'owing to')

Note: 由于 Yóuyú may often be used in the first clause without any conjunction or conjunctive in the second clause.

In cause and effect sentences, the 'effect' may be expressed before the 'cause'. The first (main) clause is then unmarked, and the second (subordinate) clause begins with 因为 yīnwèi 'because'. Sometimes 因为 yīnwèi is preceded by 是 shì 'to be':

我没(有)去	Wǒ méi(yǒu)	(lit. I not go see them (be)
见他们,	qù jiàn tāmen,	because I have another one
(是)因为	(shì) yīnwèi	mw appointment) I didn't go
我有另外	wǒ yǒu lìngwài	and see them because I had
一个约会。	yī gè yuēhuì.	another appointment.

| 他突然
晕倒了因为
他喝了太多
的酒。 | **Tā tūrán
yūndǎo le yīnwèi
tā hē le tài duō
de jiǔ.** | (*lit.* he suddenly faint-fall p
because he drink asp too
much p wine/spirit) He
suddenly passed out,
because he had had too
much to drink. |

(5) *Inference*:

| 既然你
不舒服，
就别来了。 | **Jìrán nǐ
bù shūfu,
jiù bié lái le.** | (*lit.* since you not comfortable,
then don't come p) *Since*
you aren't well, don't come
(*then*). |

(*conjunction*: 既然 jìrán 'since', linked with *conjunctive*: 就 jiù 'then')

| 既然他们
说不来，
我们就别
等他们了。 | **Jìrán tāmen
shuō bù lái,
wǒmen jiù bié
děng tāmen le.** | (*lit.* since they say not come,
we then don't wait-for
them p) Since they said
that they would not come,
we had better not wait for
them (*then*). |

(6) *Condition*:

| 只要你小心，
就不会出
什么问题。 | **Zhǐyào nǐ xiǎoxīn,
jiù bù huì chū
shénme wèntí.** | (*lit.* provided you small-
concern, then not likely
emerge any problem)
Provided you are careful,
there won't be any problem. |

(*conjunction*: 只要 zhǐyào 'provided', linked with *conjunctive*:
就 jiù 'then')

| 只有你学好
中文，你才能
去中国工作。 | **Zhǐyǒu nǐ xué hǎo
Zhōngwén, nǐ
cái néng qù
Zhōngguó
gōngzuò.** | (*lit.* only-if you study well
Chinese, you only-then can
go China work) *Only if* you
do well in your study of
Chinese will you (*then*)
be able to go and work in
China. |

(*conjunction*: 只有 zhǐyǒu 'only if', linked with *conjunctive*: 才 cái
'only then')

191

除非你去 说服他们， 他们才会 同意合作。	*Chúfēi* nǐ qù shuōfú tāmen, tāmen *cái* huì tóngyì hézuò.	(*lit.* unless you go convince them, they only-then likely agree cooperate) *Only if* you go and convince them will they (*then*) agree to cooperate.

(*conjunction*: 除非 chúfēi 'unless', linked with *conjunctive*: 才 cái 'only then')

Note: 除非 chúfēi is also regularly paired with 否则/不然 fǒuzé/bùrán 'otherwise':

除非你去说服 他们, 否则/ 不然他们不会 同意合作。	*Chúfēi* nǐ qù shuōfú tāmen, *fǒuzé/* *bùrán* tāmen bù huì tóngyì hézuò.	(*lit.* unless you go convince them, otherwise they not likely agree cooperate) You must go and convince them, *otherwise* they won't agree to cooperate.

(7) '*Non-condition*':

不管她 来不来, 我们 也按照计划 出发。	*Bùguǎn* tā lái bù lái, wǒmen *yě* ànzhào jìhuà chūfā.	(*lit.* no-matter she come not come, we also according-to plan set-out) *No matter* whether she turns up or not, we'll *still* set out according to plan.

(*conjunction*: 不管 bùguǎn 'no matter', linked with *conjunctive*: 也 yě 'also')

无论天晴 还是下雨, 我都走路去。	*Wúlùn* tiān qíng háishi xià yǔ, wǒ *dōu* zǒulù qù.	(*lit.* regardless sky fine or fall rain, I all walk-road go) *Whether* it's fine or raining, I'm going on foot.

(*conjunction*: 无论 wúlùn 'regardless', linked with *conjunctive*: 都 dōu 'all')

(8) *Supposition*:

你如果愿意, 我就替你 写回信。	*Nǐ rúguǒ* yuànyì, wǒ *jiù* tì nǐ xiě huíxìn.	(*lit.* you if willing, I then for you write reply-letter) I'll reply to the letter for you *if* you want.

(*conjunction*: 如果 rúguǒ 'if', linked with *conjunctive*: 就 jiù 'then')

要是他们家 没有电话， 我就去 电话亭打。	*Yàoshi* tāmen jiā méi yǒu diànhuà, wǒ *jiù* qù diànhuàtíng dǎ.	(*lit.* if their home not-have telephone, I then go telephone-booth make-a-call) I'll go and use the public telephone *if* there isn't one at their place.

(*conjunction*: 要是 yàoshi 'if', linked with *conjunctive*: 就 jiù 'then')

假如冬天 没有暖气， 你怎么办？	*Jiǎrú* dōngtiān méi yǒu nuǎnqì, nǐ zěnme bàn?	(*lit.* suppose winter there-isn't heating, you how manage) How do you manage *if* there isn't any heating in winter?

(*conjunction*: 假如 jiǎrú 'if'; since the second clause is a question, no linking conjunction or conjunctive is necessary)

Note: The phrase . . . 的话 . . . de huà 'if' may be used at the end of the first clause, either alone or with one of the conjunctions 如果 rúguǒ, 假如 jiǎrú, 要是 yàoshi earlier in the clause.

明天(如果) 下雪的话， 我们就去 滑雪。	**Míngtiān (*rúguǒ*)** **xià xuě *de huà*,** **wǒmen jiù qù** **huáxuě.**	(*lit.* tomorrow (if) fall snow that-is-the-case, we then go ski) We'll go skiing *if* it snows tomorrow.

(9)   *Concession*:

(a)   referring to the past:

尽管天气 不好，比赛 还是照常 进行。	*Jìnguǎn* tiānqì bù hǎo, bǐsài *háishi* zhàocháng jìnxíng.	(*lit.* though weather not good, contest still as-usual go-on) Though the weather was not good, the match was held as planned.

(*conjunction*: 尽管 jìnguǎn 'although', linked with *conjunctive*: 还是 háishi 'still')

(b)   referring to the future:

即使/就算 很危险， 我也不怕。	*Jíshǐ/jiùsuàn* hěn wēixiǎn, wǒ *yě* bù pà.	(*lit.* even-if very dangerous, I also not afraid) Even *if* it is dangerous, I'm (*still*) not afraid.

(*conjunction*: 即使/就算 jíshǐ/jiùsuàn 'even if/though', linked with *conjunctive*: 也 yě 'also')

哪怕事情 再多, 我也 要抽时间 学中文。	*Nǎpà shìqing zài duō, wǒ yě yào chōu shíjiān xué Zhōngwén.*	(*lit.* even-though affairs more much, I also want find time study Chinese) *Even* if things get even busier, I will *still* find time to study Chinese.

(*conjunction*: 哪怕 nǎpà 'even if/though', linked with *conjunctive*: 也 yě 'also')

(10) *Preference*:

与其在家里 呆着, 不如 出去走走。	*Yǔqí zài jiā li dāizhe, bùrú chū qù zǒuzǒu.*	(*lit.* rather-than at home-in stay asp, better-to go-out walk-walk) (I) would *rather* go out for a walk *than* stay at home.

(*paired conjunction*: 与其 yǔqí 'rather than' and 不如 bùrú 'better to')

我宁可饿死, 也不吃狗肉。	*Wǒ nìngkě è sǐ, yě bù chī gǒuròu.*	(*lit.* I would-rather hungry die, also never eat dog-meat) I would *rather* starve to death *than* eat dog-meat.

(*conjunction*: 宁可 nìngkě 'would rather', linked with *conjunctive*: 也不 yě bù 'and definitely not')

(11) *Time relations*:

(a) as soon as

我一洗完澡 就上床 睡觉了。	*Wǒ yī xǐ wán zǎo jiù shàng chuáng shuìjiào le.*	(*lit.* I as-soon-as wash finish bath then up bed sleep p) *As soon as* I had finished my bath/shower, I (*then*) went to bed.

(*paired conjunctives*: 一 yī 'once' and 就 jiù 'then')

(b) not yet

我等到下午 两点(钟), 他还没 (有)来。	*Wǒ děng dào xiàwǔ liǎng diǎn (zhōng), tā hái méi(yǒu) lái.*	(*lit.* I wait till afternoon two o'clock, he still not come) I waited till two o'clock in the afternoon [but] he *still* had not turned up.

(*conjunctive*: 还 hái 'still')

(c)   only then

我做完功课 才下楼去 看电视。	**Wǒ zuò wán gōngkè *cái* xià lóu qù kàn diànshì.**	(*lit.* I do finish coursework only-then down stairs go watch television) I did *not* go downstairs to watch television *until* I had finished my coursework.

(*conjunctive*: 才 cái 'only then')

(d)   then

她哭起来, 于是我就 走过去。	**Tā kū qǐlái, *yúshì* wǒ *jiù* zǒu guòqù.**	(*lit.* she cry/weep start, so I then go across) She started weeping, *so* (then) I went over (to her).

(*conjunction*: 于是 yúshì 'thereupon', reinforced by *conjunctive*: 就 jiù 'then')

我们好好地 睡了一觉, 然后就 去游泳。	**Wǒmen hǎohāo de shuì le yī jiào, *ránhòu jiù* qù yóuyǒng.**	(*lit.* we well-well p sleep asp one sleep, after-that then go swim) We had a good sleep, and then we went swimming.

(*conjunction*: 然后 ránhòu 'after that', reinforced by *conjunctive*: 就 jiù 'then')

Note 1: 于是 Yúshì and 然后 ránhòu are often accompanied by the conjunctive 就 jiù.

Note 2: The expressions . . . 的时候 . . . de shíhou 'when . . .', . . . 以后 . . . yǐhòu 'after . . .' and . . . 以前 . . . yǐqián 'before . . .' (see 10.3) are also regularly linked with 就 jiù 'then' in the main clause:

戏演完以前 观众就喝 倒彩了。	**Xì yǎn wán *yǐqián* guānzhòng *jiù* hē dàocǎi le.**	*Before* the performance (of the play) had ended, the audience booed.
法官进来的 时候, 大家就 站起来了。	**Fǎguān jìn lái *de shíhou*, dàjiā *jiù* zhàn qǐlái le.**	*When* the judge entered, everyone (*then*) stood up.
你到了以后就 给我打电话。	**Nǐ dào le *yǐhòu jiù* gěi wǒ dǎ diànhuà.**	*After* you've arrived, telephone me.

24.2.2 Paired conjunctives

There are a few *conjunctives* which repeat to form related pairs. In a sentence, these are placed immediately before two verbal predicates/comments sharing the same subject/topic:

他们一边/ 一面喝酒 一边/一面 谈天。	**Tāmen yībiān/** **yīmiàn hē jiǔ** **yībiān/yīmiàn** **tán tiān.**	(*lit.* they one-side drink wine one-side chat) They drank as they chatted.

Note: Other commonly used conjunctives of this type are:

又...又... 我又饿又渴。	**yòu...yòu...** **Wǒ yòu è yòu kě.**	I was *both* hungry *and* thirsty.
越...越... 他越跑越快。	**yuè...yuè...** **Tā yuè pǎo yuè kuài.**	He ran fast*er* and fast*er*.

Some conjunctions are used in a similar way:

咱们或者去 滑雪或者 去游泳。	**Zánmen huòzhě qù** **huáxuě huòzhě** **qù yóuyǒng.**	(*lit.* inclusive: we or go ski or go swim) We either go skiing or go swimming.

24.3 Composite sentences as parallel structures

Composite sentences can also be formed without using conjunctions or conjunctives, by placing clauses in parallel with each other. This is done in a number of ways:

(1) By repeating the same interrogative adverb or pronoun in the second clause:

谁输， 谁请客。	**Shéi shū,** **shéi qǐngkè.**	(*lit.* who lose, who invite-guest) Whoever loses will pay for the meal.
哪儿便宜 到哪儿 去买。	**Nǎr piányi dào** **nǎr qù mǎi.**	(*lit.* where cheap to where go buy) We'll go and buy wherever is cheaper.
怎么好 怎么做。	**Zěnme hǎo** **zěnme zuò.**	(*lit* how good how do) We'll do it whichever way seems best.

(2)   By posing a condition in the first clause and then answering or countering it in the second:

东西太贵， 我不买。	**Dōngxi tài guì,** **wǒ bù mǎi.**	(*lit.* thing too expensive, I not buy) If things are too expensive, I won't buy (anything).
天气不好， 我们不来了。	**Tiānqì bù hǎo,** **wǒmen bù lái le.**	(*lit.* weather not good, we not come p) If the weather isn't good, we won't come.
他们去， 我不去。	**Tāmen qù,** **wǒ bù qù.**	(*lit.* they go, I not go) If they are going, I won't go.
不把文章 写完， 我不睡觉。	**Bù bǎ wénzhāng** **xiě wán,** **wǒ bù shuìjiào.**	(*lit.* not grasp essay/article write finish, I not sleep) I won't go to bed before I finish the essay/article.

It would, of course, be acceptable to use one of the conditional conjunctions 如果 rúguǒ, 假如 jiǎrú, 要是 yàoshi (or . . . 的话 de huà) or the conjunctive 就 jiù, or both a conjunction and the conjunctive in these sentences:

<u>如果</u>东西 太贵(<u>的话</u>)， 我<u>就</u>不买了。	*Rúguǒ dōngxi* *tài guì (de huà),* *wǒ jiù bù mǎi le.*	If things are too expensive, I won't buy (anything).

(3)   By binding the two clauses in a rhythmic and semantic balance:

吃中餐 用筷子， 吃西餐 用刀叉。	**Chī zhōngcān** **yòng kuàizi,** **chī xīcān** **yòng dāochā.**	(*lit.* eat Chinese food use chopsticks, eat Western food use knife and fork) (You) eat Chinese food with chopsticks (and) Western-style food with knives and forks.
他看看我， 我看看他。	**Tā kànkàn wǒ,** **wǒ kànkàn tā.**	(*lit.* he look-look me, I look-look him) He looked at me (and) I looked at him.

24.4   *Verbs taking object clauses*

Finally, there are a few verbs which take *object clauses* and form sentences that may be regarded as composite. We list some of these verbs in categories of meaning:

(1)   Estimation, thought:

| 我认为你
是对的。 | **Wǒ rènwéi nǐ**
shì duì de. | (*lit.* I think you be right p)
I think you are right. |
| 我觉得时间
不早了。 | **Wǒ juéde**
shíjiān bù zǎo le. | (*lit.* I feel time not early p)
I feel it's getting late. |

In these examples, 你是对的 nǐ shì duì de and 时间不早了shíjiān bù zǎo le are the object clauses.

(2)   Suggestion and promise:

我说你 应该坐 火车去。	**Wǒ shuō nǐ** **yīnggāi zuò** **huǒchē qù.**	(*lit.* I say you should travel-by train go) I say (that) you should go by train.
我建议大家 一起干。	**Wǒ jiànyì dàjiā** **yīqǐ gàn.**	(*lit.* I suggest everyone together work) I suggest we should do it together.
我答应 明天去 看她。	**Wǒ dāying** **míngtiān qù** **kàn tā.**	(*lit.* I promise tomorrow go see her) I promised to go and see her tomorrow.

Note: From this last example, it can be seen that if the object clause has the same subject as the main clause, the subject need not be repeated.

(3)   Belief:

| 我相信
地球是
圆的。 | **Wǒ xiāngxìn**
dìqiú shì
yuán de. | (*lit.* I believe earth be
round p) I believe that
the earth is round. |

(4)   Wish:

| 我希望你
能来参加
我们的晚会。 | **Wǒ xīwàng nǐ**
néng lái cānjiā
wǒmen de
wǎnhuì. | (*lit.* I hope you can come
attend our evening-gathering)
I hope you will be able to
come to our party. |

(5)   Worry:

| 我担心
明天
会下雨。 | **Wǒ dānxīn**
míngtiān
huì xià yǔ. | (*lit.* I worry tomorrow possible
fall rain) I am worried that it
might rain tomorrow. |

Object clauses also naturally take the form of direct speech:

| 他说: | **Tā** *shuō*: | (*lit.* he say: not important) |
| '不要紧!' | '**Bù yàojǐn!**' | He said: 'It doesn't matter.' |

孩子问爸爸:	**Háizi** *wèn* **bàba:**	(*lit.* child ask father: you can
'你能买	'**Nǐ néng mǎi**	buy one mw toy-bear give
一只玩具熊	**yī zhsī wánjùxióng**	me p) The child asked his
给我吗?'	**gěi wǒ ma?**'	father: 'Can you buy a teddy
		bear for me?'

25 Exclamations and interjections; appositions; and apostrophes

25.1 Exclamations

Exclamations in Chinese, as in most languages, can be partial or full statements. Vehemence or emphasis is normally expressed by adding the particle 啊 **a** to the end of the exclamation. Degree adverbs such as 多么 **duō(me)** 'how'/'what' or 真 **zhēn** 'really' regularly occur before adjectives to intensify emotions.

(1) Partial statements (i.e. only the comment is present):

| 多(么)美丽 | *Duō(me)* **měilì** | (*lit.* how beautiful p scenery p) |
| 的景色啊! | **de jǐngsè a!** | What a beautiful view! |

| 真棒啊! | *Zhēn* **bàng a!** | (*lit.* really great p) Really |
| | | great! |

(2) Full statements:

| 这个箱子 | **Zhèi gè xiāngzi** | (*lit.* this mw box really heavy |
| 真重啊! | *zhēn* **zhòng a!** | p) This case is really heavy! |

| 这儿的空气 | **Zhèr de kōngqì** | (*lit.* here p air how fresh p) |
| 多么新鲜啊! | **duōme xīnxiān a!** | How fresh the air is here. |

Note: The pronunciation of the particle 啊 **a** may be influenced by the vowel or consonant that precedes it:

(1) 啊 **a** > 哇 **wa** following **ao**, etc.

| 多好哇! | **Duō hǎo** *wa!* | (*lit.* how good p) How good it is! |

(2) 啊 **a** > 呀 **ya** after **i, ai**, etc.

| 真奇怪呀! | **Zhēn qíguài** *ya!* | (*lit.* really strange p) How strange! |

(3)　啊 **a** > 哪 **na** after words ending with **n**, etc.

| 天<u>哪</u>! | **Tiān na!** | (*lit.* heaven p) Good heavens! |

(4)　了 **le** + 啊 **a** > 啦 **la**:

| 完<u>啦</u>! | **Wán la!** | (originally: 完了啊 **wán le a**!)
(*lit.* finish p) All over! |

<u>25.1.1</u>　Exclamations with **tài**

In another regular formulation, the adverb 太 **tài** 'too' is placed before an adjectival or verbal predicate followed by 了 **le**:

太好<u>了</u>!	**Tài hǎo le!**	(*lit.* too good p) Terrific!
太美<u>了</u>!	**Tài měi le!**	(*lit.* too beautiful p) How beautiful!
太感谢你<u>了</u>!	**Tài gǎnxiè nǐ le!**	(*lit.* too thank you p) I'm truly grateful!

<u>25.1.2</u>　Question-word questions as exclamations

Exclamations may also be shaped as question-word questions, generally ending with 啊 **a**, 呀 **ya**, etc.

| 你昨天
为什么
不来<u>呀</u>? | **Nǐ zuótiān**
wèi shénme
bù lái ya? | (*lit.* you yesterday for-what not come p) Why didn't you come yesterday?! |

Note: 不 **Bù** is used here instead of 没 **méi** because, although the action is in the past, the speaker wants to emphasise not the *fact* but the *intention* of the listener, who didn't turn up the day before.

你怎么没 帮忙<u>啊</u>?	**Nǐ zěnme méi** **bāngmáng a?**	(*lit.* you how not help p) How come you didn't help?
我怎么办<u>哪</u>?	**Wǒ zěnme** **bàn na?**	(*lit.* I how deal p) What am I to do?
你怎么说 这样的话<u>呀</u>?	**Nǐ zěnme shuō** **zhèyàng de** **huà ya?**	(*lit.* you how say like-this p words p) How could you say such a thing?!

Exclama-
tions and
interjec-
tions;
apposi-
tions; and
apostrophes

Chinese has a wide range of *interjections* used at the beginning of
sentences to express various kinds of emotion or attitude:

啊, 雨停了。	**Ā, yǔ tíng le.**	(*lit.* oh, rain stop p) Hey! It's stopped raining.
呸, 真卑鄙!	**Pèi, zhēn bēibǐ!**	(*lit.* bah really base) Gosh! How mean!
喂, 你去哪儿?	**Wèi, nǐ qù nǎr?**	(*lit.* hello, you go where) Hello there! Where are you going?
嗨, 下雪了。	**Hèi, xià xuě le.**	(*lit.* hey, fall snow p) Why, it's snowing.

Note: Other commonly used interjections include:

哎呀 **Āiyā**	for impatience	哎呀, 别烦我! **Āiyā! Bié fán wǒ!** Dammit! Don't bother me. (see 25.2.1 below)	
哎 **Āi**	for remorse or regret	哎, 我又弄错了。 **Āi, wǒ yòu nòng cuò le.** Oh dear, I've got it wrong again.	
哼 **Hng**	for dissatisfaction	哼, 他想骗我。 **Hng, tā xiǎng piàn wǒ.** Huh, s/he wants to fool me.	
嗯 **Ǹg**	for agreement	嗯, 行。 **Ǹg, xíng.** Mm. OK.	
哎哟 **Āiyō**	for pain	哎哟! 黄蜂蜇了我了。 **Āiyō! Huángfēng zhēle wǒ le.** Ouch, I've been stung by a wasp.	

25.2.1 Tone variations in interjections

Tones are important for interjections in Chinese, and the same interjection
with different tones can convey different feelings:

A   1st tone (pleasant surprise):

啊, 出太阳啦!	**Ā, chū tàiyáng la!**	(*lit.* interj come-out sun p) Hey! The sun has come out.

A   2nd tone (pressing a point):

| 啊, 你到底
去不去? | **Á, nǐ dàodǐ**
qù bù qù? | (*lit.* interj you after-all go not
go) Well, are you going or not? |

A   3rd tone (doubt or suspicion):

| 啊, 这是怎么
(一)回事啊? | **Ǎ, zhè shì zěnme**
(yī) huí shì a? | (*lit.* interj this be how (one)
mw matter p) What?
What is this all about? |

A   4th tone (sudden enlightenment):

| 啊, 我明白了。 | **À, wǒ míngbai le.** | (*lit.* interj I understand p) Oh,
I think I understand it now. |

An interjection may also, in different contexts, convey different feelings with no change of tone:

| 哎呀, 这个
孩子长得
这么高啦! | **Āiyā, zhèi gè**
háizi zhǎng de
zhème gāo la! | (*lit.* interj this mw child grow
p so tall p) *Goodness*, this
child has grown so tall. |
| 哎呀, 你怎么
把我的衣服
弄脏了。 | **Āiyā, nǐ zěnme**
bǎ wǒ de yīfu
nòng zāng le. | (*lit.* interj you how p grasp
my clothes handle dirty p)
Oh dear, how could you
have dirtied my clothes. |

25.3 *Appositions*

Appositions are another form of independent element in Chinese sentences. They function in a way similar to appositions in English, being placed immediately after the word or words they refer to:

| 大家都
佩服小李,
一个出色的
工程师。 | **Dàjiā dōu**
pèifú Xiǎo Lǐ,
yī gè chūsè de
gōngchéngshī. | (*lit.* everybody all admire
Xiao Li, one mw outstanding
p engineer) Everybody
admires Xiao Li, *an*
outstanding engineer. |
| 她是独生女,
她妈妈的
掌上明珠。 | **Tā shì dúshēngnǚ,**
tā māma de
zhǎngshang
míngzhū. | (*lit.* she be only-daughter,
her mother's palm-on
bright-pearl) She is an only
daughter, *the apple of her*
mother's eye. |

Pronouns or pronominal expressions such as 自己 zìjǐ 'self', 一个人 yī gè rén (*lit*. one mw person) 'alone'/'by myself', 俩 liǎ 'both'/'the two', etc., are commonly used appositions:

我自己来。	**Wǒ zìjǐ lái.**	(*lit*. I self come) I'll help myself. (i.e. to food, etc.)
他一个人走了。	**Tā yī gè rén zǒu le.**	(*lit*. he one mw person go p) He left by himself.
他们俩吵起来了。	**Tāmen liǎ chǎo qǐlái le.**	(*lit*. they two quarrel start p) The two of them started to quarrel.

25.4 *Apostrophe*

Apostrophe is another independent element, which in Chinese normally comes at the beginning of a sentence rather than at the end:

李先生，你早!	**Lǐ xiānsheng, nǐ zǎo!**	(*lit*. Li Mr, you early) Good morning, Mr Li!
张教授，请您讲话。	**Zhāng jiàoshòu, qǐng nín jiǎng huà.**	(*lit*. Zhang professor, please polite: you say words) *Professor Zhang*, please say a few words.
小陈，你上哪儿去?	**Xiǎo Chén, nǐ shàng nǎr qù?**	(*lit*. little Chen, you to where go) *Little Chen*, where are you going to?
老王，近来怎样?	**Lǎo Wáng, jìnlái zěnyàng?**	(*lit*. old Wang, recently what-like) How are things with you lately, *Old Wang*?

Part IV

Paragraphs

 Introduction

We have so far looked at the features of Chinese grammar within the structure of the sentence. However, other factors come into play in longer passages when sentences occur in sequence within the framework of a paragraph. In this final section, we will draw attention to these factors and illustrate their impact through a number of short passages in different styles.

We have already seen in our discussion of conjunctions and serial constructions that correlative and referential devices, which are apparently essential to the structure of a sentence, may be rendered superfluous by meaningful clues provided by context or cotext. For instance, in our discussion of topic-comment structures, we have encountered such meaning-dictated and form-saving tendencies as 信寄走了。**Xìn jì zǒu le.** rather than *信被寄走了。**Xìn bèi jì zǒu le.** (see 18.4.1). As we will see, Chinese is fundamentally oriented towards meaning rather than dictated by form. In the following we will explore these tendencies in more detail and consider the grammatical strategies the Chinese language employs to change or nullify certain formal ingredients of sentences when they are brought together in longer passages. Prime among these are: pronominal and conjunctional omission; elastic sentential configuration; conventional rhythmic cohesion; preferential treatment of repetition; etc. Through the exploitation of contextual meaning, the elimination of formal elements, and the employment of rhythmic balance, a Chinese speaker/writer is able to weave together sentences, which might seem incomplete to speakers of English, into paragraphs that are in fact grammatically coherent.

We will start our discussion with the diary form, essentially a narrative, and follow it with a letter, a dialogue, a speech, a description, a piece of expository writing, and a short argumentative essay. Each example will consist of the Chinese text (including a pinyin version) and a translation into colloquial English, followed by an analysis of syntactic and, in some cases, stylistic features. Where necessary we will also provide literal translations.

A diary

日记

2005年5月25日　晴/(阴)/(雨)

今晚在电视上看了一场足球比赛,是英国利物浦足球队与意大利AC米兰足球队争夺2005年欧洲杯冠军的决赛。

上半场开始不到几分钟,米兰队就进了一球,上半场结束时,比分已经是三比零,米兰队占了上风/领先。

人人都以为这回利物浦队是输定了的。可是谁也没料到,下半场一开始,利物浦队急剧进攻,并在同样戏剧性的情况下,连续踢进三球,扳成三平。

加时再赛,双方势均力敌,始终保持三比三。最后只能靠(罚)点球来决定胜负。

结果倒是利物浦队赢了,成为2005年欧洲杯的冠军。从这场比赛中,我得到了不少启发:做任何事情都一样,暂时的挫折是不足为道的,只要坚持不懈,最终定能取得胜利。

Rìjì

Èrlínglíngwǔ nián wǔyuè
èrshí wǔ rì　qíng/(yīn)/(yǔ)

Jīn wǎn zài diànshì shang kànle yī chǎng zújiú bǐsài, shì Yīngguó lìwùpǔ zúqiúduì yǔ Yìdàlì AC mǐlán zúqiúduì zhēngduó èrlínglíngwǔ nián ōuzhōubēi guànjūn de juésài.

Shàngbànchǎng kāishǐ bù dào jǐ fēn zhōng, mǐlán duì jiù jìnle yī qiú, shàngbànchǎng jiēshù shí, bǐfēn yǐjīng shì sān bǐ líng, mǐlán duì zhànle shàngfēng/lǐngxiān.

Rénrén dōu yǐwéi zhè huí lìwùpǔ duì shì shūdìng le de. Kěshì shéi yě méi liàodào, xiàbànchǎng yī kāishǐ, lìwùpǔ duì jíjù jìngōng, bìng zài tóngyàng xìjùxìng de qíngkuàng xià, liánxù tījìn sān qiú, bānchéng sān píng.

Jiā shí zài sài, shuāngfāng shìjūnlìdí, shǐzhōng bǎochí sān bǐ sān. Zuìhòu zhǐnéng kào (fá) diǎnqiú lái juédìng shèngfù.

Jiéguǒ dào shì lìwùpǔ duì yíng le, chéngwéi èrlínglíngwǔ nián ōuzhōubēi de guànjūn. Cóng zhèi chǎng bǐsài zhōng, wǒ dédàole bùshǎo qǐfā: zuò rènhé shìqíng dōu yīyang, zànshí de cuòzhé shì bùzúwéidào de, zhǐyào jiānchíbùxiè, zuìzhōng dìng néng qǔde shènglì.

Translation:

25 May, 2005 fine/cloudy/rain

This evening I watched a football match on television. It was the 2005 European Cup Final between Liverpool and AC Milan. Within a few minutes of the first half beginning Milan scored, and by the end of the half, the score was already three nil with Milan in the ascendance. Everyone thought Liverpool were bound to lose. But against all expectations, once the second half started, Liverpool attacked furiously and in similar dramatic circumstances scored three goals in succession, pulling back to three all. In extra time both sides were equally matched and the score remained three all. In the end they had to resort to penalty kicks to decide the winner. The result was that Liverpool turned out to be victorious, and became the 2005 European Cup champions. The match inspired a few thoughts in me: it's the same whatever you do – temporary setbacks should not be taken too seriously, and as long as you persevere, you are sure to win in the end.

Analysis:

This diary is essentially a narrative with the author recounting what takes place in a football match he watched on television that day. Towards the end he expresses his feelings about the result of the match by relating it to his personal experience and philosophy. The main points we need to consider here are:

(a)   contextual omission of the subject in clauses or sentences, e.g.:

今晚在电视上看了一场足球比赛 . . .

Jīn wǎn zài diànshì shang kànle yī chǎng zújiú bǐsài . . .

'This evening (I) watched a football match on television.'

As the keeper of the diary, the subject here is naturally understood as the initiator of the action, and he does not need to identify himself as 我 **wǒ** 'I'. It would therefore be superfluous, though not wrong, to introduce the pronoun, but if it were included, the tone would be somewhat unnatural. As we shall see later, the object of a verb may be left out for similar reasons.

是英国利物浦足球队与意大利AC米兰足球队争夺2005年欧洲杯冠军的决赛。

shì Yīngguó lìwùpǔ zúqiúduì yǔ yìdàlì AC mǐlán zúqiúduì zhēngduó èrlínglíngwǔ nián ōuzhōubēi guànjūn de juésài.

'(It) was the 2005 European Cup Final between Liverpool and AC Milan.'

This illustrates the discourse feature of Chinese to drop, where possible, a nominal subject (or object) that is contextually obvious, without any implications for the structural completeness of the sentence. In general, this explains why the third person neuter pronoun 它 'it' is something of a rarity in Chinese.

> 做任何事情都一样...只要坚持不懈, 最终定能取得胜利。
>
> **zuò rènhé shìqíng dōu yīyang ... zhǐyào jiānchíbùxiè, zuìzhōng dìng néng qǔde shènglì.**
>
> 'it's the same whatever (you) do – ... as long as (you) persevere, (you) are sure to win in the end'.

The subjects of the clauses in this case are of generic reference and are therefore readily omitted. Proverbial expressions in Chinese are more than likely to follow this pattern.

(b)   conventional omission of conjunctions, e.g.:

> 上半场开始不到几分钟, 米兰队就进了一球, 上半场结束时, 比分已经是三比零, 米兰队占了上风。
>
> **Shàngbànchǎng kāishǐ bù dào jǐ fēn zhōng, mǐlán duì jiù jìnle yī qiú, shàngbànchǎng jiēshù shí, bǐfēn yǐjīng shì sān bǐ líng, mǐlán duì zhànle shàngfēng.**
>
> 'Within a few minutes of the first half beginning Milan scored, (and) by the end of the half, the score was already three nil (with) Milan in the ascendance.'

All the clauses here are complete with their subjects and predicate verbs and are strung together in the sentence with commas as clausal boundaries rather than conjunctions. Chinese sentences are in fact semantic units, where sentential considerations are not confined entirely to the grammatical centrality of a 'subject-predicate' form, but focus on the linking of ideas featured sequentially but coherently in a composite unit of expression. In this case, the speaker/writer has taken five 'subject-predicate' clauses to form the unit of expression, which presents the central theme of what happens in the first half of the match. (Other speakers/writers might have shaped the same sequence into two or three sentences with, for example, full stops after the second and possibly the fourth clause. These elastic sentential configurations demonstrate the flexibility of a meaning-oriented language like Chinese.)

The English translation is obliged to introduce the conjunction 'and', but it uses other language forms to deal with the verb-dominant tendency of Chinese, of which this sentence is an example. (See (d) below.)

(c)   insertion of conjunctions contributing to the cadence of the sentence, e.g.:

下半场一开始，利物浦队急剧进攻，并在同样戏剧性的情况下，连续踢进三球，扳成三平。

xiàbànchǎng yī kāishǐ, lìwùpǔ duì jíjù jìngōng, bìng zài tóngyàng xìjùxìng de qíngkuàng xià, liánxù tījìn sān qiú, bānchéng sān píng.

'once the second half started, Liverpool attacked furiously and in similar dramatic circumstances scored three goals in succession, pulling back to three all'.

Here the clausal conjunction 并(且) **bìng(qiě)** 'and' provides the cadence for a two-part structure: it serves to highlight what is to come, introducing a commentary dimension into the narrative. Without the conjunction, the sentence becomes more of a factual report.

(d) verbal versus prepositional preponderance: a literal translation of the sentence in (b) above would be as follows:

'first half **begin** not **reach** several minutes, Milan team then **score** a goal, **arrive** first half **finish** time, score already is three-nil, Milan team **occupy** upper position'

This translation demonstrates clearly that Chinese is a language which relies heavily on verbs. We have seen that subjects and objects can readily be omitted in a defined context but a predicate verb must always be present. English, on the other hand, tends to employ nominal and prepositional expressions. This is apparent from the colloquial rendition provided in (b), where the first, third, and final clauses in Chinese all become prepositional phrases in English.

26.2 A letter

书信

志明兄：

　　您好！很久没有给您去信了，请原谅。想近来一切均好，学业上也有长足的进步吧。我也一切如常，只是小孩有时有点淘气，不太听话，多说他几句就生起气来，把门关了，叫吃饭也不下来。大概是这个年龄小孩都有点乖戾吧。再说，我和妻子也都工作繁忙，没有太多时间照顾他，跟他一起搞些有益身心的活动，所以也很难全怪他。

shūxìn

Zhìmíng xiōng:

　　Nín hǎo! hěn jiǔ méiyǒu gěi nín qù xìn le, qǐng yuánliàng. Xiǎng jìnlái yīqiè jūn hǎo, xuéyè shang yě yǒu zhǎngzú de jìnbù ba. Wǒ yě yīqiè rúcháng, zhǐshì xiǎohái yǒushí yǒu diǎn táoqì, bù tài tīnghuà, duō shuō tā jǐ jù jiù shēng qǐ qì lái, bǎ mén guān le, jiào chīfàn yě bù xià lái. Dàgài shì zhèi gè niánlíng xiǎohái dōu yǒu diǎn guāilì ba. Zài shuō, wǒ hé qīzi yě dōu

希望过了这个年龄能懂起事来, 渐渐有所改变。哦, 对了, 小李要我转告您一声, 他下个月要去澳洲访问, 为期一年, 临走时咱们三个人能否找个时间聚一聚, 还是到我家来好, 不知兄意下如何, 请覆。祝您和您家人安好! 请代问候您双亲。

弟　灵强　上

六月二十三日

gōngzuò fánmáng, méiyǒu tài duō shíjiān zhàogù tā, gēn tā yīqǐ gǎo xiē yǒuyī shēnxīn de huódòng, suǒyǐ yě hěn nán quán guài tā. Xīwàng guòle zhèi gè niánlíng néng dǒng qǐ shì lái, jiànjiàn yǒu suǒ gǎibiàn. Ò, duì le, Xiǎolǐ yào wǒ zhuǎngào nín yī shēng, tā xià gè yuè yào qù Àozhōu fǎngwèn, wéiqī yīnián, lín zǒu shí zánmen sān gè rén néngfǒu zhǎo gè shíjiān jù yī jù, háishi dào wǒ jiā lái hǎo, bù zhī xiōng yìxià rúhé, qǐng fù. Zhù nín hé nín jiārén ān hǎo! Qǐng dài wènhòu nín shuāngqīn.

Dì　Língqiáng　shàng

Liù yuè èrshí sān rì

Translation:

Dear Zhiming,

How are you? I am sorry I haven't written for ages. Hope things have gone well for you lately, and you've made good progress with your studies. Things remain the same with me and it's just that the child is sometimes a bit naughty, doesn't do as he is told, frets the more I tell him off, shuts himself away, and won't even come down when I call him to eat. Probably it's the contrariness of a child of his age. What's more, my wife and I are both busy at work and don't have too much time to look after him or do interesting things with him, and so it's very difficult to blame him entirely. We hope that when he gets past this age, he will grow up and gradually change for the better. Oh yes, young Li wants me to pass on to you that he is going for a year's visit to Australia next month, and before he goes we are wondering whether the three of us can find time to get together, perhaps better at my place. Please let me know what you think. Best wishes to you and your family, and please pass on my regards to your parents.

Yours, Lingqiang
23 June

Analysis:

The main purpose of this letter is to pass on a message to arrange a meeting of the three friends. It is customary for the writer of a Chinese letter not to come straight to the point, but politely to put in a few preliminaries to add some substance. Here there are initial statements: 'expressing good will' (e.g. 你好 **Nǐ hǎo!** 'How are you?') and 'asking for forgiveness for not writing too often' (e.g. 您好! 很久没有给您去信了, 请原谅。 **Nín hǎo! hěn jiǔ méiyǒu gěi nín qùxìn le, qǐng yuánliàng.** 'I am sorry I haven't written for ages', etc.) In addition, something like 请代问候您双亲。 **Qǐng dài wènhòu nín shuāngqīn.** 'Please pass on my regards to your parents', etc. is more often than not a concluding sentence. The address code amongst friends is usually 兄 **xiōng** 'elder brother' for someone older and 弟 **dì** 'younger brother' for someone younger in the case of men, and for women 姐 **jiě** 'elder sister' and 妹 **mèi** 'younger sister' respectively. A letter invariably ends with 上 **shàng** 'submit respectfully' after one's signature. When writing to a superior, however, one would use formal titles (e.g. 局长 **júzhǎng** 'head of the bureau', 教授 **jiàoshòu** 'professor', 主任 **zhǔrèn** 'director', etc.) or polite addresses (e.g. 先生 **Xiānsheng** 'Mr', 太太 **Tàitai** 'Mrs.', 小姐 **Xiǎojie** 'Miss', etc.).

In this letter we see linguistic characteristics already observed in the diary above: omission of clausal or sentential subjects or objects where the context eliminates any possible misunderstanding, and of conjunctional devices, when the ideas expressed belong to the same central theme, e.g.:

很久没有给您去信了, 请原谅。
hěn jiǔ méiyǒu gěi nín qùxìn le, qǐng yuánliàng.
'(I) haven't written to you for a long time.
Please forgive/excuse (me).'

想近来一切均好 . . .
Xiǎng jìnlái yīqiè jūnhǎo . . .
'Hope things have gone well (for you) lately'

只是小孩有时有点淘气, 不太听话, 多说他几句就生起气来, 把门关了, 叫吃饭也不下来。
zhǐshì xiǎohái yǒushí yǒu diǎn táoqì, bù tài tīnghuà, duō shuō tā jǐ jù jiù shēng qǐ qì lái, bǎ mén guān le, jiào chīfàn yě bù xià lái.
'it's just that the child is sometimes a bit naughty, doesn't do as (he) is told, frets the more (I) tell him off, shuts (himself) away, and won't even come down when (I) call (him) to eat.'

In fact, the suppressed subjects (in brackets) of the predicate verbs in the clauses change from first person to third person and vice versa without any problem retrieving meaning from the text (see also 23.4.3). The clauses are separated by commas alone without any need for conjunctions – a further proof that Chinese sentences are semantic units of expression. As long as the component elements contribute to the same central idea of 'the child's contrariness', they naturally belong together.

我和妻子也都工作繁忙, 没有太多时间照顾他, 跟他一起搞些有益身心的活动, 所以也很难全怪他。希望过了这个年龄, 能懂起事来, 渐渐有所改变。

Wǒ hé qīzi yě dōu gōngzuò fánmáng, méiyǒu tài duō shíjiān zhàogù tā, gēn tā yīqǐ gǎo xiē yǒuyī shēnxīn de huódòng, suǒyǐ yě hěn nán quán guài tā. Xīwàng guòle zhèi gè niánlíng, néng dǒng qǐ shì lái, jiànjiàn yǒu suǒ gǎibiàn.

'my wife and I are both busy at work and don't have too much time to look after him or do interesting things with him, and so it's very difficult to blame him entirely. (We) hope that when (he) gets past this age, (he) will grow up and gradually change for the better.'

Once again, we see that, for the same reasons noted in the previous sentence, subjects and objects, as well as conjunctions, are omitted in the Chinese text.

| **26.3** | *A dialogue* |

对话

市政府门口

小李: 老张, 老张! 想不到在这儿见到你。你来这儿干啥?

老张: 啊, 小李, 原来是你。我还以为是谁呢! 近来怎么样?

小李: 还可以。你呢?

老张: 不错, 不错。只是前几天着了点儿凉, 有点儿咳嗽, 已经差不多好了。你呢? 还在考试吧?

小李: 不, 早就考完了。

老张: 成绩怎么样?

小李: 还没公布, 估计不会太理想。有的科目很可能不及格呢。

老张: 为什么?

小李: 主要是考试前那段时间, 天气太热, 晚上也没有睡好。加上心情紧张, 饭也吃不下, 所以复习得不好。

Duìhuà

Shìzhèngfǔ ménkǒu

Xiǎo Lǐ: Lǎo Zhāng, Lǎo Zhāng! Xiǎngbudào zài zhèr jiàndào nǐ. Nǐ lái zhèr gàn shá?

Lǎo Zhāng: Ā, Xiǎo Lǐ, yuánlái shì nǐ. Wǒ hái yǐwéi shì shéi ne! Jìnlái zěnmeyàng?

Lǐ: Hái kěyǐ. Nǐ ne?

Zhāng: Bù cuò, bù cuò. Zhǐshì qián jǐ tiān zháole diǎnr liáng, yǒudiǎnr késòu, yǐjīng chàbuduō hǎo le. Nǐ ne? Hái zài kǎoshì ba?

Lǐ: Bù, zǎo jiù kǎo wán le.

Zhāng: Chéngjì zěnmeyàng?

Lǐ: Hái méi gōngbù, gūjì bù huì tài lǐxiǎng. Yǒude kēmù hěn kěnéng bù jígé ne.

Zhāng: Wèi shénme?

Lǐ: Zhǔyào shì kǎoshì qián nèi duàn shíjiān, tiānqì tài rè, wǎnshàng yě méiyǒu shuì hǎo. Jiāshàng xīnqíng jǐnzhāng, fàn yě chībuxià, suǒyǐ fùxí de bù hǎo.

老张: 别担心，可能情况没有你想象得那么糟糕。

小李: 但愿如此。

老张: 好吧，咱们先谈到这儿。今天有中国代表团来这儿访问，我是来替市长当翻译的。我还是赶快去见他吧。

小李: 好吧，那就再见了。祝你一切顺利。

老张: 谢谢，再见。

小李: 再见。

Zhāng: Bié dānxīn, kěnéng qíngkuàng méiyǒu nǐ xiǎngxiàng de nàme zāogāo.

Lǐ: Dànyuàn rúcǐ.

Zhāng: Hǎo ba, zánmen xiān tán dào zhèr. Jīntiān yǒu Zhōngguó dàibiǎotuán lái zhèr fǎngwèn, wǒ shì lái tì shìzhǎng dāng fānyì de. Wǒ háishi gǎnkuài qù jiàn tā ba.

Lǐ: Hǎo ba, nà jiù zàijiàn le. Zhù nǐ yīqiè shùnlì.

Zhāng: Xièxiè, zàijiàn.

Lǐ: Zàijiàn.

Translation:

At the door of the Municipal Government Office

Young Li: Old Zhang, old Zhang! I didn't expect to meet you here. What have you come for?

Old Zhang: Ah, Young Li, so it's you. I didn't realize it was you. How have things been for you lately?

Young Li: Quite good. What about you?

Old Zhang: Not bad, not bad. It's just that I caught a bit of a cold a few days ago, and have a bit of a cough. It's almost better now. How about you? You're still taking exams, aren't you?

Young Li: No. They finished some time ago.

Old Zhang: What were your results?

Young Li: They've not been published yet. I guess they won't be too brilliant. It's very probable that I haven't passed some subjects.

Old Zhang: Why?

Young Li: Mainly because in the period before the exam, it was too hot, and I didn't sleep well at night. On top of that, I was nervous and could not eat, so my revision didn't go well.

Old Zhang: Don't worry. Probably things won't be as bad as you imagine.

Young Li: I hope so.

Old Zhang: OK, let's leave it at that. Today a Chinese delegation is visiting here. I am interpreting for the Mayor. I must dash off to see him now.

Young Li: OK, so we'll say goodbye. Hope everything goes smoothly for you.

Old Zhang: Thank you. Goodbye for now.

Young Li: Goodbye.

Analysis:

In a dialogue or conversation, omissions are all the more common because the context is made immediately apparent by the ongoing exchange, e.g.:

老张: 成绩怎么样?
小李: 还没公布, 估计不会太理想。有的科目很可能不及格呢。

Lǎo Zhāng: Chéngjì zěnmeyàng?

Xiǎo Lǐ: Hái méi gōngbù, gūjì bù huì tài lǐxiǎng. Yǒude kěmù hěn kěnéng bù jígé ne.

'**Old Zhang**: What were your results?

Young Li: (They've) not been published yet. (I) guess (they) won't be too brilliant. It's very probable that (I) haven't passed some subjects.'

'Results' is obviously the topic of this exchange and, as it has been the keyword in the question, there is no need to reiterate it in the answer. Likewise, it is clear that 'I' have taken the examination and there is therefore no need for me to identify myself.

老张: 为什么?
小李: 主要是考试前那段时间, 天气太热, 晚上也没(有)睡好。加上心情紧张, 饭也吃不下, 所以复习得不好。

Lǎo Zhāng: Wèishéme?

Xiǎo Lǐ: Zhǔyào shì kǎoshì qián nèi duàn shíjiān, tiānqì tài rè, wǎnshàng yě méi(yǒu) shuì hǎo. Jiāshàng xīnqíng jǐnzhāng, fàn yě chībuxià, suǒyǐ fùxí de bù hǎo.

'**Old Zhang**: Why?

Young Li: Mainly because in the period before the exam, it was too hot, and (I) didn't sleep well at night. On top of that, (I) was nervous (and) could not eat, so (my) revision didn't go well.'

Once again there is no doubt that the answer relates to the candidate himself and the subject is consequently omitted.

It is also worth pointing out that in informal Chinese, as in a conversation like this, there is a tendency for speakers to use the sentence particle 了 **le**. This is because in everyday conversation (or letters) one says things as they come to mind: thus the sentences of the speaker (or writer) are less structured and tend more often than usual to round up ideas at every step. When this happens, 了 **le** becomes a natural mechanism to bring an idea to a close before the speaker goes on to another. For instance, in 已经差不多好了 **yǐjīng chàbuduō hǎo le** 'It's almost better now', 早就考完了 **zǎo jiù kǎo wán le** 'The exams finished some time ago', and 那就再见了 **nà jiù zàijiàn le** 'so we'll say goodbye', the speaker indicates that he has no doubt in his mind that what he has just verbalised represents a situation which has already been or will soon be actualised and 了 le helps him to signal that, by bringing the idea to conclusion. We can illustrate this further by adding 了 le to other sentences in the dialogue. For example, 成绩怎么样 Chéngjì zěnmeyàng? 'What were your results?' is a straightforward question, but 成绩怎么样了 Chéngjì zěnmeyàng le introduces an anxious tone into the query and indicates concern for the impending outcome; 天气太热 tiānqì tài rè 'it was too hot' is a factual statement, but 天气太热了 tiānqì tài rè le emphasises a situational change where the heat is hardly ideal for exams; if 饭也吃不下 fàn yě chībuxià 'could not eat' is again a factual report, 饭也吃不下了 fàn yě chībuxià le becomes a comment highlighting a disturbing change in appetite; if 别担心 bié dānxīn 'don't worry' is a forthright request, 别担心了 bié dānxīn le 'stop worrying' gently urges the listener to change his present state of anxiety.

We can see from the above that wherever 了 le occurs, it is an indication that what the speaker has in mind is, or will soon be, a different situation, which the listener is invited to think about. In the unstructured, and almost anarchic, sequence of such sentences, 了 le is a natural marker between them; this means that the less structured the speech (or writing), the more frequent the use of 了 le. In more structured expository or argumentative writing, as we shall see, 了 le appears far less frequently.

26.4 A welcome speech

欢迎词

张院长, 张夫人:

我代表XX大学, 对你们到敝校来访问, 表示热烈的欢迎。自从咱们两校互派留学生与访问学者以来, 双方在学术上互相促进, 取得了不少成绩。我想特别指出的是贵校派来的学生与老师, 勤奋好学, 遵守纪律, 助人为乐, 每一批都给我们留下了深刻的印象, 希望他们回到本校之后, 能够多做贡献, 进一步加强我们之间的友谊。张院长这次到来, 可以亲眼看到贵校学生与老师学习与生活的实况。在我们这儿, 他们是贵宾, 是最受欢迎的人。我们尽了一切努力, 使他们身心愉快, 学有所成。当然, 我们也得感谢张院长对我校派去的学生与

Huānyíngcí

Zhāngyuànzhǎng, Zhāngfūren:

Wǒ dàibiǎo XX dàxué, duì nǐmen dào bì xiào lái fǎngwèn, biǎoshì rèliè de huānyíng. Zìcóng zánmen liǎng xiào hù pài liúxuéshēng yǔ fǎngwèn xuézhě yǐlái, shuāngfāng zài xuéshù shang hùxiāng cùjìn, qǔdé le bùshǎo chéngjì. Wǒ xiǎng tèbié zhǐchū de shì guì xiào pài lái de xuésheng yǔ lǎoshī, qínfèn hàoxué, zūnshǒu jìlǜ, zhù rén wéi lè, měi yī pī dōu gěi wǒmen liú xià le shēnkè de yìnxiàng, xīwàng tāmen huí dào běn xiào zhīhòu, nénggòu duō zuò gòngxiàn, jìnyíbù jiāqiáng wǒmen zhījiān de yǒuyì. Zhāngyuànzhǎng zhèi cì dàolái, kěyǐ qīnyǎn kàndào guì xiào xuésheng

215

老师的无微不至的关怀与照顾, 他们归来后都众口一词地说, 在贵校学习与生活期间, 比在家里还要愉快与舒适。在此, 我谨代表本校再次向张院长表示衷心的感谢。让我也借此机会, 请在座的各位, 共同举杯对张院长和院长夫人表示敬意, 祝愿他们身体健康, 万事如意, 并在此访问期间, 有所收获。

yǔ lǎoshī xuéxí yǔ shēnghuó de shíkuàng. Zài wǒmen zhèr, tāmen shì guìbīn, shì zuì shòu huānyíng de rén. Wǒmen jìn le yīqiè nǔlì, shǐ tāmen shēnxīn yúkuài, xué yǒu suǒ chéng. Dāngrán, wǒmen yě děi gǎnxiè Zhāngyuànzhǎng duì wǒ xiào pài qù de xuésheng yǔ lǎoshī de wúwēibùzhì de guānhuái yǔ zhàogù, tāmen guīlái hòu dōu zhòngkǒuyīcí de shuō, zài guì xiào xuéxí yǔ shēnghuó qījiān, bǐ zài jiā lǐ háiyào yúkuài yǔ shūshì. Zài cǐ, wǒ jǐn dàibiǎo běn xiào zài cì xiàng Zhāngyuànzhǎng biǎoshì zhōngxīn de gǎnxiè. Ràng wǒ yě jiè cǐ jīhuì, qǐng zài zuò de gèwèi, gòngtóng jǔ bēi duì Zhāngyuànzhǎng hé yuànzhǎng fūren biǎoshì jìngyì, zhùyuàn tāmen shēntǐ jiànkāng, wànshì rúyì, bìng zài cǐ fǎngwèn qījiān, yǒu suǒ shōuhuò.

Translation:

President Zhang and Mrs Zhang,

On behalf of XX university, I express a warm welcome to you on your visit to our humble university. Ever since our two universities have been exchanging students and visiting scholars both sides have achieved considerable results in promoting mutual academic progress. What I would like to point out in particular is that the students and teachers sent by your honourable university have been diligent and committed to their studies, have observed discipline, and have taken pleasure in helping others. Every cohort has left us with a deep impression, and I hope that after their return to their own university, they are able to make wider contributions and further strengthen the friendship between us. President Zhang, you will be able to see with your own eyes during this visit the actual conditions in which the students and teachers sent by your honourable university live and study. Here they are honoured guests and the most welcome of people. We have done our utmost to ensure that they are happy in every way and successful in their studies. Of course we must also thank President Zhang for the meticulous care and concern shown to the students and teachers we have sent (to your university). When they return they say unanimously that the period when they studied at your university was even more happy and comfortable than at home. At this point, on behalf of our humble university I would like to express once again our heartfelt thanks to President Zhang. Let me take this opportunity to ask everybody present to raise their glasses together in a toast to President Zhang and Mrs Zhang and wish them good health, all success, and marked achievements during this visit.

Analysis:
A welcome speech, like other formal addresses, is likely to incorporate standard clichés, and a number of them can be seen here (e.g. 敝校 **bì xiào** 'our humble university', 贵校 **guì xiào** 'your honourable university', 谨代表 **jǐn dàibiǎo** 'on behalf of', 借此机会 **jiè cǐ jīhuì** 'take this opportunity', etc.). Another prominent feature of this style is an inclination to use rhythmic patterns and parallelisms (e.g. 勤奋好学, 遵守纪律, 助人为乐 **qínfèn hàoxué, zūnshǒu jìlǜ, zhù rén wéi lè** 'have been diligent and committed to their studies, have observed discipline, and have taken pleasure in helping others', 身心愉快, 学有所成 **shēnxīn yúkuài, xué yǒu suǒ chéng** 'are happy in every way and successful in their studies', 关怀与照顾 **guānhuái yǔ zhàogù** 'care and concern', 愉快与舒适 **yúkuài yǔ shūshì** 'happy and comfortable', etc.

26.5 A description

描述文

利兹市

    利兹是英格兰北部西约克郡的一个城市。据说是英格兰第四大城市。英格兰最大的城市当然是伦敦, 其次是伯明翰, 曼彻斯特排第三, 第四就轮到利兹了。

    近十几年来, 利兹在城市建筑上, 有很大的发展。尤其是市中心, 街道两旁的建筑愈来愈新颖别致, 步行街更是明净宽敞, 这儿行人不用担心车辆的来往。可是最有特色的还要数那一条条的拱廊街, 其他城市里并不多见。这里的拱廊街, 每条都有独特的风格, 其中有一条还有美丽的小花坛和怡人的小喷泉, 旁边摆着可供行人随时休憩的长凳, 两旁商店的橱窗里, 陈列着琳

Miáoshùwén

Lìzīshì

    Lìzī shì Yīnggélán běibù xī Yuèkèjùn de yī gè chéngshì. Jùshuō shì Yīnggélán dì sì dà chéngshì. Yīnggélán zuì dà de chéngshì dāngrán shì Lúndūn, qícì shì Bómínghàn, Mànchèsītè pái dì sān, dì sì jiù lún dào Lìzī le.

    Jìn shí jǐ nián lái, Lìzī zài chéngshì jiànzhù shang, yǒu hěn dà de fāzhǎn. Yóuqí shì shìzhōngxīn, jiēdào liǎngpáng de jiànzhù yù lái yù xīnyǐng biézhì, bùxíngjiē gèng shì míngjìng kuānchang, zhèr xíngrén bùyòng dānxīn chēliàng de láiwǎng. Kěshì zuì yǒu tèsè de háiyào shǔ nà yītiáotiáo de gǒng láng jiē, qítā chéngshìli bìng bù duō jiàn. Zhèlǐ de gǒnglángjiē, měi tiáo dōu yǒu dútè de fēnggé, qízhōng

217

琅满目的商品, 吸引了不少外地来
的游客。这条拱廊街上的咖啡馆,
还把桌椅移到街中央, 可让顾客们
坐下来舒心惬意地喝杯咖啡呢。

yǒu yī tiáo háiyǒu měilì de xiǎo
huātán hé yírén de xiǎo pēnquán,
pángbian bǎi zhe kě gōng xíngrén
suíshí xiūqì de chángdèng, liǎngpáng
shāngdiàn de chúchuāng li, chénliè
zhe línlángmǎnmù de shāngpǐn, xīyǐn
le bùshǎo wàidì lái de yóukè. Zhèi
tiáo gǒnglángjiē shang de kāfēiguǎn,
hái bǎ zhuōyǐ yí dào jiē zhōngyāng,
kě ràng gùkè mén zuò xiàlai shūxīn
qièyì de hē kāfēi ne.

Translation:

Leeds is a city in West Yorkshire in northern Britain, said to be the
fourth biggest city in England. England's largest city is of course London,
with Birmingham next, Manchester third, and Leeds coming fourth.

In the last ten years or so, there have been major developments
in urban construction in Leeds. In the city centre in particular, the
buildings along the streets are looking increasingly original and attrac-
tive. The pedestrian precincts are even more bright and spacious with
people not needing to worry about traffic. But more distinctive are the
many arcades, which are not often found in other cities. Each arcade
has its unique style. One of them even has beautiful flowerbeds and
pleasing fountains with benches beside them where people can sit and
rest any time they like. The shop-windows on either side are full of
eye-catching goods, attracting visitors from outside. The coffee shops
here also have tables and chairs in the middle of the arcade, where
customers can sit at their leisure and enjoy a cup of coffee.

Analysis:

A description in Chinese is naturally drawn to sequences of words and
phrases expressing similar meanings. For example, in this passage, to
attain variety, four different verbs are used to indicate comparison:
是 **shì** in 英格兰最大的城市当然是伦敦, 其次是伯明翰 **Yīnggélán zuì dà
de chéngshì dāngrán shì Lúndūn, qícì shì Bómínghàn**, 'England's largest city is of course London, with Birmingham next'; 排 **pái** in 曼彻斯
特排第三 **Mànchèsītè pái dì sān**, 'Manchester third', 轮到 **lún dào**
in 第四就轮到利兹了 **dì sì jiù lún dào Lìzī le**, 'Leeds coming fourth';
数 **shǔ** in 最有特色的还要数那一条条的拱廊街 **zuì yǒu tèsè de háiyào
shǔ nà yītiáotiáo de gǒnglángjiē**, 'more distinctive are the many arcades'; likewise, a variety of verbs, adjectives, and nominal expressions
is used – 摆着 **bǎi zhe** 'placed', 陈列着 **chénliè zhe** 'displayed', 移到 **yí
dào** 'moved to', 别致 **biézhì** 'original', 独特 **dútè** 'unique', 市中心
shìzhōngxīn 'city centre', 街中央 **jiē zhōngyāng**, 'middle of the street'

– to indicate position, arrangement and special quality; and in order to acquire a cadential rhythm, four character phrases are coined, e.g. 新颖别致 **xīnyǐng biézhì** from 新颖 **xīnyǐng** 'refreshingly new' and 别致 **biézhì** 'original', 明净宽敞 **míngjìng kuānchang** from 明净 **míngjìng** 'bright and clean' and 宽敞 **kuānchang** 'wide and spacious', 舒心惬意 **shūxīn qièyì** from 舒心 **shūxīn** 'relaxing one's mind' and 惬意 **qièyì** 'pleasing one's heart'; and parallel structures are formed, e.g. 美丽的小花坛 **měilì de xiǎo huātán** 'beautiful flowerbeds', 怡人的小喷泉 **yírén de xiǎo pēnquán** 'pleasing fountains', (可供行人)随时休憩的长凳, 琳琅满目的商品, 陈列着, 吸引了, (**kě gōng xíngrén**) **suíshí xiūqì de chángdèng, línlángmǎnmù de shāngpǐn, chénliè zhe, xīyǐn le**, etc. Descriptions are generally intent on achieving variety in usage and vibrancy in rhythm.

26.6 An explanatory piece of writing

说明文

识记中文单词的方法

　学中文, 除了学发音与语法之外, 还得识记一定数量的单词。一门语言的发音与语法, 都是封闭的系统, 其规则是有限的, 而且在短期内不会发生很大的变化, 所以并不难学。单词却不一样, 是永远也学不完的, 因为一门语言的词汇是一个开放的系统, 在不断更新, 不断增加。可是不要这么一说就恐慌起来。其实一门语言中常用的词儿并不多, 无非是那么几千个, 只要方法对头, 要掌握这几千个词儿倒并不难。至于那些不常用的词儿, 可以慢慢来, 等到需要的时候, 再一个一个地学。

　现在我们来谈谈学中文词儿的方法。大家都知道, 每个单词都有自己独特的发音与用法, 所以在识记一个单词的时候, 除了要知道意

Shuōmíngwén

Shíjì zhōngwén dāncí de fāngfǎ

　Xué Zhōngwén, chú le xué fāyīn yǔ yǔfǎ zhīwài, háiděi shíjì yīdìng shùliàng de dāncí. Yī mén yǔyán de fāyīn yǔ yǔfǎ, dōushì fēngbì de xìtǒng, qí guīzé shì yǒuxiàn de, érqiě zài duǎnqī nèi bù huì fāshēng hěn dà de biànhuà, suǒyǐ bìng bù nán xué. Dāncí què bù yīyàng, shì yǒngyuǎn yě xué bù wán de, yīnwèi yī mén yǔyán de cíhuì shì yī gè kāifàng de xìtǒng, zài bùduàn gēngxīn, bùduàn zēngjiā. Kěshì bùyào zhème yī shuō jiù kǒnghuāng qǐlái. Qíshí yī mén yǔyán zhōng chángyòng de cír bìng bù duō, wúfēi shì nàme jǐ qiān gè, zhǐyào fāngfǎ duìtóu, yào zhǎngwò zhè jǐ qiān gè cír dào bìng bù nán. Zhìyú nèixiē bù chángyòng de cír, kěyǐ mànman lái, děng dào xūyào de shíhou, zài yī gè yī gè de xué.

　Xiànzài wǒmen lái tántan xué zhōngwén cír de fāngfǎ. Dàjiā dōu zhīdao, měi gè dāncí dōu yǒu zìjǐ dútè de fāyīn yǔ yòngfǎ, suǒyǐ zài

思之外, 一定要把音调发准, 把有关的搭配弄清。例如'见面'一词, 意思是 '(*lit.* see face) meet', 音调是 jiànmiàn, 搭配则是'跟他见面' 'meet him' 和'见过他一面' 'met him once'。这样就不会根据英文 meet 一词的用法而说出'*见面他'这样的话来了。

记中文单词还有一个窍门, 这里值得一提, 学中文的人听了一定会高兴的。其实中文里几乎所有的词儿都是由单音节的字构成的。当代中文的字汇, 象语音语法一样, 也是一个封闭系统, 一般情况下是不会再造出什么新的字来了。常用的字也只有两千五百到三千个, 几乎所有的词儿都是由这几千个字组合而成的, 而且往往是由两个这样的字组成的。上面提到的'见面'一词就是由'见'与'面'两个字构成的, 学会了这两个字, 还可以帮助你掌握不少其他如'再见' zàijiàn '(*lit.* again see) goodbye', 见证 jiànzhèng '(*lit.* see prove) witness', '面试' miànshì '(*lit.* face test) interview' 这类词儿。

shíjì yī gè dāncí de shíhou, chú le yào zhīdao yìsi zhīwài, yīdìng yào bǎ yīndiào fā zhǔn, bǎ yǒuguān de dāpèi nòng qīng. Lìrú 'jiànmiàn' yī cí, yìsi shì 'meet', yīndiào shì 'jiànmiàn', dāpèi zé shì 'gēn tā jiànmiàn', hé 'jiàn guò tā yī miàn'. zhèyàng jiù bù huì gēnjù yīngwén 'meet'. yī cí de yòngfǎ ér shuō chū 'jiànmiàn tā' zhèyàng de huà lái le.

Jì zhōngwén dāncí háiyǒu yī gè qiàomén, zhèlǐ zhíde yī tí, xué zhōngwén de rén tīng le yīdìng huì gāoxìng de. Qíshí zhōngwén li jīhū suǒyǒu de cír dōushì yóu dānyīnjié de zì gòuchéng de. Dāngdài zhōngwén de zìhuì, xiàng yǔyīn yǔfǎ yīyàng, yěshì yī gè fēngbì xìtǒng, yībān qíngkuàng xià shì bù huì zài zàochū shénme xīn de zì lái le. Chángyòng de zì yě zhǐyǒu liǎng qiān wǔ bǎi dào sān qiān gè, jīhū suǒyǒu de cír dōushì yóu zhè jǐ qiān gè zì zǔhé érchéng de, érqiě wǎngwǎng shì yóu liǎng gè zhèyàng de zì zǔchéng de. Shàngmiàn tídào de 'jiànmiàn' yī cí jiùshì yóu 'jiàn' yǔ 'miàn' liǎng gè zì gòuchéng de, xué huì le zhè liǎng gè zì, hái kěyǐ bāngzhù nǐ zhǎngwò bùshǎo qítā rú 'zàijiàn' ('goodbye'), jiànzhèng, ('witness'), 'miànshì' ('interview') zhèi lèi cír.

Translation:

The Way to Learn Chinese Words

In studying Chinese, apart from pronunciation and grammar, you also have to learn a sufficient number of words. The pronunciation and grammar of a language are closed systems, and their rules are limited in number and moreover these rules are unlikely to change significantly over a short period of time. They are therefore certainly not difficult to learn. Words on the other hand are different. You can never stop learning them because the vocabulary of a language is an open system, forever being renewed and extended. But don't panic because I say this. In fact, there aren't many commonly used words in a language and usually no more than a few thousand. As long as you go about it properly, you'll certainly have no difficulty mastering these few thousand words. As for less commonly used words, you can take them slowly and learn them one by one when the time comes.

Now let's talk about how to learn Chinese words. Everyone knows that each word has its own unique pronunciation and usage, and therefore when learning a word, in addition to its meaning, you have to be clear about its pronunciation and collocation. For example, the word 见面 jiànmiàn, which means 'meet (*lit.* see face)', has the pronunciation (i.e. tone as well as sound) 'jiànmiàn' and the collocations of 跟他见面 gēn tā jiànmiàn 'meet him (*lit.* with him see face)' and 见过他一面 jiàn guò tā yī miàn 'met him once (*lit.* see p him one face)', etc. Thus you wouldn't say something like *见面他 jiànmiàn tā '(*lit.*) meet him' in the way you would use 'meet' in English.

There is a knack for remembering Chinese words, which is also worth mentioning here, and people learning the language will definitely be pleased to hear about it. The fact is that all Chinese words are made up of monosyllabic characters. The character set of contemporary Chinese, like its pronunciation and grammar, is a closed system too, and in normal circumstances no new characters will be created. There are only 2,500 to 3,000 commonly used characters in Chinese, and most words are combinations of two of those characters. The word 见面 jiànmiàn mentioned above is formed from the two characters 见 jiàn 'see' and 面 miàn 'face', and learning these two characters will help you to grasp many other words such as 再见 zàijiàn 'goodbye (*lit.* again see)', 见证 jiànzhèng 'witness (*lit.* see prove)', 面试 miànshì 'interview (*lit.* face test)', etc.

Analysis:
Expository writing naturally exhibits some of the features noted above in the diary, letter, dialogue and description sections. Here we will concentrate on repetitional strategies.

A piece of expository writing has to have an internal logic and coherence (see also the analysis of argumentative writing below) and focuses throughout on a particular thematic concept or concepts. One therefore finds considerable repetition of key words. This unique feature of expository writing can be seen in both the Chinese original and also the relatively literal English translation. For example, note the frequent presence of key concepts like pronunciation and grammar, closed and open systems, words, characters, collocation, etc. However, there is a marked difference in the strategies adopted by the two languages. In

English, repetition is normally avoided by the use of pronouns and a wide range of synonyms, though in practice, where the writing is more oriented towards meaning and content rather than style, repetition becomes more acceptable. In Chinese, however, which is not comfortable with nominal or pronominal substitution, repetition is more readily tolerated and, where the context is clear, meaning takes over, allowing for simple omission. For example:

大家都知道, 每个单词都有自己独特的发音与用法, 所以在识记一个单词的时候, 除了要知道意思之外, 一定要把音调发准, 把有关的搭配弄清。

Dàjiā dōu zhīdao, měi gè dāncí dōu yǒu zìjǐ dútè de fāyīn yǔ yòngfǎ, suǒyǐ zài shíjì yī gè dāncí de shíhou, chú le yào zhīdao yìsi zhīwài, yīdìng yào bǎ yīndiào fā zhǔn, bǎ yǒuguān de dāpèi nòng qīng.

Everyone knows that each word has its own unique pronunciation and usage, and therefore when learning a word, in addition to <u>its</u> meaning, you have to be clear about <u>its</u> pronunciation and collocation.

26.7 *An argumentative piece of writing*

议论文

Yìlùnwén

健康之我见

Jiànkāng zhī wǒ jiàn

　　有人说: '健康是财富中的财富。' 我觉得这个说法是十分正确的。其实道理很简单。试想一下, 一个人, 如果身体不好, 一年到头病病歪歪的, 就算再有钱, 又怎样去享受美好的人生呢?

　　要说明健康的重要, 我还可以举出一个例子: 上中学时有个同班同学, 他确实是个数学奇才, 老师不懂的习题, 他也能解答, 可是由于身体不好, 年纪轻轻的就夭折了。我一直认为, 要是今天他还活着, 定能像爱因斯坦那样为社会和人类造福的。由此可见, 无论是什么, 都要以健康为基础。

　　Yǒu rén shuō: 'Jiànkāng shì cáifù zhōng de cáifù.' Wǒ juéde zhèi gè shuōfǎ shì shífēn zhèngquè de. Qíshí, dàoli hěn jiǎndān. Shì xiǎng yīxià, yī gè rén, rúguǒ shēntǐ bù hǎo, yī nián dào tóu bìng bìng wāi wāi de, jiùsuàn zài yǒu qián, yòu zěnyàng qù xiǎngshòu měihǎo de rénshēng ne?

　　Yào shuōmíng jiànkāng de zhòngyào, wǒ hái kěyǐ jǔchū yī gè lìzi: Shàng zhōngxué shí yǒu gè tóng bān tóngxué, tā quèshí shì gè shùxué qícái, lǎoshī bù dǒng de xítí, tā yě néng jiědá, kěshì yóuyú shēntǐ bù hǎo, niánjì qīngqīngde jiù yāozhé le. Wǒ yīzhí rènwéi, yàoshi jīntiān tā hái huó zhe, dìng néng xiàng Àiyīnsītǎn nèiyàng wèi shèhuì hé rénlèi zàofú de. Yóucǐ kějiàn, wúlùn shì shénme, dōu yào yǐ jiànkāng wéi jīchǔ.

那么说,怎样才能使自己健康起来呢?在我看来,使身体健康的因素,不外五个方面:(一) 要经常锻炼身体,使自己血脉畅通,筋骨壮健,增强对疾病的抵抗力;(二) 起居饮食有度,保证适量的睡眠,多吃蔬菜水果,少吃肥腻荤腥;(三) 不抽烟、酗酒、或吸毒,介绝一切危害生命与健康的陋习;(四) 注意冷暖,讲究卫生,减少患病的机会;(五) 时刻保持心情愉快,为人公正、善良、慷慨,遇事沉着、冷静,不动肝火,考虑与处理问题,均从正面出发。

如果我们能做到以上五点的话,健康也就有了基本的保障。有了健康,也就有了一切:从事学习研究也好,完成工作任务也好,外出度假旅游也好,无论进行什么活动,你都能从中得到最充分的乐趣。

上面所说的只是我个人的看法。说得不对的地方/如有不当之处,欢迎大家批评指正。

Nàme shuō, zěnyàng cáinéng shǐ zìjǐ jiànkāng qǐlái ne? Zài wǒ kànlái, shǐ shēntǐ jiànkāng de yīnsù, bùwài wǔ gè fāngmiàn: **yī**, yào jīngcháng duànliàn shēntǐ, shǐ zìjǐ xuèmài chàngtōng, jīngǔ zhuàngjiàn, zēngqiáng duì jíbìng de dǐkànglì; **èr**, qǐjū yǐnshí yǒudù, bǎozhèng shìliàng de shuìmián, duō chī sūcài shuǐguǒ, shǎo chī féi nì hūn xīng; **sān**, bù chōuyān, xùjiǔ, huò xīdú, jièjué yīqiè wēihài shēngmìng yǔ jiànkāng de lòuxí; **sì**, zhùyì lěngnuǎn, jiǎngjiu wèishēng, jiǎnshǎo huànbìng de jīhuì; **wǔ**, shíkè bǎochí xīnqíng yúkuài, wéi rén gōngzhèng, shànliáng, kāngkǎi, yù shì chénzhuó, lěngjìng, bù dòng gānhuǒ, kǎolǜ yǔ chǔlǐ wèntí, jūn cóng zhèngmiàn chūfā.

Rǔguǒ wǒmen néng zuò dào yǐ shàng wǔ diǎn de huà, jiànkāng yě jiù yǒu le jīběn de bǎozhàng. Yǒu le jiànkāng, yě jiù yǒu le yīqiè: cóngshì xuéxí yánjiū yě hǎo, wánchéng gōngzuò rènwù yě hǎo, wàichū dùjià lǚyóu yě hǎo, wúlùn jìnxíng shénme huódòng, nǐ dōu néng cóngzhōng dédào zuì chōngfèn de lèqù.

Shàngmiàn suǒ shuō de zhǐshì wǒ gèrén de kànfǎ. Shuō de bù duì de dìfang/rúyǒu bùdàng zhī chù, huānyíng dàjiā pīpíng zhǐzhèng.

Translation:
People say 'Health is the richest of riches'. I feel this is entirely correct. The reason in fact is quite simple. Just think for a moment, if a person is in poor condition and is sickly all year long, even if he is wealthy, how can he enjoy a happy life? To illustrate the importance of good health, I can cite an example: at middle school I had a fellow student who was a mathematics genius. He could even solve equations that the teacher couldn't. However, because he was in poor health he died very young. I have always thought that, if he were still alive today, he would have been able like Einstein to bring benefits to society and mankind.

From this it can be seen that, no matter what the circumstances, good health must be the foundation.

This being the case, how can you make yourself healthy? As far as I am concerned, the factors for ensuring good health lie in five areas: (1) You should take regular exercise to achieve good blood circulation and physical strength and increase resistance to disease; (2) Your daily diet and lifestyle should be controlled to guarantee an appropriate amount of sleep, and you should eat more vegetables and fruit and less greasy food; (3) Don't smoke, drink excessively or take drugs, and give up all bad habits that endanger life and health; (4) Pay attention to temperature change and be particular about hygiene, to reduce chances of falling ill; (5) Always maintain a cheerful frame of mind. When treating people, be kind, fair, and generous, and in dealing with matters stay cool and calm, don't lose your temper, and always start from the positive.

If we can accomplish these five points, our health will basically be guaranteed. If you have health, you have everything: whether you are pursuing study and research, completing tasks at work, going off for holiday travel, or engaging in any activity no matter what, you can always derive the greatest pleasure from what you are doing.

What I have said above is just my own opinion. If any of it is wrong or inappropriate, I would welcome criticisms or comments.

Analysis:

A piece of argumentation like this is likewise more structured than more informal speech or writing. In this case we want to draw attention to logical links provided by the presence of paired conjunctions and conjunctives between different parts of the argument. See for example 如果...就算...又 **rúguǒ ... jiùsuàn ... yòu** 'if... even if...', 要是...定能 **yàoshi ... dìngnéng** 'if...', 无论...都要 **wúlùn ... dōuyào** 'no matter...', 如果...也就 **rúguǒ ... yějiù** 'if...', 无论...都能 **wúlùn ... dōunéng** 'no matter...', 可是 **kěshì** 'however', etc. Also present are those idiomatic phrases commonly found in any piece of argument, which serve as signposts of progression from one idea to another (e.g. 其实 **qíshí** 'in fact', 试想一下 **shìxiǎng yīxià** 'just think for a moment', 由此可见 **yóu cǐ kě jiàn** 'from this it can be seen', 那么说 **nàme shuō** 'this being the case', 在我看来 **zài wǒ kàn lái** 'as far as I am concerned', etc.). A sentence like the last one is virtually a cliché which occurs as a modest gesture at the end of a presentation:

上面所说的只是我个人的看法。说得不对的地方/如有不当之处，欢迎大家批评指正。

Shàngmiàn suǒ shuō de zhǐshì wǒ gèrén de kànfǎ. Shuō de bù duì de dìfang/rúyǒu bùdàng zhī chù, huānyíng dàjiā pīpíng zhǐzhèng.

'What I have said above is just my own opinion. If any of it is wrong or inappropriate, I would welcome criticisms or comments.'

The translation, more literal than colloquial in this case, reveals precisely the lexis and steps of argument in the Chinese original. Again, as regards other features such as the omission of subjects and objects, etc., please see the analyses given for earlier sections.

Glossary of grammatical terms

adjectives	Words used to describe, define or evaluate qualities or characteristics associated with nouns, such as 'big, green, good'. Gradable adjectives are adjectives that generally can be modified by a degree adverb. That is, they can be graded to varying degrees using a range of adverbs such as 'very, extremely', etc. Non-gradable adjectives are usually not modifiable by degree adverbs as they have more absolute meanings (e.g. 'male, female, square, black') and define rather than describe.
adverbial	In Chinese, a word or phrase placed directly before a verb to modify it, usually providing background information such as time, location, means, method, manner, etc. (e.g. 'yesterday, in London, by train, with chopsticks, slowly', etc.).
aspect markers	The functional words 了 **le**, 过 **guo**, 着 **zhe** and 在 **zài** which are closely associated with verbs. 了 **Le**, 过 **guo** and 着 **zhe** are suffixed to the verb, and 在 **zài** immediately precedes it; they indicate the aspectual notions of completion, immediate or past experience, simultaneousness, persistence, and continuation. Chinese aspect markers are NOT indicators of tense. Tense is specified by time expressions placed before the verb or at the beginning of the sentence.
attitudinal verb	In Chinese, a verb which reflects the speaker's attitude. It may be followed by verbal as well as nominal objects (e.g. 'I *like* tea, I *like* to drink tea').
attributive	In Chinese, a word, phrase or clause placed before a noun to qualify or identify it (e.g. '*nice* weather, a *very useful* book', or – a clause – 'a *nobody-will-ever-forget* experience').

causative verb	A verb which causes its object to produce an action or to change state (e.g. '*ask* him to come, *make* him happy', etc.).
clause	A term employed to describe a subject-predicate or topic-comment construction which relates to other similar constructions, with or without conjunctional devices, to constitute a *sentence* in Chinese.
comment	The part of a sentence in a topic-comment sentence which follows the *topic*. The topic establishes the theme or focus of interest in the sentence, while the comment describes, defines, explains or contends, etc. In contrast with a subject-predicate sentence which narrates an incident (e.g. somebody did something), a *topic-comment* sentence makes observations, provides descriptions, offers explanations, etc. The verb 是 **shì** 'to be', adjectives, modal verbs and the particle 了 **le** are all regular elements in a comment.
complement	A word, phrase or clause which comes directly either after a verb (i.e. a *verbal complement*) to indicate the duration, frequency, terminal location or destination, result, manner or consequential state of the action expressed by the verb, or after an adjective (i.e. an *adjectival complement*) to indicate its degree or extent.
composite sentence	A general term referring to a sentence which consists of more than one clause or predicate linked together by (a) conjunction(s) or conjunctive(s). A composite sentence may therefore be of a compound or complex nature, using coordinate or subordinate conjunctions.
conjunctions	Words used to join two words, phrases or clauses (e.g. 'and, otherwise, because', etc.). Conjunctions in Chinese often form related pairs (e.g. 'because . . . therefore, though . . . however', etc.).
conjunctives	*Referential adverbs* used to link two clauses or predicates/comments.
context	The extralinguistic situation or environment in which a verbal event takes place.
cotext	The verbal text (in speech or in writing) that goes before or after the verbal event under consideration.

coverb	In Chinese, a preposition-like verb which is not normally used on its own but is followed by another verb (or other verbs). A coverb with its object forms a *coverbal phrase*, which indicates location, method, instrument, reference, etc.
dative verb	A verb which requires two objects: a direct object and an indirect object (e.g. give him a present, in which 'him' is the indirect object and 'a present' is the direct object).
definite reference and indefinite reference	Terms used in connection with nominal or pronominal items. The difference between definite and indefinite reference may be illustrated by the use of the definite article 'the' and the indefinite article 'a(n)' in English.
degree adverb	See *adjective*.
direction indicators	A set of *motion verbs* which follow other verbs as direction complements to indicate the spatial direction or, sometimes, the temporal orientation (i.e. beginning, continuing or ending) of the actions expressed by those verbs.
indefinite reference	See *definite reference*.
intensifier	A word used to emphasise or highlight elements in a sentence.
intentional verb	A verb which expresses the speaker's intentions. It is generally followed by another verb indicating the action which the speaker intends to take (e.g. 'I plan to study Chinese').
location phrase	A location word or postpositional phrase preceded by the *coverb* 在 zài '(be) in, at'.
measure words	Also known as *classifiers*, these are words which must be used between a numeral or demonstrative and the noun it qualifies. English equivalents are 'a *piece* of cake, a *glass* of beer', but in Chinese measure words are used with all nouns.
modal verbs	A set of verbs which are used directly before other verbs to indicate possibility, probability, necessity, obligation, permission, willingness, daring, etc. (e.g. 'can, must, should, may, dare', etc.).
notional passive	A term used to refer to a construction in which the object of the verb is brought forward to a subject position before the verb, while the verb is still encoded in its active form. Hence the passive voice is not realised in its actual form but can only be notional.

onomatopoeia	A word which is used to approximate to a natural sound in real life. There are a considerable number of conventionalised onomatopoeic words in Chinese, but they are also regularly created spontaneously.
particle	In Chinese, a monosyllabic item which has no independent meaning of its own but serves to deliver a structural or functional grammatical message. The sentence particle 吗 **ma**, for example, has no independent semantic significance, but its presence has the function of changing a statement into a general question.
phonaesthemes	Two-syllabled items which are suffixed to an adjective to add to its descriptive power by introducing some kind of sound connotation.
postposition	A word placed after a noun to indicate a part of the noun or a spatial/temporal relationship to the noun (e.g. 'on, in, outside, above', etc.), A noun followed by a postposition is called a *postpositional phrase*, which usually indicates location or time, and resembles a *prepositional phrase* in English (e.g. the prepositional phrase 'on the table' in English is rendered in the word order 'the table on' in Chinese).
predicate	The part of a sentence that follows the *subject*. The subject is usually the initiator or recipient of the action expressed by the verb or verb phrase in the predicate. In a Chinese *subject-predicate* sentence, the subject is generally of *definite reference*.
referential adverbs	A set of monosyllabic adverbs such as 就 **jiù**, 才 **cái**, 都 **dōu**, 也 **yě**, 又 **yòu**, 再 **zài**, 还 **hái**, 倒 **dào**, 却 **què**, etc., which in a sentence refer either backwards to elements before them or forward to elements after them, echoing or reinforcing the meaning of those elements.
serial construction	A type of Chinese sentence in which more than one verb occurs in succession without any conjunctional devices.
state verb	In Chinese, a verb which is formed by placing the particle 了 **le** after an adjective. A state verb indicates a state of affairs rather than an action or an event.
subject	See *predicate*.
tense	See *aspect markers*.
topic	See *comment*.

Index